D0810344

WITHDRAWN

AMERICAN THEATRE HISTORY

THE
MAGILL
BIBLIOGRAPHIES

AMERICAN THEATRE HISTORY

An Annotated Bibliography

Thomas J. Taylor

SALEM PRESS

Pasadena, California   Englewood Cliffs, New Jersey

∞ The paper used in these volumes conforms to the American National Standard for Permanence of Paper for Printed Library Materials, Z39.48-1984.

Library of Congress Cataloging-in-Publication Data

Taylor, Thomas J. (Thomas James), 1937-
   American theatre history / Thomas J. Taylor
      p. cm.—(Magill bibliographies)
   Includes bibliographical references and index
   ISBN 0-89356-672-1
   1. Theatre—United States—History—Bibliography.
I. Title. II. Series.
Z5781.T25   1992
[PN2221]   91-43961
016.792'0973—dc20   CIP

I wish to dedicate this work to my son Beckett, for his enthusiasm for theatre and his daring to pursue the stage in disdain of all the horror stories. May he someday become part of American theatre history himself.

EDITORIAL STAFF

CONTENTS

ACKNOWLEDGMENTS

I would like to acknowledge the help of Don Appleby, who made available the University of Akron library theatre collection for this project. I would also like to thank professors Ed Williams and John Ross of the University of Alabama for beginning my education in theatre history by teaching me patiently and by example.

AMERICAN
THEATRE
HISTORY

INTRODUCTION
Finding the Voice of the American Stage

The history of the stage in America parallels, in many respects, the history of the country's impulses for freedom, expansion, and experimentation. The dynamics that made the country unique gradually enabled American theatre to develop its distinct character—iconoclastic, daring, celebratory, and expansionist.

The "colonies" knew only their European predecessors—especially French and English theatre—and copied their rules and traditions faithfully, as though achieving a kind of respectability by emulating the continental masters. The first encyclopedists of American theatre, such as George Seilhamer, report the frequent borrowing of whole productions from Europe by the stages of Philadelphia (the city that almost became the U.S. theatre center) and the regular passage of English actors and actresses over the Atlantic to the sister colonies.

As the East Coast became civilized and perhaps even overcrowded, the expansion to the West included riverboat theatre up and down the Mississippi, featuring troupes such as Noah Ludlow's and Sol Smith's. Pioneer theatre brought the most entertaining theatre to the outposts of the Gold Rush, while San Francisco boasted active productions very early in its development, as reported in Joseph Gaer's checklist.

Boston, New York, Philadelphia, and Baltimore vied for theatrical prominence. William Clapp's records of the Boston stage list all the famous companies and actors from the Continent, as well as the distinctly American characters and home-grown acting talent of people such as Danforth Marble, the "Stage Yankee." It was only a matter of time before Europe saw the best of the American talent, such as Edwin Forrest.

Once New York established itself as the center of theatrical activity, it grew rapidly. At first, that center was not on "Broadway" but in lower Manhattan, as John Frick has described in his study of the Rialto at Union Square. The Astor Place Riot in 1849 served as a watershed for change; new theatres were being built in the mid-1840's, and what is called "Broadway" today began to take shape. The long and colorful history of New York theatre has been chronicled well by Stanley Appelbaum and T. Allston Brown.

A major change occurred after World War I, partly because of the chaotic social changes brought about by that conflict, but more dramatically by the revolt of the theatre professional against the exploitation of the nonartistic producers and theatre building owners, represented best by the Syndicate of Charles Frohman. With the organization of actors in 1918 and the successful challenge to monopoly by the Shuberts, the tide shifted from commerce to art. Prompted by the "new theatre" of Europe, American theatre artists began to experiment with smaller, more personal and naturalistic styles, and found a unique voice in Eugene O'Neill and the Provincetown Players, as described in Robert Sarlos' study.

As a measure of the variety of American theatre, O'Neill's plays were being discovered at the same time that Flo Ziegfeld was presenting his long, lavish, and profitable Follies, which are so well depicted in Robert Baral's book on revues. The last of the "well-made plays" were being seen, and touring of the larger American cities had become commonplace, bringing theatre to a gradually changing working class. The 1930's, a time of great social reexamination, brought political theatre to the American stage, again both a reflection of European expressionism and agitprop theatre and a unique expression of its own. The Group Theatre, recalled in Harold Clurman's *The Fervent Years*, was one manifestation of this new spirit, and Clifford Odets wrote plays that said something for them all.

The Federal Theatre Project, 1935-1939, was as close as America came to a national theatre, and its record of accomplishment, as chronicled in Hallie Flanagan's *Arena* and Tony Buttitta's *Uncle Sam Presents*, was considerable. Broadway theatre survived through World War II, although its artistry declined, and its commercialism increased.

After World War II, theatre at first tried to return to its old formulas, but the world had changed too much. With the decline of Broadway experimentation and risk, the off-Broadway movement gained momentum. Perhaps Jose Quintero's career is a good focus for examining the impulses that brought off-Broadway to light, as described in Stuart Little's *Off-Broadway: The Prophetic Theater*.

The 1960's—socially and political volatile in many ways—saw the spread of regional theatre, whose history can be found not only in such overviews as Julius Novick's *Beyond Broadway* and Stuart Vaughan's autobiographical *The Possible Theatre*, but also in the company histories of individual efforts, such as Bernard Coyne's history of the Arena Stage and Carl Marder's history of the Dallas Theater Center. Usually driven by a strongly artistic woman or man from whose energies whole cities draw creative imagination, these regional theatres, despite their geographical distance, are joined by the official League of Resident Theatres (LORT) and by their mutual desire to build the best theatre companies and repertories for their communities. With the support of private corporations, state funding agencies, and federal organizations such as the National Endowment for the Arts, they are becoming America's national theatre.

How to Use this Book

This bibliography is annotated to serve readers in their search for the right source for American theatre history. Descriptions of each entry include the contents of the book, the style, the range (both generically and chronologically), and the presence or absence of critical apparatus and illustration. Roughly divided by periods, the entries often cross these artificial boundaries. Major encyclopedias and multivolume works that deal with all periods are placed in the first section with which they deal. When histories of actors, companies, playwrights, and so on cross sections, they are placed where the celebrity did his or her best work. Thus, George Abbott's and Helen Hayes's autobiographies are found in the chapter on theatre between the wars, even though their careers stretched well into the three decades beyond that period.

Another important case in point is the history of musical theatre. Broad studies cross the chronological barriers and are placed where they begin. The musical *Oklahoma!* holds a unique place in theatre history, however, and when possible, studies have been placed on either side of that watershed production of 1943.

One distinct value of an annotated bibliography is its accessibility for browsing. By browsing through the entries, the reader can get an idea of what kind of material is available and can pursue a distinct line of inquiry through the section's offerings. The student in pursuit of a specific piece of information may scan the general category and find new and inviting lines of inquiry not suggested by book titles alone. For example, in pursuit of New York experimental theatre information, the student may discover Chicago's Compass Theatre, as described in Janet Coleman's book; a search through regional theatre entries may uncover new material on funding for the arts, as described in Ron Bergin's practical guide to corporate sponsorship.

This bibliography lists only book-length studies and sources, and I have tried to separate theatre from drama by omitting books that deal with the script as literature rather than as theatrical "recipe." Thus, long lists of books on Tennessee Williams, for example, are not found here because many of them deal strictly with the literary quality of the work, giving virtually no attention to the pieces as stage script. Nevertheless, rather than neglect these playwrights completely (for they are essential to the theatre), the bibliography includes two or three books on each of the major playwrights as a sort of introduction to further examination of the works as literature. Where possible, these few entries contain bibliographies. Of course, studies of playwrights that pay particular attention to questions of staging, directional history, scene design, or other theatrical matters are fully represented here.

Special notice should be made of the dissertation entries, a rich source of theatre history, published in exact duplication of the originals by University Microfilms. These make available studies that were formerly confined to the libraries of the originating institutions. These dissertations, which are definitely not esoteric specializations useful only to advanced research, often present the first collections of materials on such intriguing subjects as the origins and development of regional theatres (such as William Clark's study of the Cleveland Play House, or David Emmes's analysis of South Coast Rep), the producing or directing styles of influential theatre personalities (as in Dorothy Laming's study of Ellis Rabb), and the exhaustive chronological sifting of old newspapers and periodicals to extract pertinent information about performances and acting careers, such as Albert Asermely's study of Augustin Daly, and Mary Curtis' exhaustive study of the Charleston Stage. All contain full bibliographies as well, making them doubly valuable even to the student researcher.

What is American Theatre's Future?

What is the future of American theatre? The gradual establishment of "new play development" systems, as practiced at the National Playwrights' Conference (the

"O'Neill"), the Midwest Playlabs of Minneapolis, and scores of other workshops and festivals, has forever changed the relationship of the playwright to the producing company, ensuring a better level of communication between them. In addition, university theatre training programs are increasingly making use of local professional not-for-profit theatre as part of the training of actors, designers, directors, and technicians. This marriage can only be good for American theatre. Finally, the existence of the Theatre Communications Group, with its many publications—especially the very popular *American Theatre* magazine—is a sign that the theatre is alive and well across the continent.

Conversely, the stage cannot dismiss film and television as viable funding sources for live theatre, nor can playwrights, directors, and actors survive on stage revenue alone. Consequently, the future seems to hold a continued and expanded relationship between live theatre and the media, with the media gradually forming whole partnerships in the production endeavors. Playwrights will look toward the media as they write their plays, and producers will evaluate a play's potential for film and television before investing in it as a stage work. What this "marriage" will do to drama is anyone's guess, but it may spell the end of live theatre as a pure medium. It may, however, be the very reason for the survival of live theatre, and the experience of going to see a play will never be duplicated in film and television. Futuristic talk of holographic performances simultaneously projected on many stages at once is just that—futuristic daydreaming.

Does American theatre have a future? Yes, because in the final analysis, American theatre history is the history of individuality, of daring, of irreverence toward the Establishment, of Dionysian impertinence. The most pessimistic among the doomsayers of live theatre must still admit that these qualities are present in abundance in American theatre's next generation.

Thomas J. Taylor

THE BEGINNINGS TO 1914

Alger, William Rounseville. *Life of Edwin Forrest: The American Tragedian*. 1877. Reprint. New York: Arno, 1977.
A reprint of an early biographical analysis of Forrest: his parentage, apprenticeship, early New Orleans years, and gradual rise to fame as the foremost American actor of the nineteenth century. Strong biography for its type, with about a dozen engravings of Forrest in various roles. Alternates between factual information and critical examination. Appendices contain Forrest's will and facsimiles of medals struck in his honor: "Just to opposers and to friends sincere." Index.

Anderson, John. *The American Theatre: An Interpretive History*. New York: Dial, 1938. Reprint. Ann Arbor, Mich.: University Microfilms, 1969.
A plain-spoken little book that begins with the premise that, far from being "transplanted European theatre," American theatre quickly and convincingly developed a unique character in the 140 years from *The Contrast* to Eugene O'Neill's *Strange Interlude*. During that period, "a continent had been spanned, a wilderness opened, and an industrial oligarchy raised," providing unique conditions for a unique theatrical phenomenon. Anderson laments, however, contemporary (1938) trends toward "journalistic" theatre that wants plays "hot off the griddle."

Andrew, Richard Harlan. *Augustin Daly's Big Four: John Drew, Ada Rehan, James Lewis, and Mrs. G. H. Gilbert*. Ann Arbor, Mich.: University Microfilms, 1976 (Ph.D. dissertation, University of Illinois at Urbana-Champaign, 1971).
This greatest of American *regisseurs* from the last quarter of the nineteenth century specialized in light comedies often loosely adapted (stolen) from European second-rate farce. The four principal actors of Daly's New York theatre worked together so often and so closely that they merit a study and a special term all by themselves. Ensemble acting, American producer style, during a nongolden era, but interesting as part of the history of acting in America. Bibliography.

Appelbaum, Stanley, ed. *The New York Stage: Famous Productions in Photographs*. Mineola, N.Y.: Dover, 1976.
From the Theatre and Music Collection of the Museum of the City of New York, this pictorial review of the years 1883-1939 contains reprints of 148 production stills with perhaps a hundred words each of cast identification, scene description, and similar information. The buzz-saw scene from *Blue Jeans* (1890) and the "deus ex excavating crane" scene from *High Tor* (1939) are worth the browsing. A good source for students of stage design, costuming, large-cast blocking, and the fine art of posing for production shots.

Arant, Fairlie. *A Biography of the Actor Thomas Abthorpe Cooper.* Ann Arbor,
  Mich.: University Microfilms, 1976 (Ph.D. dissertation, University of Minnesota,
  1971).
  Active in American theatre from before the nineteenth century (he was born in
  England in 1775) to 1849, Cooper was a "find" of Thomas Wignell of the
  Chestnut Street Theatre (Philadelphia), who was in England looking for actors
  in 1796. After his break with Wignell in 1798, he continued to act in Philadelphia
  and New York. An interesting study of the life of the British-imported actor
  seeking a permanent home in early American theatre and of New York's gradual
  displacement of Philadelphia as the center of American stage activity. Strong
  bibliography and impressive scholarly research into obscure collections.

Asermely, Albert A. *Daly's Initial Decade in the American Theatre, 1860-1869.*
  Ann Arbor, Mich.: University Microfilms, 1975 (Ph.D. dissertation, University
  of New York, 1973).
  By concentrating on the first ten years of Augustin Daly's career, Asermely
  shows how Daly's ideas, theatrical style, and connections were formed. Daly is
  called here a "transitional" figure between the "orientation from romance to
  realism and from star to director." The seeds of his aesthetics were in the "social
  and theatrical ferment of New York before the Civil War; they were watered
  during the conflict and flowered shortly thereafter." Selected bibliography of
  newspaper sources and William Winter memoirs.

Barber, Rupert T., Jr. *An Historical Study of the Theatre in Charlotte, North
  Carolina, from 1873-1902.* Ann Arbor, Mich.: University Microfilms, 1976
  (Ph.D. dissertation, Louisiana State University, 1970).
  In large part a history of the Charlotte Opera House, this study divides into five
  periods a volatile time in southern theatre, when the local stock company was
  being replaced by the touring companies of Charles Frohman's Theatrical
  Syndicate. Charlotte's history is representative of other southern and midwestern
  cities that shared the same theatrical fate when the economics of legitimate theatre
  forced a dissolution of regional creative energy, only recently rectified in the
  renewed health of regional theatre. Lacks exhaustive play lists and other reference
  summaries of dissertations. Photograph and floor plan of the Opera House;
  bibliography.

Barnabee, Henry Clay. *Reminiscences of Henry Clay Barnabee: Being an Attempt
  to Account for His Life, with Some Excuses for His Professional Career.* Boston:
  Chapple Publishing, 1913.
  Sometimes called "My Wanderings," this memoir of the singer and "king of
  comic opera" of the nineteenth-century stage and leader of The Bostonians is both
  a record of real events and a re-creation of the mood of the times. The Barnabee
  concert troupe, arriving home in Boston in 1871, met expenses by singing for

a funeral, even "counting the house" on that somber occasion. Delightful reading; no critical apparatus but some illustrations.

Barnes, Eric Wollencott. *Anna Cora: The Life and Theatre of Anna Cora Mowatt*. London: Secker & Warburg, 1954. Printed in the United States as *The Lady of Fashion: The Life and Theatre of Anna Cora Mowatt*. New York: Charles Scribner's Sons, 1954.
By quoting extensively from the actress' autobiography, Barnes lets her tell her own story, but with annotation and comment about the theatre during her time (the mid-nineteenth century). "Lily" (her family's name for her) was also a successful playwright (*Fashion* is still anthologized), so her insights into the workings of the theatre are doubly valuable. This appreciative biography illustrates the excitement of the American version of Victorian theatre, chronicling the successes of its best-known author and actress from her childhood to her death in 1870 at the age of 50. Eleven illustrations and a rich narrative style enlighten the subject; however, the text lacks sufficient dates or a chronicle and is difficult to follow in this respect. Notes and index.

Barrett, Lawrence. *Charlotte Cushman*. New York: Burt Franklin, 1889.
Originally a lecture delivered to the Dunlap Society, this booklet includes a list of characters played by Miss Cushman and a chronological list of her performances in New York from 1836 to 1841. "Her earnestness of nature shone through all her dramatic work," claims Mr. Barrett, but the frontispiece shows a formidable face more suited to Ma Barker than to the Green Room. A graceful but all too brief introduction to a remarkable nineteenth century actress.

Bauland, Peter. *The Hooded Eagle: Modern German Drama on the New York Stage*. Syracuse, N.Y.: Syracuse University Press, 1968.
From von Kotzebue's *Menschenhass und Reue* in 1798, German drama has found an audience in New York even when, during the "new theatre" era, "American managers were less than eager to undertake the importation of German naturalism." Valuable for comparing American expressionism with its German roots, brought to the United States by traveling companies and reflected in the work of e. e. cummings, Sophie Treadwell, John Howard Lawson, Paul Sifton, and others. Excellent appendix listing all originally German plays to find an audience in New York from 1894 to 1965.

Belasco, David. *The Theatre Through Its Stage Door*. New York: Harper & Brothers, 1919.
Part autobiography but, more important, a statement of principles by the master of stage realism, this early self-portrait features several dozen illustrations of Belasco at work ("The Shops Where Mr. Belasco's Lighting Apparatus Is Manufactured and Experiments in Stage-lighting Are Constantly Being Carried

On") and of his colleagues—notably, David Warfield and Leslie Carter. Belasco pays attention to detail in life as in art, pointing out that his fireplace contains seventy-three tiles taken from the Alhambra at Granada, Spain. Good reading; Belasco proves himself a keen observer of the details of human discourse as well. No critical apparatus.

Bibee, Jack Loren. *The Acting of Richard Mansfield*. Ann Arbor, Mich.: University Microfilms, 1978 (Ph.D. dissertation, University of Illinois at Urbana-Champaign, 1974).
This study of Mansfield concentrates on his acting style and gives him credit for "not so much his talent, which was considerable, but rather . . . his overwhelming ambition." Good study for Mansfield's non-Shakespearean contributions, notably in *Arms and the Man* (1894) and *Peer Gynt* (1906), which "helped introduce symbolism as a dramatic style." Augments William Winter's biography (and newspaper reviews) and other previous studies.

Binns, Archie. *Mrs. Fiske and the American Theatre*. New York: Crown, 1955.
Binns's book, written in cooperation with Olive Kooken, is a thorough and well-written biography of this first lady of the theatre at the beginning of America's version of "new theatre," roughly 1875-1915. Many illustrations, both of portraits and of productions, add to the colorful descriptions of this apparently magnetic stage figure. Mrs. Fiske also was a formidable company manager, bringing her tour to Chicago, Cleveland, Kansas City, and elsewhere. Informative and readable account of her life and her theatre.

Bordman, Gerald. *The Oxford Companion to American Theatre*. New York: Oxford University Press, 1984.
Like all the Oxford companions, this reference work helps sort out the salient facts on every theatre subject, from producer Alex Aarons to Edward Albee's *The Zoo Story*. More a dictionary than a full reference work, it serves best as the starting point for a more thorough subsequent inquiry. Plays summarized and critiqued (excluding musicals, for some reason) enjoyed fairly long runs, usually on Broadway. Plot and character summaries for thousands of plays, biographical sketches of every major player, producer, director, and designer, along with profiles of important American theatres and (too briefly for the regional theatres) theatre companies. Some limitations: Howard Sackler is found only under *Great White Hope*, for example. Other odd choices as well: Martin Beck but not Julian Beck. No illustrations or lists; no cross-referencing except for a "which see" signal in the text.

Bost, James S. *Monarchs of the Mimic World: Or, The American Theatre of the Eighteenth Century Through the Managers—The Men Who Made It*. Orono: University of Maine at Orono Press, 1977.

Good biographical sketches and outlines of methodologies for Lewis Hallam (Senior and Junior), David Douglass, John Henry, Thomas Wignell, John Hodgkinson, and William Dunlap from 1752 to 1805. In this rendition, these brave men held the theatre on their shoulders for the actor, the audience, and the age "despite the threat of theatre fires," "despite rowdyism and rioting, dirty benches and candle drippings," "despite inadequate heating," "despite wretched ventilation," the crowds kept coming. Good introduction to the history of management. Index.

Bousliman, Charles William. *The Mabel Tainter Memorial Theatre: A Pictorial Case Study of a Late Nineteenth-Century American Playhouse.* Ann Arbor, Mich.: University Microfilms, 1976 (Ph.D. dissertation, Ohio State University, 1969).
The Tainter Theatre is in Menomonie, Wisconsin—not a theatre hotbed, but a pioneer town built on the white-pine logging industry. Constructed in 1890, the theatre was restored and maintained meticulously and today serves as an architectural museum piece for the study of stage practices during this period. Unfortunately, the 170 illustrations of every detail, from fly winches to statuary, do not reproduce well enough to serve the text. Nevertheless, important for the history of such stage hardware as gas lighting (never used for illuminating theatrical production here) and catwalks, the alterations of which were newsworthy in 1906.

Brett, Roger. *Temples of Illusion: The Golden Age of Theaters in an American City.* East Providence, R.I.: Brett Theatrical, 1976.
A privately printed account of several Providence theatre buildings of the last quarter of the nineteenth century and first half of the twentieth, from the Providence Opera House to the less venerable Westminster ("the Sink of burlesque's heyday") to early movie houses. Rare photos of façades and interiors, packed and empty houses, buildings in bloom and in ruin, including the Theatre Comique the day after it burned in 1888, "as dismal a morning-after as ever was seen by its beery patrons." Well collected and written and historically valuable in portraying what happened to theatres everywhere.

Brown, T. Allston. *A History of the New York Stage from the First Performance in 1732 to 1901.* 5 vols. 1903. Reprint. New York: Benjamin Blom, 1964.
The most authoritative and exhaustively detailed chronicle of New York theatre ever attempted (William Dunlap's ends in 1832), with every cast list of every play, revue, musical, and farce to tread the boards, along with details of openings, closings, changes of cast, management, venue, and more. Details are organized by theatre house, then by date. For serious scholars; includes a forty-eight-page index that covers only plays and characters.

_____. *History of the American Stage.* 1870. Reprint. New York: Benjamin Blom, 1969.

Biographical outlines of virtually every actor and actress (along with some musicians, managers, and sundry hangers-on) appearing on the American stage between 1733 and 1870. A prodigious undertaking in one volume. Dedicated to Joseph Jefferson, who "made his great reputation as an actor in the part of Rip Van Winkle." About one hundred illustrations, engravings apparently done anonymously and expressly for this book. Sometimes (as with Miss Eaton, who gets one sentence) the entries are exasperatingly short and incomplete; at other times (as with Thomas D. Rice, known as "Jim Crow"), quite thorough. Last entry in an appendix is Charles Fechter, who debuted as the book was going to press.

Burr, David Holcomb. *Richard Mansfield: A Re-Evaluation of His Artistic Career.* Ann Arbor, Mich.: University Microfilms, 1978 (Ph.D. Dissertation, University of Michigan, 1972).
Mansfield "embodied the characteristics of the nineteenth century star actors" and was also an excellent manager "widely recognized and acclaimed for exceptional and innovative productions." One of the last great actor-managers to survive what Burr and others refer to as "an era of transition" to modern drama, Mansfield is not frequently mentioned in theatre history anthologies. An appendix provides a chronology of Mansfield's characterizations but is not detailed enough to be of much use. Bibliography.

Carson, William G. B. *Managers in Distress: The St. Louis Stage, 1840-1844.* St. Louis: St. Louis Historical Documents Foundation, 1949.
Continuing his readable series on the St. Louis theatre scene in the nineteenth century, Carson tells the tales of city-slicker managers (Noah Ludlow and Sol Smith contracted debts in at least five states), the pioneer ventures they conceived, and the woe they came to. A good picture of what theatre producing must have been like everywhere during the period: "[Smith] derived a certain pleasure from the fracas. But poor Ludlow seems to have been blessed with no such knack." Play performances, index, and bibliography.

_____. *The Theatre of the Frontier: The Early Years of the St. Louis Stage.* 1932. Reprint. New York: Benjamin Blom, 1965.
An introduction summarizes the historical evidence for the book's premise: Human beings will endure anything to see theatre. Pioneers, in the middle of a precarious existence and in the face of institutional disapproval, took their theatre as it came to them, rough but ready. The theatre years 1815-1840 in the unlikely city of St. Louis are discussed in this very readable chronicle. Play list appendix, bibliography, and index.

Cassady, Marshall G. *The History of Professional Theatre in Salem, Ohio, 1847-1894.* Ann Arbor, Mich.: University Microfilms, 1975 (Ph.D. dissertation, Kent State University, 1972).

Although Salem was not an important theatre scene, its professional theatre history is typical of the Midwest's acceptance and reluctant adoption of the late-nineteenth century touring companies' notion of what made "legitimate" theatre. Perhaps the most valuable element is the description of elocutionists, minstrels, and other variety entertainments of the period. Documented thoroughly and illustrated well but poorly duplicated in this edition. Appendices of daybooks, with selective index (performers, plays, companies); bibliography of works cited.

Churchill, Allen. *The Great White Way: A Re-Creation of Broadway's Golden Era of Theatrical Entertainment*. New York: E. P. Dutton, 1962.
The years 1900 to 1919 are entertainingly re-created here, from London import *Florodora* (often misspelled) to *Lightnin'*, the first play to close as a result of an Actors Equity strike. Inner workings of the Syndicate, the separation of vaudeville from "legit" theatre, and the star method of Broadway success are discussed in anecdotal style; Edward F. Albee's system of milking theatre: "Albee's UBO took five per cent of an actor's salary, plus a five-per-cent agent's fee, for booking *into Albee theatres*!" (Emphasis in original.) Bibliography and index.

Clapp, Henry Austin. *Reminiscences of a Dramatic Critic*. Boston: Houghton Mifflin, 1902.
From a large collection of drama critiques published in the *Boston Daily Advertiser* (1870-1900), Clapp selects some reminiscences to recall, revise, and retell. Far more interested in the lost arts and artists than in the present (1902) predicament of the stage, Clapp, like T. S. Eliot's theatre cat, has seen all the great ones come and go and is ready to embellish his brief memories of contact with ruminations of his own. Special attention is paid to the Booths and, in an attached essay, to Henry Irving. Difficult reading and unpliable as a research source; index.

Clapp, William, Jr. *A Record of the Boston Stage*. 1853. Reprint. New York: Benjamin Blom, 1968.
A collection from the *Boston Evening Gazette* "for reference and perusal," according to the preface. Clapp was in his prime during this decade, and his history of Boston's dramatic entertainments from 1749 to 1850 or so is quick-witted and incisive, if not altogether informative. Increase Mather warned against the theatre-devil as early as 1686, but a 1750 law put teeth into the injunction by imposing a five-pound fine. One hundred years later, the drama was "firmly planted in New England for good or for evil," as Thomas Barry writes and Clapp reports. Details of early American theatre (offstage pranks, ticket prices, shared billings, and bitter company rivalries) culled from the author's considerable research prevent historical formality from invading this fascinating account and remind the scholar that not all theatre existed in New York. No critical apparatus, but an index was published in *Theatre Documentation* (volume 1, number 1).

Cohan, George M. *Twenty Years on Broadway and the Years It Took to Get There: The True Story of a Trouper's Life from the Cradle to the "Closed Shop."* 1925. Reprint. Westport, Conn.: Greenwood Press, 1971.
Cohan reports on his struggle for good theatre and against unionized houses in this thirty-four-chapter self-examination written at the height of his career but not long after losing his battle with Actors Equity. He addresses readers as though they were young playwrights, sardonically advising, "First, think of something to say. Then say it the way the theatergoer wants to hear it said, meaning, of course, that you must lie like the dickens." A certain bitterness or combativeness intrudes into this superficially modest but actually rather self-promoting piece; valuable as a first-person defense of Cohan's practices.

Corbin, Sister Germaine. *The Acting of Otis Skinner.* Ann Arbor, Mich.: University Microfilms, 1976 (Ph.D. dissertation, University of Illinois at Urbana-Champaign, 1971).
Skinner's more famous daughter Cornelia left his "papers" to the Harvard Theatre Collection in 1969. Sister Corbin pored over the Skinner letters, original manuscripts, contracts and business agreements, and other material to research this nineteenth century "transition" actor who, for fifty years (1877-1933), played beside Edwin Booth, Joseph Jefferson, and others, toured extensively from 1881, was a staple in Augustin Daly's theatre company, and survived professionally well past World War I. He wrote on his acting theories and espoused "the necessity for artistic control in the actor's use of emotion." Thorough study; appendices of Skinner's tours, portraits.

Craig, William Scott. *The Theatrical Management of Sol Smith: Organization, Operation, Methods, and Techniques.* Ann Arbor, Mich.: University Microfilms, 1972 (Ph.D. dissertation, University of Illinois, 1963).
Smith began his thirty-year career in 1832, joining Noah Ludlow in 1835 to form Smith and Ludlow, Theatrical Managers. Makes use of materials in the Missouri Historical Society archives, St. Louis, the center of Smith's professional activity and his place of burial. After a chapter of biography, concentrates on the conditions of performance and the composition of the companies. Business and finance take a final chapter. Valuable source for theatre study west of the Alleghenies. Full chronology, season roster, and the original partnership agreement.

Crawford, Mary Caroline. *The Romance of the American Theatre.* 1913. Rev. ed. Boston: Little, Brown, 1925.
Claims a debt to two more thorough treatments of American theatre: William Dunlap's *History of the American Stage* (1832) and Arthur Hornblow's 1919 *History of the Theatre in America from Its Beginnings to the Present Time*, which filled the gap between editions of Crawford's study. This is a "somewhat eclectic survey of the whole field," focusing on "dominant personalities and general

tendencies." A good, early, subjective yet knowledgeable appreciation of American theatre's youthfully romantic character. Illustrations are mostly portraits of actors in their most famous character poses. Notes that Eugene O'Neill's "career is certainly full of interest," and "John Barrymore [has] recently given us a highly creditable Hamlet."

Curtis, Mary Julia. *The Early Charleston Stage: 1703-1798.* Ann Arbor, Mich.: University Microfilms, 1972 (Ph.D. dissertation, Indiana University, 1968). It is difficult to imagine what this study could add to Eola Willis' account (*The Charleston Stage in the XVIII Century with Social Settings of the Time*), but Curtis claims that she incorporates "information gathered in more recent histories of American Theatre," includes legal documents that Willis had overlooked, and corrects errors. One addition: The managers' role is given more weight than Willis gave it. Together (perhaps adding Stanley Hoole), these studies say all there is to say on the subject.

Cutler, Jean Valjean. *Realism in Augustin Daly's Productions of Contemporary Plays.* Ann Arbor, Mich.: University Microfilms, 1972 (Ph.D. dissertation, University of Illinois, 1962).
"The first American regisseur" is the subject of this study on stage realism as it emerged as a theatrical style (often in contrast to the "romantic" style) from 1866 to 1899, the years of Daly's active participation in American theatre's development. He not only implemented stage design innovations but also, as an actor trainer, changed the production from a "star" to a "team-work" performance. By concentrating on contemporary plays rather than the standard classical repertory, Cutler focuses on Daly's contributions to realism. Bibliography; many plates of his notebooks and productions, but they are poorly reproduced in this reprint.

Daly, Charles P. *First Theater in America.* 1896. Reprint. Port Washington, N.Y.: Kennikat Press, 1968.
A brief, stately essay answering the question, "When was the drama first introduced in America?" Arguing against William Dunlap's suggestion (1752), Daly finds evidence for a New York theatre as early as 1733 and a more active company in 1750. His research methods and attention to detail serve as models for subsequent theatre history scholarship. The Dunlap Society, founded in 1885, originally published this essay and appended an even shorter one in which Daly considers "the objections made to the stage," faulting Jeremy Collier for citing "pagan writers."

Day, Susan Stockbridge. *Productions at Niblo's Garden Theatre, 1862-1868, During the Management of William Wheatley.* Ann Arbor, Mich.: University Microfilms, 1978 (Ph.D. dissertation, University of Oregon, 1972).

After the Park Theatre burned down in 1848, Niblo's Garden Theatre became New York's main attraction during the Civil War years under the guidance of William Wheatley, a Philadelphia actor-manager transported to Broadway. Wheatley introduced the burlesque spectacle to America (forerunner of the musical comedy) in the form of *The Black Crook* (by an American). This study details the production and several others, placing them in the theatre structure and in theatre history: "*The Black Crook* . . . presented large numbers of European dancers in tights for the first time in America," lit by a "newfangled" calcium spotlight.

Dickinson, Thomas H. *The Insurgent Theatre*. New York: B. W. Huebsch, 1917. Best known for his compilations of European experimental theatre during the advent of modernism, Dickinson describes the impulses of his time, when "artists, actors, painters, producers, organizers and audience have been brought together for the service of a new art for the theatre." Best for measuring the pulse of the "little theatre," where many theatre workers were impelled "to do plays . . . by the codes their own artistic sense said was right." A balanced but enthusiastic manifesto with a valuable list of representative "little theatres" and their repertories from 1906 to 1917. Index.

Dobkin, William Edward. *The Theatrical Career of Danforth Marble: Stage Yankee*. Ann Arbor, Mich.: University Microfilms, 1976 (Ph.D. dissertation, Indiana University, 1970).
After "Yankee" Hill, Marble was perhaps the most famous actor in the comic American rustic style often called "yankee." A phenomenon of the second third of the nineteenth century, the yankee character was played with great success by Marble ("Dan Marble" was his popular name) in *Sam Patch the Jumper*, the story of a great horse, from 1836 through the 1840's. This study gathers disparate and sketchy information on Marble (a chronology of the cities he was known to play in is appended) and evaluates him as "a portrayer of the Yankee and as an actor and to determine his place in American theatrical history."

Dormon, James H., Jr. *Theater in the Ante Bellum South: 1815-1861*. Chapel Hill: University of North Carolina Press, 1967.
Theatre found a more receptive audience in the "aristocratic" and Europe-loving South than in the Puritan North, and much of American theatre history began in the South. Dormon argues a more protracted, broader affection for the theatre, where traveling shows took advantage of the navigable rivers and mild climate to spread through the South. This scholarly study details that long-lasting affection, citing company after company of commercially successful theatre below what was to become the Mason-Dixon Line. Bibliography, index, and twenty-one unattractive pink-sepia illustrations.

Doty, Gresdna Ann. *The Career of Mrs. Anne Brunton Merry in the American Theatre*. Baton Rouge: Louisiana State University Press, 1971.
The Philadelphia theatre scene at the turn of the nineteenth century, specifically the Chestnut Street Theatre, was the first home of Merry, an actress neglected in some histories, though she "was the most celebrated actress to appear in this country before 1808." This study provides details of her career and, in passing, "insight into the American theatre in its infancy and the conditions under which performers worked." Clarifies some misunderstandings for the theatre history student: she is also Mrs. Wignell and Mrs. Warren, though best known by her stage name of Mrs. Merry. Good appendix of roles; bibliography and index.

Downer, Alan S., ed. *The Memoir of John Durang, American Actor: 1785-1816*. Pittsburgh: University of Pittsburgh Press, 1966.
The "pioneer" theatre of America's first few decades found John Durang, a member of Lewis Hallam's company in 1785, in his glory as he "painted scenery, built playhouses, performed acrobatic and equestrian feats, constructed a puppet show, developed summer amusement parks, organized and directed acting companies, founded a short-lived theatrical dynasty, devised transparencies, pyrotechnic displays, and pantomimes, and played minor roles in legitimate drama." In short, Durang's memoirs are the diaries of a whole era of American entertainment. Downer provides notes on the Wignell-Reinagle Company and an index.

Dunlap, James Francis. *Queen City Stages: Professional Dramatic Activity in Cincinnati, 1837-1861*. Ann Arbor, Mich.: University Microfilms, 1975 (Ph.D. dissertation, Ohio State University, 1954).
A massive catalog of every play performed over a sixteen-year period (1845-1861) listed from playbills during the great expansion of Cincinnati prior to the Civil War. Most of the chronological listings for this study are available only in three Ohio libraries, but the tables (thirty-two in all, breaking down the plays by genre), appendices, and the text itself have a wider distribution. Strictly for historical reference; thorough and impressive, but not bedside reading.

Dunlap, William. *History of the American Stage*. New York: n.p., 1832.
The earliest chronicle of the American theatre scene, largely outdated by Seilhamer's later study and T. Allston Brown's 1903 study, though more comprehensive than both. Dunlap was much respected by his peers, and this chronicle was heavily cited during the first century of theatre criticism. The Dunlap Society, named in honor of his contributions, published several tracts on theatre history as well.

Durham, Weldon B., ed. *American Theatre Companies, 1749-1887 and 1888-1930*. Westport, Conn.: Greenwood Press, 1986 and 1987.

Not exactly two volumes of the same work, since this study was published separately in two parts, but following the same format. A sensible way of digesting theatre history, these sources list theatre companies, followed by as much relevant material as history has provided. A typical entry includes a description of the impulses toward the company's founding, its location and physical plant, personnel, repertory (sometimes a massive document in its own right, as with the New Chatham Theatre Stock Company, whose list of titles alone runs some seven pages), and bibliography. Each entry is signed by its author, with a list of contributors in an appendix. Chronology of theatre companies; name and title indexes.

Eaton, Walter Prichard. *At the New Theatre and Others: The American Stage, Its Problems and Performances, 1908-1910.* Boston: Small, Maynard, 1910.
Despite the narrow time frame of this collection of papers originally published in journals of the period, it discusses "what tendencies were at work shaping our drama" during a particularly volatile period, when the theatrical Syndicate was gradually giving way to "the Fine Art" of theatre, as Eaton calls it. The small producers, many of them artists themselves, began to find theatrical outlets for their work without working under the compromises of the Syndicate's long-term monopoly on playing spaces. Summarizing a year at the New Theatre, planned and designed by Heinrich Conried, is Eaton's way of summarizing the freedom of theatrical enterprises in this new era. No critical apparatus.

Edwards, John Cornwall. *A History of Nineteenth Century Theatre Architecture in the United States.* Ann Arbor, Mich.: University Microfilms, n.d. (Ph.D. dissertation, Northwestern University, 1963).
The birth and death of theatre buildings, arranged by period and geography, before 1800, to 1837, after 1837, after the Civil War, eastern, midwestern, and western locations. More than one hundred illustrations, poorly reproduced, of exteriors, interiors, and transverse sections of some fifty theatres, with verbal descriptions of many more. Aims "to record the development of the nineteenth century American theatre as an architectural type" and "to give special attention to the physical arrangements within the building which are theatrical in disposition." Good introduction to the subject.

Ericson, Robert Edward. *Touring Entertainment in Nevada During the Peak Years of the Mining Boom, 1876-1878.* Ann Arbor, Mich.: University Microfilms, 1976 (Ph.D. dissertation, 1970).
Working from newspapers of the time ("fortunately . . . chatty, informal, and quite thorough"), the author exhausts his subject and the reader with protracted recapitulations of every review, advertisement, gossip item, and miscellaneous tidbit from some eighteen newspapers. In unhappy contrast to Margaret Watson's study of roughly the same period, this sedulous tome puts the audience to sleep. Strong bibliography, however.

Ernst, Alice Henson. *Trouping in the Oregon Country: A History of Frontier Theatre.* Portland: Oregon Historical Society, 1961.
"First Curtains in a Last Frontier" is the first chapter in this well-written account of the Oregon Territory theatrical history. The audience, consisting of "American settlers and the British personnel of the fort, . . . its trappers" and other sturdy souls, saw *The Golden Farmer* as early as 1853 and *Little Lord Fauntleroy* as late as 1890. "The New Century" presents a conclusion to the past and a look forward. A selected bibliography lists Oregon newspapers and periodicals, along with other sources; valuable index.

Ewen, David. *The Story of America's Musical Theater.* Philadelphia: Chilton, 1961.
Ewen, author of a dozen books on American musicals and their creators, offers a readable history of musical forms in entertaining, even celebratory, rhetoric. Covers the operettas ("What did matter . . . was that the scenes and costumes were nice to look at, the tunes delightful to listen to, and the performers pleasant to watch"), to the sometimes subtle difference between musical play and musical comedy ("Where musical comedy is frivolity and entertainment . . . the musical play is an art form concerned mainly with important human values."). Good index; no illustrations.

Falk, Bernard. *The Naked Lady: A Biography of Adah Isaacs Menken.* London: Hutchinson, 1934. Revised 1952.
"The Menken" is treated like a lovely, "naked" (that is, appearing in "pink silk fleshings, with the small end of a dimity nothing fastened to her waist"), lost lady of Astley's Theatre, with thirty-six illustrations and a text full of admiring anecdote. Menken's sometimes scandalous career and private life are revealed here temptingly: "her silk-draped limbs again aroused enthusiasm, but the box office receipts were the reverse of flattering." Other notables—Charles Dickens, Mark Twain, George Sand—swirl around her through several marriages, disasters, and triumphs, but she is the magnet. Good reading, and a lusty portrait of "the face, the form, the legs that sometimes had charmed, sometimes had shocked, her own [American] countrymen."

Felheim, Marvin. *The Theater of Augustin Daly: An Account of the Late Nineteenth Century American Stage.* Cambridge, Mass.: Harvard University Press, 1956.
Daly was not a run-of-the-mill theatre manager but the innovative visionary who brought "new theater" from Europe to America at the turn of the century. A theatrical biography rather than a personal one, this study nevertheless portrays Daly in a good light—not the raging megalomaniac often assumed, but a quiet, considerate, even gentle man who loved his theatre and his actors. Among other accomplishments, Daly was the "first American dramatist to deal with the divorce problem," in his play *Divorce* (1871), which enjoyed a phenomenal stage history. Index.

Fisher, Lawrence Frederick. *A Descriptive Study of the Acting Career of James O'Neill.* Ann Arbor, Mich.: University Microfilms, 1975 (Ph.D. dissertation, University of Michigan, 1969).
Many know James O'Neill from his son Eugene's depiction of him in *Long Day's Journey into Night,* or know of his "captivity" in the role of the *Count of Monte Cristo* (begun in 1883). Fisher expands and fills out that career, describing the forces that moved O'Neill in one professional direction or another—often it was concern for the welfare of his family, not some misguided sense of his own genius. The study repairs Eugene's portrait and seeks to "refute, when necessary, any myths which have come into popular acceptance since the time of [James's] death in 1920." A massive fifty-three-page table of performances; bibliography.

Ford, George D. *These Were Actors: A Story of the Chapmans and the Drakes.* New York: Library Publishers, 1955.
The time was 1705 to 1944, and their families joined in the marriage of Harry Chapman and Julia Drake. More than their biography, however, this is the story of nineteenth century American theatre told in readable, almost novelistic style. Unfortunately, the paucity of dates, the careless use of nicknames and vague references, and the overwriting get in the way of the factual history of these actors and their families. A not very helpful index.

Freeman, Benjamin Pope, Jr. *The Stage Career of Charles D. Coburn.* Ann Arbor, Mich.: University Microfilms, 1976 (Ph.D. dissertation, Tulane University, 1970).
The Coburn Players, who held the stage for a dozen years at the beginning of this century in several venues, began in Savannah in 1895. "A tough-minded, tight-fisted theatre magnate" as well as a demanding actor, Coburn is studied first in the apprentice years (1897-1904), then, as a theory of theatre emerged, with the Coburn Players between 1904 and 1916. The New York engagements section (1917-1930) details Coburn's reasons for helping to found Actors Equity; the festival years (1935-1940) "represented a dream of university theatre and professional theatre in alliance." Valuable source for study of academic theatre, Equity beginnings, and actor-manager techniques. Bibliography.

Frick, John W. *New York's First Theatrical Center: The Rialto at Union Square.* Theater and Dramatic Studies 26. Ann Arbor, Mich.: UMI Research Press, 1985.
This study makes the point that Union Square—Broadway, the Bowery, and Fourteenth Street—was the first center of theatrical activity, not the present "Broadway" near Times Square. Gathering all the available archival information, especially architectural, into one study, Frick describes the typical life of the theatre personalities of the period between 1870 and 1900. Authoritative and exhaustive; bibliography and index.

Frick, John W., and Carlton Ward, eds. *Directory of Historic American Theatres*. Westport, Conn.: Greenwood Press, 1987.

A project of the League of Historic American Theatres, from a data base created by John B. Heil, originally begun by Gene Chesley (who died in 1981). Theatres built before 1915, designed for live entertainment and still standing, are listed with (where available) opening date, opening show, physical description of façade and auditorium, stage dimensions and equipment, seating capacity and design, and similar information of interest to the historian and theatre preservationist. Major stars, types of entertainment, and other information; brief additional paragraph for some entries, such as this one describing the Fountain Theatre in Mesilla, New Mexico: "Murals depicting valley scenes were painted by Fountain in 1914 and still exist on interior walls." Center section of photographs. The buildings are all, in Antonin Artaud's words, "signalling through the flames."

Gaer, Joseph, ed. *The Theatre of the Gold Rush Decade in San Francisco*. New York: Burt Franklin, 1935.

After a brief introduction to the 1850-1860 explosion of "culture" following gold to the West, this book is a 1105-title checklist of authors, first performances, theatre openings, and dates of every recoverable play the editor could find. Many of the scripts can be found in the San Francisco Public Library, and they are well worth further inquiry. Operas and their performance language are listed as well, and playwrights' contributions are counted (John Baldwin Buckstone had thirty-four plays running during this decade).

Gaisford, John. *Drama in New Orleans*. New Orleans: J. B. Steel, 1849. Reprint. Ann Arbor, Mich.: University Microfilms, 1971.

Tongue in cheek and eye on gossip, Gaisford takes readers on a tour of the burgeoning New Orleans theatre scene as it expanded, like America itself, from "a room in St. Philip Street" (in 1817) to "the season of 1849 [which] stands alone on the records of Amateur Histrionics as one of complete success," with many a side trip between. Offstage antics "to which I will not further allude" lard the loose narrative and subjective criticism ("This favorite play, abounding as it does with clap traps for applause, was received as usual, in a favorable manner"). No critical apparatus.

Gallegly, Joseph. *Footlights on the Border: The Galveston and Houston Stage Before 1900*. The Hague: Mouton, 1962.

Local newspapers (as far away as New Orleans) supplied the raw data for this remarkably readable study of Texas theatre before the twentieth century. In five- and ten-year chapters, swinging from Galveston to Houston and back with apparent abandon, Joseph Gallegly re-creates the performance arts of this un-promising frontier land to conclude, rather surprisingly: "Essentially, the border

theatre . . . differed but little from that of the more settled and cultured regions."
With photographs and an appendix of attractions. Index and brief bibliography.

Geller, James J. *Grandfather's Follies*. New York: Macaulay, 1934.
An avid theatregoer recalls the great melodramas and theatre stories of the past
fifty years and retells them in a cracker-barrel style that is accompanied by simple
cartoon cuts by John Held, Jr., Geller "describes the epoch making plays; tells
how they came to be written, and the amazing career that each of the plays had."
Recollections of *Lady of Lyons, Uncle Tom's Cabin, Ticket-of-Leave Man*, and
three dozen more are told without scholarly pretense (and very few stabilizing
dates). Best used to find a firsthand account of a well-known, long-running drama
(table of contents serves as a menu).

Georges, Corwin Augustin. *Augustin Daly's Shakespearean Productions*. Ann
Arbor, Mich.: University Microfilms, 1975 (Ph.D. dissertation, Ohio State
University, 1972).
One way to cut through the amazingly varied career of Daly is to separate his
classical productions from his new plays; Georges concentrates on Shakespearean
works under Daly's thumb, "not only scenic elements, but also the use of music,
the adaptation of scripts, realistic and special effects in lighting, and the acting
style of his company" from 1869 to 1899. Special emphasis on his 1887 "mis-
cast" and "farcical" production of *Taming of the Shrew*, but revealing "the
emergence of the modern director in the United States."

Gilder, Rosamond, and George Freedley. *Theatre Collections in Libraries and
Museums: An International Handbook*. New York: Theatre Arts, 1936.
Not as out of date as first suspected because the collections hold still and grow;
witness the New York City Library Collection and the Folger Shakespeare
Library. The first section concentrates on the United States, Canada, Mexico,
and South America. Annotated descriptions, approximate sizes, degrees of
availability to the public, and more are provided. Freedley adds an essay on the
care and preservation of fugitive material. Index.

Gould, Thomas R. *The Tragedian: An Essay on the Histrionic Genius of Junius
Brutus Booth*. 1868. Reprint. New York: Benjamin Blom, 1971.
Short sketches of about twenty roles in the "elder Booth" repertory told by a
"fan" and friend who, in a sort of posthumous publicity brochure, published this
literary sculpture of the work. "In the hope of giving body to the vision . . . we
proceed to record our impressions of Mr. Booth's genius for dramatic imperson-
ation. . . . An actor's posthumous fame is, by the nature of his art, visionary and
traditional." Good for studying the rhetorical style of such flattering essays of
the time.

Graham, Philip. *Showboats: The History of an American Institution.* Austin: University of Texas Press, 1951.
An excellent introduction to the floating theatres of William Chapman, Gilbert Spaulding and Charles Rogers, Capt. A. B. French, and a dozen others who brought theatre to the American pioneer river cities from 1831 to the 1930's. "Always Good—Now Better than Ever" was French's motto, echoing the competitive spirit of these enterprising showboats, illustrated here with thirty portraits of boats, people, and productions. Parade of showboats appended, an invaluable checklist of riverboat theatre activity; bibliography and index.

Grau, Robert. *The Stage in the Twentieth Century.* 1912. Reprint. New York: Benjamin Blom, 1969.
Continuing a detailed account of the American stage, Grau covers the first dozen years of the twentieth century without really noticing the changes around him. The Syndicate is treated as a permanent (even benevolent) fixture; vaudeville and burlesque are legitimate representatives; one chapter asks, "The Stage of tomorrow—Who will perpetuate the classics of the theatre?" Hundreds of probably unique photographs, mostly portraits of producers. The really new event, predicted in his previous volumes, is that "the Stage as a theme no longer is confined to the player in the flesh." In other words, the "irresistible moving picture" is here. Compare this volume with Dickinson's *The Insurgent Theatre.*

Green, Elvena Marion. *Theatre and Other Entertainments in Savannah, Georgia, from 1810 to 1865.* 2 vols. Ann Arbor, Mich.: University Microfilms, 1977 (Ph.D. dissertation, University of Iowa, 1971).
A thorough study of fifty-five years of Savannah theatre organized by proprietorship, managerial operations, licenses, companies, stars, salaries, admission prices, and several other criteria. Volume 1 is an analytical essay; volume 2 contains indexes of plays, playwrights, actors, entertainers, and production personnel. Most of this material is drawn from George Odell's *Annals of the New York Stage* and Savannah court and municipal documents.

Green, Richard Louis. *The Shakespearean Acting of Edwin Forrest.* Ann Arbor, Mich.: University Microfilms, 1975 (Ph.D. dissertation, University of Illinois, 1969).
Forrest, with his manly, "American" style of acting, played many parts of a uniquely American nature but also excelled in Shakespearean roles. It was in these roles that he was compared and contrasted with his English rivals, notably William Charles Macready. Three characters—Othello, King Lear, and Hamlet—are examined in detail in order to reconstruct the acting style of Forrest, as well as his interpretation of the roles. Working with stock companies of varying talent, Forrest, a perfectionist and believer in using the original texts, could only lament: "One woman . . . got through Desdemona, knowing only about fifteen lines of

the . . . text, all the rest being improvised" in several languages! Interesting account of the long-suffering theatrical hero.

Grossmann, Edwina Booth. *Edwin Booth: Recollections by His Daughter.* 1894. Reprint. New York: Benjamin Blom, 1969.
The Booth family, as represented here, especially in the list of illustrations, was a theatrical dynasty stretching well past the nineteenth century. The daughter who wrote these memoirs was very close to Edwin, named for him, and a substitute "woman of the house" after the death of her mother in 1860: "I think, indeed, that his own sorrows made him cling more closely to the child who had been left so suddenly in his care." A portrait of Edwin and his grandchild in 1887 captures much of what the daughter's relationship must have been like. Well-written but very short "recollections," followed by a publication of "letters to his daughter" and "letters to his friends." Index, and illustrations of "articles belonging to Edwin Booth," an odd assortment of stage-jewel swords, crowns, and rings.

Harvey, Ruth. *Curtain Time.* Boston: Houghton Mifflin, 1949.
Written in the style of a girl's reminiscences of a happy childhood between "house" and "house" and chronicling the life of a traveling show family in the late nineteenth century. This fictionalized history drops real names—Grand Opera House, Daly's Theatre, Wallack's, Booth's, Tony Pastor's Variety Theatre, Niblo's Garden—but avoids exact dates. Not quite right for theatre history, but extremely accurate on details of the life itself: "An orange!" the waitress said in loud, withering scorn. "You're an *actress*—you get *prunes*!" Recommended for young readers.

Henderson, Mary C. *The City and the Theatre: New York Playhouses from Bowling Green to Times Square.* Clifton, N.J.: James T. White, 1973.
The architecture, the façades—the real estate end of New York theatre history is presented here with valuable photos and facts, arranged moving uptown and up the calendar. Henderson places the theatre buildings in their expanding surroundings as the city grows to its present impossible configuration. Her affection for these old structures is apparent in Henderson's obituaries of those that have fallen victim to the wrecking ball or have been reduced to movie houses, as are her fears for the future of those edifices that are still standing but in trouble. Notes, bibliography, index.

Herbert, Ian, ed. *Who's Who in the Theatre: A Biographical Record of the Contemporary Stage.* 17th ed. Detroit: Gale Research, 1981.
A continuation of the 1912 *Who's Who*, with additional volumes. Volume 2 contains playbills, and volume 3 covers contemporary theatre, film, and television. A good first stop in researching celebrities from the past or present, but not the final word. The "playbills" volume is limited by staying with London and

New York theatre at a time when regional theatre deserved a closer look. Several indexes, but lacks a list of players tied into their performances. Volume 1 (biography) explains the editors' procedures for admission and updates, along with an interesting history. Much material is dropped from each edition, so past editions may be more valuable to the historian than the current one.

Hewitt, Barnard. *Theatre U.S.A.: 1665 to 1957*. New York: McGraw-Hill, 1959.
Professional theatre recounted in contemporary documents, mostly newspaper commentaries, with substantial amplification by Hewitt, toward a discernment of patterns in historical development. Even though chapters are divided at certain decades, the thrust of the arrangement is the maturation of American theatre from its European roots to its own aesthetic signature. Sacrifices chronology for thematic organization. More than one hundred illustrations; bibliography and index. "The Selections and Their Authors" provides textual and biographical information on plays cited in the text.

Hill, West T., Jr. *The Theatre in Early Kentucky: 1790-1820*. Lexington: University Press of Kentucky, 1971.
Samuel Drake, possibly the first producer to bring a theatre company beyond Pittsburgh, is credited with creating Kentucky's "Western Theatrical Empire," in this interesting study of "The Athens of the West" and its theatrical heritage. According to the record of performances during the thirty-year explosion of cultural activity, Kentucky recorded 560 performances, about 90 percent of the total "western" theatrical activity during this time. George Colman the younger was the most popular playwright, with sixty-five performances of sixteen plays. Appendix and index.

Hill, Yankee. *Scenes from the Life of an Actor*. 1853. Reprint. New York: Benjamin Blom, 1972.
"Compiled from the journals, letters, and memoranda of the late Yankee Hill," who was a great comic actor and lecturer of the mid-nineteenth century. The anonymous compiler is indebted to "the restoration of a lost trunk, containing manuscripts and letters connected with Mr. Hill's professional journeyings," and which were to have been the beginning of George Handel Hill's own autobiography. He died at age 40, however, in 1849. This early biography is a great source of lectures and anecdotes from his repertory, along with engravings of some of his antics.

Hodge, Francis. *Yankee Theatre: The Image of America on the Stage, 1825-1850*. Austin: University of Texas Press, 1964.
American comedy emerged and developed during a relatively short period in the middle of the nineteenth century, largely in tandem with the "Yankee" character, a stereotype pleasing to both American and European audiences. Traces the

careers of four actors famous for their depictions of the Yankee: James Hackett, George Hill, Dan Marble, and Joshua Silsbee. Although this subject has been treated elsewhere, it is viewed here in a historical perspective and with a respect not always proffered the comic character. Long bibliography, index, and an appendix giving a facsimile of a "Yankee talk" dictionary ("critturs" = "creatures").

Honaker, Gerald Leon. *Edwin Booth, Producer: A Study of Four Productions at Booth's Theatre.* Ann Arbor, Mich.: University Microfilms, 1975 (Ph.D. dissertation, Indiana University, 1969).
Another way to divide and examine Booth's career is to concentrate on his skills as a producer: handling money matters, making administrative decisions, and then taking the stage as the guarantee of the sold-out house. Four productions—*Romeo and Juliet, Hamlet, Richelieu* (less often analyzed than the Shakespearean productions), and *Julius Caesar*—are examined in detail from the production point of view. That after strenuous production duties the great man could play the great roles is a tribute to his energy. Strong scholarship; bibliography.

Hoole, W. Stanley. *The Ante-Bellum Charleston Theatre.* Tuscaloosa: University of Alabama Press, 1946.
Hoole begins in 1800 and ends in 1861, complementing the work of Eola Willis (*The Charleston Stage in the XVIII Century with Social Settings of the Time*). The play, player, and playwright lists and chronological records, organized so that no one need ever scour the original periodical documents again, make this study both thorough and usable. Interesting, too, to compare the Douglass Company with the Placide Company of Comedians that dominated the nineteenth century stage in South Carolina. Hoole's introduction recaps the arguments in favor of more attention to southern theatre "as a distinct factor in the molding of public opinion and character," attention that has been paid since his study.

Hornblow, Arthur. *A History of the Theatre in America from its Beginnings to the Present Time.* 1919. Reprint. New York: Benjamin Blom, 1965.
A good, early, two-volume history drawing from previous sources and acknowledging the work of George O. Seilhamer to 1797. Critical of William Dunlap's *History of the American Theatre*, claiming it is more autobiography than history. Hornblow has a tendency to concentrate on theatre buildings rather than on actors or companies, and illustrations are either formal portraits or architectural exteriors. Authoritative as a reference, but not very interesting to read from cover to cover. Strong index of names and plays.

Hossalla, Richard J. *Henry E. Abbey, Commercial-Manager: A Study of Producing Management in the Theatre of the Late Nineteenth Century (1870-1900).* Ann Arbor, Mich.: University Microfilms, 1975 (Ph.D. dissertation, Kent State University, 1972).

Hossalla is right to concentrate on the manager of the theatre during this period because, even more than the resident or traveling star, managers such as Abbey determined the success or failure of every theatrical enterprise. Marrying art with commerce, these geniuses in their own right had distinct signatures of management that marked every show on their ledger. Part biography, part study of the money side of early theatre, this study concludes with a précis of Abbey's activities as a manager in chart form.

Hoyt, Harlowe R. *Town Hall Tonight*. Englewood Cliffs, N.J.: Prentice-Hall, 1955.
The story of the country theater of the 1880's and 1890's, told from a Wisconsin (Beaver Dam) perspective but applicable to all similar halls for hire. Touring shows, counting on local standardized scenery and a ready-made naïve audience willing to see anything from "the big city," moved from town to town. This informal study, rather than following a show, watches the changing scene at the local town hall, whose bill also changed from night to night. The birth of the repertory companies, the touring shows, the circuit, told from the small-town standpoint, captures the atmosphere of early theatre better than could a library of scholarly studies.

Hughes, Glenn. *A History of the American Theatre, 1700-1950*. New York: Samuel French, 1951.
Admittedly dependent on secondary sources, this informative and usable survey of American theatre serves as a handy reference. Thorough descriptions in full paragraph form, with transitions between sections, but lacking any pretense at a thematic foundation. Occasionally top-heavy on dramatic literature, as when summarizing a season, but dealing with the finances and practicalities of theatre as well. A friendly overview of American theatre in twenty- to twenty-five-year leaps, sprinkled with illustrations and told with a vigorous, affectionate, but not overawed anecdotal style. For example, "Let us conclude our account of the first half-century of American theatricals (1700-1750), a period decorated with quaint shadows and fitful lights, a period of tentative gestures and fugitive events. A period of beginnings." A good way to find the flavor of early American theatre; less thorough after World War I but still very readable. Strong index and selected bibliography. Recommended as an overview.

Hunter, Frederick J., comp. *A Guide to the Theatre and Drama Collections at the University of Texas*. Austin: University of Texas Humanities Research Center, 1967.
In this most unlikely place are some of the best theatre collections in the world, starting with the Wrenn, Aitken, and Stark Collections. An impressive list of collections, with descriptions of contents, illustrated with rare stage designs and costume plates. For example, includes the manuscript holdings of plays by Maxwell Anderson, Lillian Hellman, Arthur Miller, and Tennessee Williams (but

Glass Menagerie is at the University of Virginia). Most impressive, this guide is more than twenty years old.

Hutton, Laurence. *Curiosities of the American Stage.* New York: Harper & Brothers, 1891.
An uncritical survey of American stage characters "in their less familiar aspects," by which Hutton means Indians, African Americans, children, frontiersmen, and the "stage American" in character plays. Wonderful chapters on "the infant phenomena" (such as Master Betty, the Infant Roscius) and "a century of American Hamlets." Two indexes, cleverly called "The Cast of Characters" and "The Synopsis of Scenery."

Ireland, Joseph N. *Records Of the New York Stage from 1750 to 1860.* 2 vols. 1866. Reprint. New York: Benjamin Blom, 1966.
The kind of sedulous record-keeping that gives theatre history a bad name, this tersely written recitation of events is as undramatic as theatrical history gets ("Richard II was also produced . . . its characters thus distributed"). Some opinion, however, accompanies the chronicle ("and his performances continued to attract and gratify the public"), but Ireland's enthusiasm for theatre is suspect. Interesting to compare with William Dunlap's and T. Allston Brown's similar checklists—Dunlap's to 1832, Brown's to 1901.

Isaacs, Edith J. R. *The Negro in the American Theatre.* New York: Theatre Arts, 1947.
A fairly early "photo album" of successful African-American entertainers from nineteenth century figures to Pearl Bailey. Particularly fascinating are the portraits of African dance-theatre figures exotically depicted in African operas and native traditional rituals. Strong chapter on Federal Theatre, and good pictorial documentation of Edna Thomas as Lady Macbeth in Orson Welles's production, and Patricia Roberts and Sadie Brown in Owen Dodson's production of *Mourning Becomes Electra* at Howard University. Good source of unusual documentation.

Jacobsen, Bruce Carl. *A Historical Study of the Bozeman, Montana, Opera House.* Ann Arbor, Mich.: University Microfilms, 1975 (Ph.D. dissertation, University of Minnesota, 1969).
A fairly brief history of the Bozeman Opera House, beginning in 1890 and declining in the 1920's, culled from sparse material and stitched together via "considerable speculation based upon the available material." Much of the activity in the Opera House was social and political rather than theatrical, but the parade of stars who graced the stage, even if only for a night, speaks almost sadly about the itinerant life of the actor. Reproductions of illustrations are mostly too faded to count; house attractions listed in appendix.

James, Reese Davis. *Old Drury of Philadelphia: A History of the Philadelphia Stage, 1800-1835*. 1932. Reprint. New York: Greenwood Press, 1968.
Philadelphia almost became the theatre capital of the U.S., and the Old Drury, officially the "Chesnut [sic] Street Theatre," was its most exciting venue. William Burke Wood and William Warren managed as professional and ambitious a theatre as the early nineteenth century had to offer, and left behind in the nine-volume "Diary or Daily Account Book" carefully detailed records of box office receipts, contractual transactions, seasons, and other documents of their history; James published this book out of chronological sequence with Thomas Pollock's study of the century before (*The Philadelphia Theatre in the Eighteenth Century*). Condensed with general introduction, and indexes to plays and players.

_____. *Cradle of Culture, 1800-1810: The Philadelphia Stage*. Philadelphia: University of Pennsylvania Press, 1957.
Season by season from 1800 to 1810, the Chestnut Street Theatre of Philadelphia is honored in this chronology of one of America's oldest theatre houses. A book about "actors and actresses . . . roles . . . dancers . . . artists . . . managers," it is even more about "the growth of a city and a country and the role the Chestnut played" in building a national spirit in this "cradle of culture." Appendices of performances and performers; index.

Jefferson, Joseph. *"Rip Van Winkle": The Autobiography of Joseph Jefferson*. London: Reinhardt and Evans, 1949.
Among several generations of Joseph Jeffersons who were actors is this one (1829-1905), who became famous in three roles: Rip Van Winkle, Dr. Pangloss, and Bob Acres. A light comic actor greatly respected by his peers for his gentle disposition and rare talent, Jefferson purportedly wrote this autobiography, edited and with a foreword by his granddaughter Eleanor Farjeon. The style and the vagueness regarding dates, however, leave much bibliographical history in question; better to go to the original edition (New York: Century, 1889) or to Alan S. Downer's 1964 edition, which includes a helpful introductory essay.

Jordan, Harold Trice. *Thomas Cooper: A Biographical Chronology*. Ann Arbor, Mich.: University Microfilms, 1972 (Ph.D. dissertation, Tulane University, 1968).
As a chronology of the career of Thomas Cooper, this study is well organized and easy to use. It divides his career (roughly 1792-1830) by transatlantic crossings between England (his birthplace) and America—especially Philadelphia, where he performed often on the Park Theatre stage—and elsewhere. Good comparisons with George Cooke, a fellow actor who performed with Cooper in *Othello* and *Venice Preserved* in 1811. Informative on Cooper's "retirement" career as a customs inspector in New York. Bibliography.

Kanellos, Nicolas. *A History of Hispanic Theatre in the United States: Origins to 1940*. Austin: University of Texas Press, 1990.
A long-needed and well-done history of Hispanic theatre, from mid-nineteenth century California to leading man Pepe Luiz's touring companies in the 1930's. Kanellos is describing not folk drama leading to Luiz Valdez's Teatro Campesino, but fully professional touring and resident companies, building from a long Spanish formal tradition at first aimed toward the large urban Chicano populations but eventually favored by all discerning theatregoers. This entry could be in chapter 5 (ethnic theatre) as well. Glossary, references, and index.

Kaufman, Edward Kenneth. *A History of the Development of Professional Theatrical Activity in Los Angeles, 1880-1895*. Ann Arbor, Mich.: University Microfilms, 1978 (Ph.D. dissertation, University of Southern California, 1972).
Almost a companion volume to Woods's study (*The Interaction of Los Angeles Theatre and Society Between 1895 and 1906*) of the next ten years, this study is less sociological and more economical and architectural in its focus. The conditions were right for local theatrical activity during these years, before big business found this market. More readable than most theses of this nature.

Kendall, John S. *The Golden Age of the New Orleans Theater*. Baton Rouge: Louisiana State University Press, 1952.
The French theatres lie outside this work, which covers much of the same material as Nelle Smither's *A History of The English Theatre in New Orleans* but with a much livelier style. The opening line: "Somewhere in the distance a clock sounds the hour of eight." All the great entertainments came to New Orleans, once the country had established its identity, and the play list reads like a history of nineteenth century East Coast theatre. Kendall cites Smither's work in a bibliographical note.

Kimmel, Stanley. *The Mad Booths of Maryland*. Mineola, N.Y.: Dover, 1940. Revised and enlarged, 1964.
At the center of this fascinating biography of the Booth brothers—Edwin, Junius and Wilkes—is a singular photograph of John Wilkes Booth, distracted and angry about something. This is the story of the stage success of two Booths and the tragic place in history of the third. The best biography of Wilkes because it places him in the nineteenth-century theatrical milieu where his frustrations began and his act of self-loathing was consummated. Highly recommended to American historians as well as theatre researchers. Index and scores of rare illustrations, including twenty-three of Wilkes's escape route.

Kolin, Philip C., ed. *Shakespeare in the South: Essays on Performance*. Jackson: University Press of Mississippi, 1983.
The performance history of William Shakespeare's plays south of the Mason-

Dixon line. Repairs inattention by traditional American theatre history books to the contributions of the South to classical drama. Arnold Aronson supplies details of Virginia theatre, including the earliest performance (1752), *Merchant of Venice* in Williamsburg; the last essay describes a Florida production of *Midsummer Night's Dream* in 1979. Part 1 (history) covers Shakespeare productions by region, state, and city; part 2 covers festivals but stops short of the Alabama Shakespeare Festival's move to Montgomery.

Krows, Arthur Edwin. *Play Production in America.* New York: Holt, 1916.
"Presented . . . mainly to remark America's contribution to international development," this pre-O'Neill assessment of American theatre emphasizes technical advances, backstage innovations, and lighting breakthroughs. Follows the play production chronologically, from first reading to a description of audience types. More than forty photographs and illustrations of the then-modern stagecraft.

Krumm, Walter Courtney. *The San Francisco Stage, 1869-1879.* Ann Arbor, Mich.: University Microfilms, 1972 (Ph.D. dissertation, Stanford University, 1961).
After the Gold Rush drew the next generation of entrepreneurs and tradespeople, San Francisco expanded from 150,000 to 234,000 residents, and theatre refined itself into a glittering scene, ready for the innovations of such theatre legends as David Belasco. This study of the interim "transitional" period corrects and updates the previously written recollections of "aging San Franciscans recalling former days, and travelling actors who appeared on the local stages." Bibliography but no index.

Landau, Penny Maya. *The Career of Mary Ann Duff, the American Siddons: 1810-1839.* Ann Arbor, Mich.: University Microfilms, 1982 (Ph.D. dissertation, Bowling Green State University, 1979).
Although born in London in 1794, Duff was an American tragic actress in partnership with her actor husband John R. Duff, who also performed with greats such as Edwin Forrest, Edmund Kean, and Junius Brutus Booth. Popular in Boston, New York, and Philadelphia, she was often compared in acting style to the famous English actress Mrs. Sarah Siddons. She played more than two hundred characters in her almost thirty-year career. Bibliography and appendices of biographical documents, including a chronology.

Leach, Joseph. *Bright Particular Star: The Life and Times of Charlotte Cushman.* New Haven, Conn.: Yale University Press, 1970.
A definitive modern biography of the nineteenth century's most famous American actress. Leach tells Cushman's story and provides an informed overview of the theatrical mise-en-scène in which she thrived. As Lady Macbeth, Cushman represented all women who were anxious to take power into their own hands; Leach deals with the comparison in a chapter on the Civil War entitled "A

Woman's Power in the National Struggle (1861-1863)." An odd adulation pervades the study, however: "The years had shown in lives like Miss Cushman's that a pure spirit could 'go stainless,' even in the theatre." Notes and index.

Lee, Douglas Bennett, Roger L. Meersman, Donn B. Murphy. *Stage for a Nation: The National Theatre—150 Years.* Lanham, Md.: University Press of America, 1985.
A coffee-table book celebrating the National Theatre of Washington, D.C.—a tryout and touring house rather than a company of actors—where the presidents and first ladies see their theatre. After early theatres burned or met other demises, the National was built in 1835: "And the long survival of the National Theatre itself is a drama as stirring and grand as any yet acted on this remarkable stage for a nation." Not to be confused with a "national theatre," which resides, if anywhere, in the League of Resident Theatres (LORT) regionals.

Leonard, William Everett. *The Professional Career of George Becks in the American Theatre of the Nineteenth Century.* Ann Arbor, Mich.: University Microfilms, 1976 (Ph.D. dissertation, Ohio State University, 1970).
Becks collected theatrical materials from the Civil War to the end of the century as he managed American productions and British imports. His promptbooks in particular are valuable sources of information for historians of the post-Civil War period. Leonard uses the collection, housed in the New York Public Library, to draw a picture of the theatre world Becks worked in professionally. Good documentation, but illustrations are not reproduced in the University Microfilms edition—they are available at Ohio State University.

Lesser, Allen. *Enchanting Rebel: The Secret of Adah Isaacs Menken.* 1947. Reprint. Port Washington, N.Y.: Kennikat Press, 1973.
This study was prompted by the discovery of a small book of diary notes, sketches, and poems by the actress. New Orleans-born Menken (claimed to be "the most famous actress in the world of the 1860s") found success in the vaudeville footlights of San Francisco, Paris, and New York. She was celebrated not only for "legitimate roles" but also for light comedy, comic opera, equestrian extravaganzas (notably *Mazeppa* in 1864), and on the pages of gossip newspapers, "bare-faced, bare-limbed, reckless, erratic, ostracized, but gifted, kindhearted, successful." George Sand was her son's godmother, and "the Menken" was photographed with Alexander Dumas in his shirtsleeves! Strong photograph section, and a good account of life among the happier denizens of American theatre.

Leuchs, Fritz A. H. *The Early German Theatre in New York: 1840-1872.* New York: Columbia University Press, 1928. Reprint. New York: AMS Press, 1966.
Not to be confused with a study such as Peter Bauland's, this book examines the distinctly German theatre—mostly German-language theatre—catering to a

German New York population. Theatres and theatre companies such as the Liebhabertheater, the Altes Stadttheater, and the Neues Stadttheater, heavily but not exclusively offering German plays, are discussed here in an authoritative and detailed account of ethnic theatre during New York's immigrant growth. Appendices for easy reference; bibliography and index.

Litto, Fredric Michael. *Edmund Simpson of the Park Theatre, New York, 1809-1848*. Ann Arbor, Mich.: University Microfilms, 1975 (Ph.D. dissertation, Indiana University, 1969).
After a fairly brief "provincial apprenticeship," in 1809 Simpson rose to act in and eventually manage the Park Theatre during the height of New York's claim to become the theatre capital of America. This study examines his contribution to that claim, as he gave his energies to the Park, working with all the great stars until his death in 1848. An appendix gives Simpson's journal entries on a talent-recruiting trip to England (1843), an insightful document on the methods and means for building a stock company. Bibliography, list of roles, and full notes.

Ludlow, Noah M. *Dramatic Life as I Found It*. 1880. Reprint. New York: Benjamin Blom, 1966.
A personal remembrance of the Mississippi Valley theatre scene by the most famous "frontier actor-manager," who brought theatre to the wilderness with Samuel Drake, Sr., after the War of 1812, and with Sol Smith as Smith and Ludlow, Theatrical Managers. Ludlow's book, which is a primary source for any subsequent study of theatre (and theatrical riverboat) life on the Ohio or Mississippi, avoids the tediousness of his peers by adopting a lively narrative style. Index.

McNamara, Brooks. *The American Playhouse in the Eighteenth Century*. Cambridge, Mass.: Harvard University Press, 1969.
Originally a 1965 dissertation, this study concentrates on architectural changes from the Christopher Wren/David Garrick models of England to their American counterparts, and on stage innovations and inventions incorporated into American staging during the incipient decades. Working from rare drawings and even models (no pure example of eighteenth century playhouses exists), McNamara attempts to "recreate the playhouses of our eighteenth century ancestors." Traces the development of the theatre building, "delineating and interpreting the major patterns of expansion and change" in the eighteenth century, and therefore not an exhaustive list of every construction. Well-illustrated with exteriors and interiors of existing and restored buildings, conjectural reconstructions, artifacts, and occasional English theatre interiors of the Georgian type that facilitate speculation about nonextant American interiors. Valuable source, not only of discrete information but also trends and directions. Fifty illustrations, notes and index.

McNeil, Barbara, and Miranda C. Herbert, eds. *Performing Arts Biography Master Index.* 2d ed. Detroit: Gale Research, 1981.
Originally published under the title *Theatre, Film, and Television Biographies Master Index* in 1979, this is a consolidated index from more than one hundred performing arts biographical dictionaries with "at least a moderate amount of biographical, critical, or career-related information on individuals connected with the performing arts," with 270,000 individual entries of persons living and dead. Lists publications by author, subject, and title. "Enables the researcher to determine, without tedious searching, in which sources biographical information on an individual can be found." A good place to start, bypassing individual indexes, for information on actors and managers, with birth and death dates given for most entries.

Maher, Dennis Michael. *The Theatre in St. Louis, 1875-1900.* Ann Arbor, Mich.: University Microfilms, 1982 (Ph.D. dissertation, University of Wisconsin at Madison, 1980).
Lotta Crabtree was a famous performer who spent a large part of her career (fourteen appearances from 1875 to 1890) in St. Louis, retiring in 1891 as "the richest actress in American stage history." This study scours the records to recap an active and profitable time for midwestern theatre tours and celebrities. Appendices give figures, percentages, and major stars; "all attractions presented at all major theatres in St. Louis" are given in handy tabular form. Bibliography.

Mammen, Edward William. *The Old Stock Company School of Acting: A Study of the Boston Museum.* Boston: Trustees of the Public Library, 1945.
Part of a larger but unrealized series on stock companies and little theatres, this brief but fascinating history of acting styles among stock companies concentrates on the Boston Museum Theatre, a nineteenth century phenomenon that, from 1843 to 1893, never allowed "damn" to be said on its stage. Otis Skinner said of stock training (Mammen reports) that "while three years of stock company experience gave him many tricks of the trade, they taught him very little of the real art of acting." Valuable bibliography for continued inquiry into the history of acting styles, an ephemeral subject.

Marcosson, Isaac F., and Daniel Frohman. *Charles Frohman: Manager and Man.* New York: Harper & Brothers, 1916.
This biography is definitive for its time but is tempered by Frohman's recent death and the hand of his son in the writing. The acerbic nature of the great but avaricious theatre magnate shows even in James M. Barrie's "appreciation": "I had only one quarrel with him, but it lasted all the sixteen years I knew him." He was "lovable," however, despite history's opinion to the contrary. Wonderful portraits of theatre greats from the period, roughly from 1877, when young Frohman became an advance agent, to his drowning on the *Lusitania* in 1915

(curiously, very few dates are given throughout this study). Appendices of Frohman productions and excerpts from letters; index.

Marker, Lise-Lone. *David Belasco: Naturalism in the American Theatre.* Princeton, N.J.: Princeton University Press, 1975.
Concentrating on Belasco's contributions to stage realism, Marker combines an explanation of his theories with a description of their practical application in his career; she successfully comes to Belasco's defense against his New Stagecraft detractors. As Marker's subtitle suggests, Belasco and stage naturalism are synonymous, not only in terms of sets and lights but also as an acting style. From purchasing the inside of a restaurant for use as a stage set to implementing a twelve-minute sunset for *Madame Butterfly*, Belasco has attempted to duplicate and expand upon the audience's perceptions of nature and life; details are documented here, but in essay form. New York chronology and an index, but few illustrations, most of which are black and white.

Marks, Patricia. *American Literary and Drama Reviews: An Index to Late Nineteenth Century Periodicals.* Boston: G. K. Hall, 1984.
A major source of information for theatre has always been the review of productions from city newspapers. Contains 177 pages of citations of drama reviews from the prolific period from about 1880 to 1900. That is, plays are listed by title, followed by lists that tell readers where to find reviews of those plays. For the reader whose library sources include back copies of *Impressionist*, *Judge*, *Truth*, *Spirit of the Times*, and other such obscure and now rare periodicals, this book is invaluable. Otherwise, it is a frustrating book indeed, and of very little use to the student researcher.

Mates, Julian. *America's Musical Stage: Two Hundred Years of Musical Theatre.* Westport, Conn.: Greenwood Press, 1985.
The strength of this study lies in Mates's comparisons of musical forms with their distinctly American product, the stage musical. Examining structures from grand opera to vaudeville, "all interrelated, all forming a part of what we refer to as the American musical stage," the work is organized in two "acts" and eight "scenes," with a photograph section, notes, index, and an interesting bibliography in essay form. Sources are divided into musical texts, biographies and diaries, histories, special studies, playbills (with programs, photographs and newspapers), and discography.

Messano-Ciesla, Mary Ann Angela. *Minnie Maddern Fiske: Her Battle with the Theatrical Syndicate.* Ann Arbor, Mich.: University Microfilms, 1985 (Ph.D. dissertation, New York University, 1982).
A fresh look at Mrs. Fiske's life, especially her company's constant battle with the monopoly of Charles Frohman's Syndicate. There is a decidedly feminist slant

to this dissertation; the author constantly refers to the fact that Mrs. Fiske, "as a woman," accomplished so much. Fiske's leadership, along with the rise of other independents (including the Shuberts, whom she opposed), is thoroughly discussed. Good source of documentation, Syndicate agreements, and the like. Appendices and bibliography.

Moody, Richard. *America Takes the Stage: Romanticism in American Drama and Theatre, 1750-1900*. Bloomington: Indiana University Press, 1955.
By concentrating on the genre of romanticism, this study offers more than average information on such phenomena as native themes and characters, romantic acting styles, and scene design, in which the panorama was both real and metaphorical: "dramatic action . . . set against a seemingly unlimited and ennobling" background. Twenty-one plates, including the poster for *Shenandoah* (1888), which promised "love-making on the stage." Particularly strong in African-American drama and music; some illustrations of minstrel songs.

_____. *The Astor Place Riot*. Bloomington: Indiana University Press, 1958.
The history of America's most famous theatre riot, May 10, 1849, near Astor Place and East Eighth Street, an "area . . . occupied by a mob of enraged citizens battering one another in what appeared to be a gigantic free-for-all." The bone of contention: which actor, British William Charles Macready or American Edwin Forrest, was a better Macbeth. This account, a cross between a police report and newspaper gossip, includes the background of the riot and its outcome (thirty-one casualties). Readable and oddly frightening; a good introduction to the sociology of theatregoing in the nineteenth century. Sources and references.

_____. *Edwin Forrest: First Star of the American Stage*. New York: Alfred A. Knopf, 1960.
A modern biography that retells the story of the nineteenth century's greatest American tragedian in a readable (if occasionally romantic) and informative style. Twenty-four illustrations, including some photos of the Edwin Forrest Home in Philadelphia, where "twelve old American actors are invited to spend their declining years"—Moody's book is dedicated to these actors. Good details of Forrest's demanding physical regimen and the William Charles Macready-Edwin Forrest theatre conflict, the latter called "A Bad Night in Astor Place." Index.

Moore, Lester L. *Outside Broadway: A History of the Professional Theater in Newark, New Jersey, from the Beginning to 1867*. Metuchen, N.J.: Scarecrow Press, 1970.
"Way off-Broadway" is how actors today describe New Jersey theatre, actually a thriving and innovative arena for new plays and budding actors. Its first professionals were recorded in 1799, its first theater was the Concert Hall (1847), and its queen was Emma Waller in roles from *Guy Mannering*, *Camille*, and

Lucretia. This study celebrates "a theater trying to find its role in the life of a growing, culturally intermixed, industrial center. It is also the story of a theater born too late." Notes, play list, and selective bibliography.

Morris, Clara. *Life on the Stage: My Personal Experiences and Recollections*. New York: McClure, Phillips & Co., 1902.
"Chapter First: I Am Born" begins this oddly self-absorbed, melodramatic telling of Morris' life and career (virtually no dates cited) as she learns "love, fear and hunger . . . and Alas! I Lose One of my Two Illusions." Soon, however, the autobiography becomes exciting: horses on stage cause trouble, "I Meet Wilkes Booth," "Contemptuous Words Arouse in Me a Dogged Determination to Become a Leading Woman Before Leaving Cleveland," and so forth. Great anecdotes told of Augustin Daly, Union Square, New York, Columbus, Ohio, and many other places in the dialogue style of Bulwer-Lytton. A detailed picture of a touring company theatre at the end of the nineteenth century.

Morris, Lloyd. *Curtain Time: The Story of the American Theater*. New York: Random House, 1953.
From George Frederick Cooke's memorial erected in 1821 to the death of Gertrude Lawrence in 1952, Morris commemorates and chronicles the progress of American theatre, from the shadow of English tradition to the emergence of its own Broadway style. Morris' "storytelling" approach is friendly but authoritative, and he plants a lively illustration on almost every page. The two-thousand-entry index could suggest considerable student scholarship on the subject.

Moses, Montrose J. *The Fabulous Forrest: The Record of an American Actor*. 1929. Reprint. New York: Benjamin Blom, 1969.
This is the fifth biography of the great American actor, who was "anxious for a published record of his career" and "anxious to be vindicated in print, though he assumed the attitude of wanting only the truth told about himself." A neutral motive is the justification for this work, which attempts to view Forrest's life "in relation to the backdrop of its national surroundings." Good for political and cultural details, and perceptive about why he was honored by but not invited into the inner circle of society. Bibliography and index.

_____. *Famous Actor-Families in America*. 1906. Reprint. New York: Benjamin Blom, 1968.
The Booths, the Jeffersons, the Sotherns, the Boucicaults, the Hacketts, the Drews and the Barrymores, the Wallacks, the Davenports, the Hollands, the Powers: a who's who of the artistic first families of American theatre, with about fifty portraits. Covers most of the nineteenth century. Theatre was a family business, the talented and ambitious master often thrusting greatness upon the reluctant apprentice, only to be outshone by the next generation. The book works

best when art imitates life: "Sothern's Dundreary was played to the Georgina of
his wife . . . Dundreary did most of the talking."

Moses, Montrose J., and John Mason Brown, eds. *The American Theatre as Seen
by its Critics: 1752-1934*. New York: W. W. Norton, 1934.
A collection with no critical apparatus save a brief introduction and a few
explanatory footnotes, this volume nevertheless stands on its own as an immediate
and straightforward appraisal of American theatre, one stage event at a time. The
strong rhetoric and rich expression of almost two centuries of firsthand theatrical
opinion, from "Criticus" through William Dunlap, Walt Whitman, William
Winter, Stark Young, and Burns Mantle, to Jack Conway. The editors do provide
a chronological table of contents and biographical sketches of cast and critics.

Murdoch, James E. *The Stage: Or, Recollections of Actors and Acting from an
Experience of Fifty Years*. Philadelphia: J. M. Stoddart, 1880. Reprint. New
York: Benjamin Blom, 1969.
After a full life on the stage, Murdoch retired to write these "recollections" of
his theatrical adventures in America and (as was necessarily the practice in the
nineteenth century) on the continent. Murdoch was not only a tragedian of some
merit but also a diarist who knew Kemble, Kean, Cooke, and many other
notables of early American theatre. From 1829 to 1879, he acted, lectured,
orated (keeping to patriotic themes throughout), and watched another generation
of actors take his place. He was an interesting writing stylist fascinated by
etymologies and wordplay. A good source of anecdotal recollections of mid-
nineteenth century American theatre. Particularly valuable in comparing and
contrasting the acting styles of famous English and American actors, and in the
brief sketches and reminiscences of actors, actresses, and managers of his time.
Index.

Nugent, J. C. *It's a Great Life*. New York: Dial Press, 1940.
"The mills in Niles, Ohio, shut down in '77, when Rutherford B. Hayes was
President. It seemed to us as though everybody was out of work except Mr.
Hayes." Nugent leaps in entertaining style from a childhood of poverty to a life
on the stage. In 1895, at age seventeen, he joined a touring company of *Woman
Against Woman*. There followed a colorful stage life and "talking picture" career,
even a stint on *Variety* as anecdotist (some of his columns appear in an appendix). Frustrating for the student because virtually no dates or other milestones
to his career are incorporated into the text, nor are they appended as a chronology. No index.

Odell, George C. D. *Annals of the New York Stage*. 15 vols. New York: Columbia
University Press, 1927.
"Amusements in the Colonies, particularly in New York, to 1750" begins this

comprehensive, thorough report on American theatre told in "annal" form—not exactly year by year, but with a definite chronological arrangement—the last entry is "Brooklyn and the suburbs," circa 1894. Often, as in volume 1 with the John Street Theatre, George Odell follows the progress of one theatre producing company or location and then retraces his steps, going back a few years. The illustrations—generally of playbills, broadsides, portraiture, journalistic cartoons, and similar historical resource material but later including photographs of actors and other celebrities—are sprinkled throughout the fifteen volumes. Full index after each volume. The essential source for theatre historians, considered authoritative even by subsequent revisers and correctors.

Overmyer, Grace. *America's First Hamlet*. New York: New York University Press, 1957.
John Howard Payne, actor, playwright, "minor poet, an original if unstable editor, a champion of the rights of the American Indian," first played Hamlet in the 1809-1810 season in Boston. Known variously as "the young Roscius" or "the American Roscius," he continued his career in London and returned to Boston and New York to act through the 1830's, dying in 1852. A good biography, slightly short on dates but with full notes, bibliography, index, and a few specimens of Payne's poetry.

Overstreet, Robert Lane. *The History of the Savannah Theater, 1865-1906*. Ann Arbor, Mich.: University Microfilms, 1976 (Ph.D. dissertation, Louisiana State University, 1970).
The Savannah Theater reopened after General William T. Sherman's capture of the city and remained at the center of theatrical activity until a fire in 1906 temporarily ended entertainment there. The history of the building itself reads like a history of professional acting—Joseph Jefferson, Edwin Booth, Edwin Forrest, and dozens of other famous actors made a point of stopping at Savannah; Oscar Wilde even lectured there. "It is probably safe to assert," says Overstreet, "that no Southern city of similar size had a more active theater." Bibliography, chronological list of attractions at the theatre, and selected cast lists.

Patrick, John Max. *Savannah's Pioneer Theater from Its Origins to 1810*. Athens: University of Georgia Press, 1953.
This beautiful almost-seaside town was a natural focus for cultured and refined Georgians in the late eighteenth and early nineteenth centuries. The best traveling companies (including French strolling players) went there with their productions. Theatrical criticism began in 1803, and drama "declined" in 1807—Patrick is much too gracious to make a connection. This short book is packed with interesting information; an indexed handlist of stage performances in Savannah from 1781 to 1810 is included.

Pinkston, Claude Alexander, Jr. *Richard Mansfield's Shakespearean Productions.*
Ann Arbor, Mich.: University Microfilms, 1982 (Ph.D. dissertation, University
of California at Los Angeles, 1980
As actor, manager, and "director" (the term was not used much at that time) for
about thirteen years at the turn of the twentieth century, Mansfield played Cyrano
de Bergerac during the "transition" to modern drama, and also restored Shakespearean authenticity to *Richard III*, *Merchant of Venice*, *Henry V*, and *Julius
Caesar*. This study offers a valuable discussion of the actor-manager function in
this period as well. Adds some information to William Winter's biography of
Mansfield; his promptbook to *Richard II* is appended.

Pollock, Thomas Clark. *The Philadelphia Theatre in the Eighteenth Century.*
Philadelphia: University of Pennsylvania Press, 1933.
Published primarily as a day book of the period with protracted introductory
theatre history summary, Pollock's record should have preceded Reese James's,
since it deals with the "Vivat Rex" period of theatre. Military historians will note
the record of "an interlude by military actors," British soldiers occupying
Philadelphia in the winter of 1777-1778, and "just outside the city the American
Army, quartered at Valley Forge, improvised a theatre and gave plays during
the spring of 1778." Details also of *Prince of Parthia*, reputedly the first American play to be done on American soil, April 1767. Play, player, and playwright
lists; general index.

Postlewait, Thomas, and Bruce A. McConachie, eds. *Interpreting the Theatrical
Past: Essays in the Historiography of Performance*. Iowa City: University of
Iowa Press, 1989.
Though not specifically related to American theatre history, this volume outlines
the many fruitful approaches to theatre history in general, justifies the discipline
as a pedagogical pursuit, and defends the methodologies of scholars who have
spent their careers preserving the theatrical heritage. Particularly valuable is
Postlewaite's own contribution, an essay on how to use autobiography as a
document of theatre history. A select but thorough bibliography of theatrical
historiography, and an index.

Quinn, Arthur Hobson. *A History of the American Drama*. 2 vols. New York:
Appleton-Century-Crofts, 1923. Rev. ed., 1936; 2d ed., 1943.
One of the first thorough studies of American theatre, concentrating on the
dramatic literature but covering stage practices, production methods, and scenography along the way. The first volume brings the study to the Civil War; the
second volume in the second edition updates to 1942 and contains the best
bibliography of critical work to that time.

Reignolds-Winslow, Catherine Mary. *Yesterdays with Actors*. Boston: Cupples and Hurd, 1887.
"A few trifling recollections that may be of some slight interest" to students of nineteenth century theatre and acting, especially the author's reactions to Charlotte Cushman, Edwin Forrest, John Brougham, Laura Keen, E. A. Sothern, and others. Chapters on the Boston Museum Theatre and photogravures and vignettes of about two dozen celebrities of the stage. The author's own stage efforts began with a small part in *Cinderella* in Chicago; specific dates not given.

Ritchey, Robert David. *A History of the Baltimore Stage in the Eighteenth Century*. Ann Arbor, Mich.: University Microfilms, 1976 (Ph.D. dissertation, Louisiana State University, 1971).
Working at Louisiana State University, Ritchey uses Thomas Clark Pollock's study, *The Philadelphia Theatre in the Eighteenth Century*, as a model, moving from John Milton's *Comus* (1772) through the rest of the century by means of playbills, newspaper advertisements and reviews, and occasional previously published material. Acknowledging his debt to similar studies of New York, Boston, Annapolis, and Charleston, Ritchey nevertheless adds considerably to what is known about "colonial theatre" in America. Exhaustive list of "every known author of plays and the titles of his plays produced in Baltimore" during this period; bibliography and a valuable player index.

Robbins, Phyllis. *Maude Adams: An Intimate Portrait*. New York: G. P. Putnam's Sons, 1956.
Miss Adams may have played alongside all the famous actors of the American stage during the Victorian and Edwardian eras as Chantecler, Joan of Arc, and Juliet, but it is as Peter Pan that she will always be remembered. Phyllis Robbins was a personal friend, and, after some small research into the first twenty-six years of Maude Adams's life, Robbins can rely on her personal remembrances. A warm, loving biography, with a section containing photographs (with one "hitherto unpublished photograph") that guarantees to win new admirers to this sweet-faced, marvelous actress. Play list of her appearances and an index.

Roman, Lisbeth Jane. *The Acting Style and Career of Junius Brutus Booth*. Ann Arbor, Mich.: University Microfilms, 1973 (Ph.D. dissertation, University of Illinois, 1968).
This study attempts to capture the elusive art of the actor, this time by examining seven major roles of Edwin Booth's less notorious but equally talented father Junius (1796-1852). "The facts must be retrieved from playbills, theatre records, diaries, letters and newspaper files," says Roman, who gives Junius back his place as "one of the foremost actors in America." Richard III, Iago, Shylock, and Hamlet, as well as Sir Giles Overreach in Philip Massinger's *A New Way to Pay Old Debts*, were "the elder Booth" Junius' stock in trade. Good for

observing the histrionic side of early nineteenth century acting styles. Bibliography and list of unpublished letters.

Ruggles, Eleanor. *Prince of Players: Edwin Booth*. New York: W. W. Norton, 1953.
Biographical styles of the mid-1950's tend to take the facts of previous biographies and novelize them into a more three-dimensional but more conjectural portrait. In this book, Ruggles turns Booth's theatrical life into a romance: "Don't you recognize him? It's Mr. Booth. Junius Brutus Booth. He's drunk again." "And the boy?" "That's his son Edwin." A good way to get into the mise-en-scène of the century's most famous actor, so long as the reader separates Ruggles' art from authentic biography. A section entitled "Notes on Sources" acknowledges Ruggles' debts to William Winter, Stanley Kimmel, Richard Lockridge, and Booth's daughter Edwina.

Russell, Charles Edward. *Julia Marlowe: Her Life and Art*. New York: D. Appleton, 1927.
The beautiful actress who played every important Shakespeare role in the early twentieth century but did not succeed in "new theatre" roles to the same degree is lovingly portrayed here. Full portraits of Julia, in many roles and at different times in her career, are scattered throughout this biography. Her gentle style as actor-manager was very effective; she would "waft an actor aside and pour into the porches of his ears the ideas she wished to have portrayed." Valuable study for the reader who wants to compare the "old" style with the new. Index.

Samples, Gordon. *Lust for Fame: The Stage Career of John Wilkes Booth*. Jefferson, N.C.: McFarland & Company, 1982.
Before he earned his place in history books, Wilkes (as biographers call him, to distinguish him from other members of this illustrious acting family) aspired to a stage career. Always in the shadow of his famous father, Edwin, and sometimes marked by an incivility of attitude that disenchanted producers, fellow actors, and audiences, Wilkes could also charm. As Richard III, he toured from Boston to New Orleans in search of stage fame. This study finds Wilkes to be a magnetic, "unforgettable" presence on stage, acting with "the fire, the abandon, the unpredictable staging" of his father. Bibliography, chronology, and cast lists.

Sampson, Henry T. *The Ghost Walks: A Chronological History of Blacks in Show Business, 1865-1910*. Metuchen, N.J.: Scarecrow Press, 1988.
Stepping back from his earlier study of the minstrel show/musical of the twentieth century, Sampson chronicles (in true chronicle style, event by event) the gradual progress, from the Civil War to the eve of World War I, of "a small number of black entertainers, who, having emerged from slavery, illiterate and handicapped by racial prejudice and discrimination, produced a brand of popular entertainment

which, by 1900, was enjoyed by audiences throughout the United States and abroad." Invaluable scholarship, rare photographs and broadsides, thorough index. A fascinating document in every respect.

Schultz, Jacqueline Ann. *The Life and Career of Frederick Belasco (1862-1920).* Ann Arbor, Mich.: University Microfilms, 1982 (Master's thesis, California State University at Long Beach, 1980).
This master's thesis discusses the contributions of a theatrical manager of the early twentieth century who should not be mistaken for his more famous brother David. A San Francisco theatre, the Alcazar (rebuilt three times), was the home of Belasco's management; later, the Belasco theatre in Los Angeles was named after the family. A good example of how West Coast theatre emulated New York models while adjusting for California cultural tastes, offering "a mixed bag of unique and varied components." Bibliography and some photographs of theatre building exteriors.

Seilhamer, George O. *History of the American Theatre.* 3 vols. 1888-1891. Reprint. New York: Benjamin Blom, 1968.
Much more expansive and detailed than earlier histories, correcting "the errors of the past" and adding new material culled from anecdotal and autobiographical accounts of stage managers, actors, and actresses. Seilhamer transforms this subjective and unreliable material into legitimate scholarship, publishing as well many of his own sources, such as cast lists, advertisements, and legal announcements of all kinds. Norman Philbrick provides an appreciative and informative introduction. Index after each volume.

Shattuck, Charles H. *The Hamlet of Edwin Booth.* Urbana: University of Illinois Press, 1969.
This is as close as words can get to describing every detail of an actor's performance—every gesture, every motivation, every facial nuance. Centers on Booth's 1870 version of the character and offers full documentation to support its claims. A landmark in performance documentation and historical reconstruction of the ephemeral Dionysian art. Index.

Shaw, Dale. *Titans of the American Stage: Edwin Forrest, the Booths, theO'Neills.* Philadelphia: Westminster Press, 1971.
Shaw surveys several American stage eccentrics, justifying their "unfortunate tendencies" such as madness, megalomania, drug addiction, womanizing, and obsession with fame by referring to their "prodigious work, and . . . true talent." A good introduction to both the accomplishments and the lost battles against the "temptations and weaknesses that daily bring ordinary people to complete destruction" of these great figures. Illustrated with some of the more famous poses; index and brief bibliography.

Shockley, Martin Staples. *The Richmond Stage: 1784-1812*. Charlottesville: University Press of Virginia, 1977.
Season by season and professional touring company by company, Shockley's organized and accurate chronicle of early Virginia theatre is presented with no prefatory remarks or introductory statement. Two valuable appendices, one listing acting companies by seasons and one describing "the theatre that was not built," B. Henry Latrobe's proposed but unrealized Richmond theatre-hotel complex. Notes; indexes of names and titles.

Simond, Ike. *Old Slack's Reminiscence and Pocket History of the Colored Profession from 1865 to 1891*. Bowling Green, Ohio: Popular Press, 1974.
A reprint, saved from deterioration by the careful attention of Francis Lee Utley in 1973, of a late nineteenth century pamphlet by a banjo comique, Ike Simond. "Filled with valuable data, drawn from Simond's own experiences as a black minstrel and from his having seen many other black entertainers." Utley adds introductory comments, remarking that Simond reported "the facts as he knew them purged of the very subjective perspectives and judgments now in such great demand," and an index to all references, as well as a chronology of black minstrelsy in the period.

Skinner, Otis. *Footlights and Spotlights: Recollections of My Life on the Stage*. New York: Blue Ribbon Books (Bobbs-Merrill), 1924.
Beginning in an East Hartford hall as "the favorite elocutionist and impersonator," Skinner found a life in the theatre for fifty years. He pauses momentarily some nine years before retirement to remember the good times and the bad. Along with the details of performances and the requisite theatre anecdotes, Skinner proposes some theories of acting that he, in his modest way, sought to practice in Augustin Daly's company and elsewhere. By his own inventory: "Three hundred and twenty-five parts; have appeared in sixteen plays of William Shakespeare, acting therein, at various times, thirty-eight parts, and I have produced under my own direction thirty-three plays."

Smith, Sol. *Theatrical Management in the West and South for Thirty Years*. New York: Harper & Brothers, 1868.
An autobiographical account, "interspersed with anecdotical sketches," by a retired actor-manager who traveled through a dozen states with companies of "country theatricals" in the middle of the nineteenth century. How some sixteen roles are played by eight actors, the methods by which a strolling company can gather an audience, the sharing system of profits versus salaries, and other secrets of the theatre of hard knocks are told in amusing style. Good on William Chapman's Floating Theatre (which he sold to Smith in 1847), Noah Ludlow (Smith's partner since 1835), and dozens of other early enterprises. An appendix of every anecdote he could not fit into the text, and a drawing of the tombstone he would

like to have when the time comes: "Exit Sol." For a saner view, see William
Scott Craig.

Smither, Nelle. *A History of the English Theatre in New Orleans.* 1944. Reprint.
New York: Benjamin Blom, 1967.
  In an unusual approach to regional theatre history, this study demonstrates how
  English (language) theatre found its audience in the highly sophisticated, even
  "European," city of New Orleans, from before 1818 to "an end of an era" in
  1842. A major figure in the history is James H. Caldwell, who, after managing
  several Virginia theatres, brought a troupe to New Orleans in 1820 and stayed.
  The most famous of the buildings, the St. Charles Theatre, figured prominently
  in the larger success of culture in general. Play, player, and playwright lists,
  standardized for theatre histories of this type and this period.

Sollers, John Ford. *The Theatrical Career of John T. Ford.* Ann Arbor, Mich.:
University Microfilms, 1983 (Ph.D. dissertation, Stanford University, 1962).
  Ford, the author's grandfather and owner of the famous Ford Theatre where
  Lincoln was shot, organized the stages of pre- and post-Civil War Baltimore and
  other parts South and North as a manager of touring companies. He took charge
  of such famous actors as Joseph Jefferson and Lotta Crabtree. Coming from a
  journalism background and succeeding far beyond other managers of the era,
  Ford once claimed, in the 1877-1878 season, to have "131 speaking actors" on
  his payroll. Discussed mainly as a businessman and against a larger background
  of Baltimore expansion during the reconstruction era. Chronology and bibliography in appendices.

Specimens of Show Printing, Being Fac-similes in Miniature of Poster Cuts. Philadelphia, 1869-1872. Reprint. Hollywood: Cherokee Books, n.d.
  This is actually an advertising catalog that offered posters to theatre managers
  who were engaged in the lucrative enterprise of presenting melodramas during
  the nineteenth century. Managers could order posters from this catalog (prices
  quoted per hundred), which has accidentally (compare with Sears catalogs as a
  source for costumers) become an outstanding source of scholarly material
  regarding the subjects and range of melodrama during this period. A one-page
  anonymous explanation of the catalog's existence and a one-page explanation of
  ordering procedures by J. H. Alexander (the company's manager) are followed
  by about three hundred reproductions of posters illustrating the most amazing
  period of American theatre history.

Spritz, Kenneth. *Theatrical Evolution: 1776-1976.* Yonkers, N.Y.: Hudson River
Museum, 1976.
  A catalog of American theatre material containing reproductions of hundreds of
  theatre documents, exhibited at the Hudson River Museum in 1976. Many

previously unreproduced production stills, sketches, and portraits (even a theatrical playing-card deck) from otherwise inaccessible collections, showing the progress of American theatre through its transition from European influence to its current identity. The text argues well for the uniqueness of American theatre, but the value of the book lies in the hundreds of stunning visual documents tracing that history. Unfortunately, all the photographs are black and white, there is no index, and the binding has failed after only fifteen years.

Stebbins, Emma. *Charlotte Cushman: Her Letters and Memories of Her Life.* Boston: Houghton, Osgood, 1878. Reprint. New York: Benjamin Blom, 1972. Claiming to be merely the editor, Stebbins turns her friendship with the famous actress into a full-length portrait not only of Cushman but also of the American theatre and theatrical life from 1816 to the publication of this book (Cushman died in 1876). Among the biographical details are analyses, as far as she can go, of Cushman's acting style. As is true of many nineteenth century biographies, the writing style often gets in the way of factual information; the work is nevertheless valuable for a summary of the conditions of working actors during this period.

Taubman, Howard. *The Making of the American Theatre.* New York: Coward-McCann, 1965. Rev. 1967. Almost a biography of American theatre, this book focuses on the forces that drove the theatre from childhood through adolescence to youth and (someday) maturity. "The events and forces that have gone into the making of American theatre must be viewed from two different points of view: in the light of what they meant, said and did for their contemporaries, and in the perspective of centuries of world theatre history." Devotes ten chapters to the period up to 1900, then moves about a half-decade per step, pausing occasionally for a closer look at Eugene O'Neill, musicals, and the rise of off-Broadway, among other things. Good reading, with Taubman's critical viewpoint for the most part held patiently in the background. A personalized memoir of the history, focusing on Taubman's own favorites. Both the critic's eye and the journalist's are called into play; the best discussions, such as those on Dion Boucicault and early "realism," reconstruct historical events using modern, present-tense rhetoric. Brief chapters, roughly chronological, assume a familiarity with the subject. Index and three groups of illustrations.

Toll, Robert C. *Blacking Up: The Minstrel Show in Nineteenth-Century America.* New York: Oxford University Press, 1974. A response to the demand of middle-class America for a "popular culture," the minstrel show followed the invention of Natty Bumppo, Davy Crockett, Yankee, Brother Jonathan, and Mike Fink, combining "the folk-based themes and lore of other forms with Barnum's flair for promotion and [adding] a compelling new figure—the black man." A sociological study and cultural essay as well as a history, dividing the minstrel form in two at the Civil War. Good chronological list of black minstrel troupes, 1885-1890, in appendix. Strong bibliography; index.

_____. *On with the Show: The First Century of Show Business in America.* New York: Oxford University Press, 1976.
The term *show business* implies the more spectacular, presentational types of entertainment, such as the circus, extravaganzas, and vaudeville stages, rather than literary and story-based dramas. Claiming to be only "the first word" on its subjects, the book celebrates the energy and flamboyance of America's early stage personality (roughly the nineteenth century). Strong on "girlie shows" and female impersonators, less satisfying on "negroes" and blackface in show business. Plenty of illustrations; a bibliographical essay and a strong comparative chronology (between society and show business); index.

Tompkins, Eugene. *The History of the Boston Theatre: 1854-1901.* 1908. Reprint. New York: Benjamin Blom, 1969.
Tompkins was "manager" of this illustrious theatre for the last twenty-three years of this history and was in a good position to supply not only the details of production but also the photographs and illustrations that accompany it, which come from a lifelong collection begun by his father. Includes a delightful photograph of Loie Fuller almost flying, in the 1891-1892 season. No stylist, Tompkins simply lists the season's accomplishments in paragraph form, eschewing the lively anecdote; a long, detailed index acts as a "who's who" of Boston theatre life.

Toscan, Richard Eric. *The Organization and Operation of the Federal Street Theatre from 1793-1806.* Ann Arbor, Mich.: University Microfilms, 1975 (Ph.D. dissertation, University of Illinois at Urbana-Champaign, 1970).
This study of the old Boston Theatre from 1793 to 1806 takes as its focus the management, organization, and operation of the theatre. It reaches past typical historical sources such as playbills and newspaper accounts to find lessons for future managers in invoices, treasurers' reports, and inventories. The single essential source for this study was "the detailed minutes of the meetings of the Boston Theatre proprietary, now in the holdings of the Boston Public Library." If the history of a theatre is in its box office, this study succeeds.

Towse, John Ranken. *Sixty Years of the Theater: An Old Critic's Memories.* New York: Funk & Wagnalls, 1916.
The value of such memoirs rests with the perspicacity and humility of the writer. In this book, the dramatic critic for forty-three years of the *New York Evening Post*, succumbing to the temptation of disorder and subjective selection, manages

to offer insights while lamenting the decline of theatre since the great days of William Charles Macready, Edwin Forrest, and others. This work may contain material not touched on in more thorough studies, but it is not likely. Interesting photographs, many arranged in triptychs.

Turner, Mary M. *Forgotten Leading Ladies of the American Theatre: Lives of Eight Female Players, Playwrights, Directors, Managers and Activists of the Eighteenth, Nineteenth and Early Twentieth Centuries.* Jefferson, N.C.: McFarland & Company, 1990.
No 140-page book can do justice to this subject, but Turner presents some preliminary areas of inquiry for further study in this essay on women as forces for change in the theatre and in the world. The two activists discussed—Minnie Maddern Fiske and Mrs. Fanny Kemble—particularly deserve deeper study, but so do Charlotte Cushman, Mrs. John Drew, Laura Keene, Anna Cora Mowatt, Susanna Haswell Rowson, and Sophia Turner. A good start for future critical work. Notes, index, bibliography.

Unterbrink, Mary. *Funny Women: American Comediennes, 1860-1985.* Jefferson, N.C.: McFarland & Company, 1987.
A much-needed overview of feminine humor on the American stage, from Lotta Crabtree (who, at eight, "made her debut entertaining saloon patrons in Rabbit Creek, California"), Marie Dressler, and Mabel Normand, through television's best—Imogene Coca and Mary Tyler Moore—to "rising stars" Whoopi Goldberg (risen by the time the book was published; Gilda Radner's death is not noted here either) and the High-Heeled Women troupe of four "vibrant" comediennes. Add a roll in the aisle with Moms Mabley, Phyllis Diller, and Totie Fields, and this book becomes a celebration of positive energy in the women's movement. There is a funny side to militant feminism and a deadly serious side to these talented entertainers. Not enough photographs. Good index and reference section. Highly recommended.

Vernon, Grenville, comp. *Yankee Doodle-Doo: A Collection of Songs of the Early American Stage.* New York: Payson & Clarke, 1927. Reprint. Detroit: Singing Tree Press, 1973.
The introduction and notes supplied by Vernon, along with melody lines and lyrics to some fifty stage songs written and performed before the Civil War, make this quite a historical resource. "Those who believe in the progressive improvement of the American theatre will not be edified by a comparison of the songs of the forties and fifties with those of an earlier date . . . the lyric stage was in the doldrums." Bright, brief biographical comments introduce each cluster of songs; some illustrations. "My love is like a raging hot volcano,/Vesuvius in a fit of indigestion."

Wade, Jere Dueffort. *The San Francisco Stage, 1859-1869*. Ann Arbor, Mich.: University Microfilms, 1978 (Ph.D. dissertation, University of Oregon, 1972). Filling in the decade between the Gold Rush "frontier theatre" and the coming of professional commercial "big-business" theatre of the young Belasco and his managerial style, this study covers the pre- and post-Civil War years. This was a period in which "the city began to shift from its position as a principal doorway, supplier, and clearing house for the gold rush pioneers, to that of a major commercial and financial center." Good discussion of the Metropolitan and Opera House competition, in which *The Black Crook* and its pirated version, *The Black Rook*, vied for audiences. Bibliography.

Watermeier, Daniel J. *Between Actor and Critic: Selected Letters of Edwin Booth and William Winter*. Princeton, N.J.: Princeton University Press, 1971.
Some three to four hundred letters passed between Edwin Booth and William Winter from 1869 to 1890 (augmented here with Winter's notes up to 1893). The letters are selected and arranged by periods, promptbooks, and European tours, including the last great performances of the Booth-Barrett tour, 1886-1890. The letters outline a professional friendship while demonstrating how the theatre worked in this period. A valuable list of birth and death dates for all persons mentioned, and a selected bibliography and index.

Watson, Margaret G. *Silver Theatre: Amusements of the Mining Frontier in Early Nevada 1850 to 1864*. Glendale, Calif.: Arthur H. Clark, 1964.
A marvelously constructed and entertaining review of the zany frontier theatre told in anecdotal form and arranged by year. From "Tarantula Juice" to "The Thirty-Sixth Gun," chapters describe in outrageous detail what can only be called the Dionysian search for wealth in the unlikely foothills of a desert stumbling toward statehood. Although such staples as *Ticket-of-Leave Man, Dick Turpin*, and *Blackeyed Susan* were the advertised entertainment, often the best show was in the audience. Bibliography (which does not include the Ericson dissertation) and exhaustive index.

Webb, Dorothy Louis Beck. *The Early History of the Arch Street Theatre, 1828-1834*. Ann Arbor, Mich.: University Microfilms, 1976 (Ph.D. dissertation, Indiana University, 1970).
This Philadelphia playhouse went through four managements and management styles during its first few years before becoming part of a theatrical monopoly. Webb analyzes the social and economic conditions that brought this theatre into being as well as the management styles of its early years. A calendar of plays and afterpieces presented there is appended.

Wemyss, Francis C. *Chronology of the American Stage, from 1752-1852*. 1852. Reprint. New York: Benjamin Blom, 1968.

After valuable lists of "all" managers, "all" theatres, the "names of the officers of His Majesty George the Third's Army, who acted as amateurs . . . when the regular Players were forced to retire to the West Indies, during the War of the Revolution" (including "Lieutenant Pennefeather, who acted many of the female parts"), the first company of comedians, and so forth, this marvelous, information-packed book becomes a brief biography of actors and actresses of the period. Occasional fascinating sidelights, such as the entry on "Riots": Wemyss lists six, the last being the famous Astor Place riot of 1849, to which he affixes sixteen "facts" of the case, very authoritatively and exhaustively discussed. Be sure to check the appendix of entries "received too late for insertion in their proper place." Another appendix lists "theatres in the United States, which have been destroyed by fire, and when."

Willis, Eola. *The Charleston Stage in the XVIII Century with Social Settings of the Time.* 1924. Reprint. New York: Benjamin Blom, 1968.
Like all regional theatre histories, this one claims that its value lies in the as-yet-unrecorded contributions of a particular community—in this case, Charleston, South Carolina—to theatre history in general. The American prologues of Mr. David Douglass' American Company of Comedians, for example, are "brought to light." Indeed, the illustrations and cast lists alone are valuable for southern theatre historians; subsequent studies of this nature cite Willis' work extensively. Index.

Wilson, Francis. *Francis Wilson's Life of Himself.* Boston: Houghton Mifflin, 1924.
Born in 1854 to a New Jersey Quaker family, Wilson forsook his pious beginnings for a life on the stage as a circus character, blackface minstrel (the team of Macklin and Wilson), wandering player, "Variety" performer, and "utility man" at the Chestnut Street Theatre in Philadelphia in 1877. Throughout his life, as he rubbed elbows with theatre (and nontheatre) greats, Wilson brought his sensitivity, love of learning, and liberal-mindedness to his notebooks, from which this autobiography grew. Illustrated with dozens of wonderful portraits. A strong subject index transforms the book into a theatre history reference of particular value.

Wilson, Garff B. *A History of American Acting.* Bloomington: Indiana University Press, 1966.
Often lost in the light of famous personality actors, and frozen in still portraits, the art of acting is difficult to chronicle and characterize. Wilson finds several "schools" in early American acting styles: the Heroic, the Classic (ladies and gentlemen), Emotionalism, Personality, and the Comic. The study does not stop with the invention of the camera; one of the best chapters deals with early movie acting styles. A valuable study combining discerning observation of sparse evidence with a broad understanding of the mise-en-scène of early theatre. About

forty illustrations, mostly formal portraits and portrait photographs of famous actors in classic poses. Index.

_____. *Three Hundred Years of American Drama and Theatre*. Englewood Cliffs, N.J.: Prentice-Hall, 1973.
A basic, organized, readable educational text with the subtitle "From *Ye Bear and Ye Cubb* to *Hair*." Credits William Dunlap with transforming playwriting into an American profession; charts New York's gradual control of theatre from 1800 to 1850; addresses the "renaissance" of 1900-1920, which was encouraged by European developments; and refers to theatre developments in the 1960's as "the phoenix in flames." Bibliography and index; about one hundred typical illustrations scattered throughout the text.

Wilstach, Paul. *Richard Mansfield: The Man and the Actor*. 1908. Reprint. Freeport, N.Y.: Books for Libraries Press, 1970.
That this book was reprinted demonstrates its importance to students of American theatre history, especially the "transitional" period. Mansfield, by excelling in Shakespearean roles (and managing companies of Shakespeare tourers) and at the same time acknowledging—even promoting—"the new theatre" of Henrik Ibsen, George Bernard Shaw, and other Europeans, ensured his place in the annals of the stage. Touching and informative chapter on Mansfield's relationship with his son Gibbs; they played imaginary improvisational games together, a clear example of Mansfield's basically imaginative spirit. Valuable bibliography of early scholarship on Mansfield; many entries out of print and rare.

Winter, William. *Ada Rehan: A Study*. 1891. Reprint. New York: Benjamin Blom, 1969.
This study of Rehan's acting style is useful because, according to Winter's preface to the second edition, "no dramatic artist of our time is more popular, and few performers of any period have served the dramatic art with such resolute zeal and such self-sacrificing devotion." In the Shakespearean roles of Viola, Beatrice, and Julia, but especially in unusual parts such as Pierrot, Rehan entertained from 1873 to well past Winter's second edition in 1898 (she migrated to London for several seasons). Good illustrations. Rehan's love of bulldogs is depicted in several photographs, one of which was taken beside Lord Byron's monument to his own dog. An adulatory but descriptive study of Rehan's acting style.

_____. *Life and Art of Edwin Booth*. New York: Macmillan, 1893. Reprint. New York: Benjamin Blom, 1972.
Winter and Booth were friends as well as professional rivals (Winter reviewed much of Booth's stage work for the *New York Tribune*). This critical review of his work builds on an earlier (1872) essay examining twelve major characters

in Booth's repertory but adds biographical material. Still considered the definitive biography of Booth, especially when supplemented with the collected letters, which Winter mentions only briefly. Poetic and epistolary memorials are added in an appendix.

_____. *Life and Art of Joseph Jefferson.* New York: Macmillan, 1894.
This study of Joseph Jefferson III, who, when it was written, was giving lectures at universities and had been elected president of The Players, succeeding Edwin Booth, is offered "together with some account of his ancestry and of the Jefferson family of actors," a task Winter took up in earnest some thirteen years earlier. Winter makes several conjectural side trips, notably regarding the infamous Bacon versus Shakespeare controversy, as he moves easily through the biography. Index.

_____. *The Jeffersons.* 1881. Reprint. New York: Benjamin Blom, 1969.
The stage Jeffersons, who have to be numbered like monarchs, had their start in England during the Garrick period. This book ends with Joseph Jefferson III's career in full swing. Winter, a critic and supporter of new theatre, covers the entire dynasty, at the same time offering an overview of American theatre itself; the Chestnut Street Theatre (1792-1820), for example, although rebuilt, was, like Jefferson, "ill almost one third of the time . . . in the season of 1823-24." Good for getting the dynasty straight and for following the fortunes of the family through early American theatre history. Index follows a good concluding chapter summarizing the family's accomplishments.

_____. *The Wallet of Time.* 1913. Reprint. Freeport, New York: Books for Libraries Press, 1969.
Winter brought European drama, especially Henrik Ibsen, to America at the turn of the century. He offers biographical essays, "personal, biographical, and critical reminiscence of the American theatre," as a sort of requiem to the era preceding Winter's own modern times. A strong encyclopedic source in two volumes, not unlike Arthur Hobson Quinn's history of the American stage, but organized around performers. Many photographs and portraits. Volumes are separately indexed; essays on Ibsenites and on American actors abroad are included in appendices.

Withers, Nan Wyatt. *The Acting Style and Career of John Wilkes Booth.* Ann Arbor, Mich.: University Microfilms, 1982 (Ph.D. dissertation, University of Wisconsin at Madison, 1979).
As "an actor in the nineteenth century," Wilkes may come closer to the norm than did his illustrious father. In this study of his style during his fairly short career (1838-1865), he takes on some of the attributes of a James Dean: "He was adored by women in his audiences as well as by professional actresses." An

interesting annotated chronology of his career and a list of roles he played; four portraits; bibliography.

Wolcott, John Rutherford. *English Influences on American Staging Practice: A Case Study of the Chestnut Street Theatre, Philadelphia, 1794-1820.* Ann Arbor, Mich.: University Microfilms, 1973 (Ph.D. dissertation, Ohio State University, 1967).
Microfilmed in two volumes, this study concentrates on a single stage house over a sixteen-year period. Examines how British designers gradually influenced and then bowed to American stage practices, which were innovative and "pioneering" in their freshness but relied on English models for their essential design. Architectural details of the Chestnut by English architect John Inigo Richards make Wolcott's point: The square shape of many American theatres differs from the "semi-circular or elliptical seating arrangement of contemporary English theatres." The Chestnut "reigned as the undisputed queen of American theatres" but burned in 1820. Volume 2 gives many interesting facts about scene-painting practices. Recommended for theatre design students.

Woll, Allen. *Black Musical Theatre: From "Coontown" to "Dreamgirls."* Baton Rouge: Louisiana Stage University Press, 1989.
Corrects the notion that Eubie Blake was the first African-American composer, conductor, and producer through a thorough and readable reexamination of African Americans in musical theatre from about 1855 to the 1980's. Compares "white critics'" opinions with actualities, discusses the financial rewards of African-American musicals before and after the Crash of 1929, and credits Arena Theatre in Washington, D.C., with the development of the musical version of *Raisin in the Sun.* Good on financial figures and the impact of African-American theatre on the box office. Bibliography, index, some photographs (mostly stills).

Woods, Alan Lambert. *The Interaction of Los Angeles Theater and Society Between 1895 and 1906: A Case Study.* Ann Arbor, Mich.: University Microfilms, 1978 (Ph.D. dissertation, University of Southern California, 1972).
Part historical sociology, part theatre history, this two-volume study concentrates on how the permanent stock companies were received by a volatile and various Los Angeles *fin-de-siècle* society. That the theatre "was responsive not to specifically local conditions but to increasingly homogeneous national trends" forms Woods's thesis. He makes the point that "the living theater successfully functioned in America as a mass entertainment medium" only during these Syndicate days. Second volume is a Los Angeles Theater Day Book appendix.

Woollcott, Alexander. *Mrs. Fiske: Her Views on the Stage.* 1917. Reprint. New York: Benjamin Blom, 1968.
"I was at supper with Hedda and Tess and Becky Sharp . . . that erect figure,

vital, alert, indefatigable, eloquently animate," says Woollcott of his friend and colleague, Minnie Maddern Fiske. He describes her reservations about the idea of repertory, Granville-Barker's "new theater" innovation. This book provides several conversations of that type, revised by Woollcott in the remembering but true to the independent and discerning theatrical sense of this star, who, from 1870 through 1916 (where the book stops), graced the stage with her charm. Good biographical sketch as a final chapter.

Yeater, James Willis. *Charlotte Cushman, American Actress*. Ann Arbor, Mich.: University Microfilms, 1973 (Ph.D. dissertation, University of Illinois, 1959). After a biographical background, Charlotte Cushman is studied as an actress of many talents whose career began around 1836 and continued for many years in Shakespearean and non-Shakespearean roles (a major division in this critical examination of her acting style). She "retired" around 1852, but several farewell engagements followed (including a "sensational" appearance at Booth's Theatre in 1871), all the way up to her last appearance on the stage (Boston, 1875). Bibliography and appendix of appearances.

Young, William C. *Famous American Playhouses, 1716-1899*. Documents of American Theater History 1. Chicago: American Library Association, 1973. An encyclopedic double-columned edition, with copious illustrations, of Young's comprehensive and possibly exhaustive survey of theatre architecture in America. The physical structure of early American theatre is the focus of the first volume of this central source for American theatre history. A well-illustrated and conveniently organized (but not by city) compendium of American theatre's "bricks and mortar." Young's text is augmented with contemporary descriptions and opinions; the buildings' major managerial occupants are sketched as well. The series "is intended as a basic reference tool for librarians, scholars, students, and others interested in the American theater." Volume 2 covers architecture up to 1971 (see chapter 2). Name, geographical, and subject indexes.

Zacek, Dennis Cyril. *The Acting Techniques of Edwin Booth*. Ann Arbor, Mich.: University Microfilms, 1976 (Ph.D. dissertation, Northwestern University, 1970). Examines not only the acting technique of the nineteenth century's most famous American actor but also the generally accepted stage presentational style of all the "stars" of the era. Zacek separates by chapter the major Shakespearean roles, after providing an opening section on art versus nature, "the vigorous myth," and defining and describing melancholia. Draws heavily on contemporary reviews, especially William Winter. Notes after each chapter; bibliography.

1914 TO 1945

Abbott, George. *"Mister Abbott."* New York: Random House, 1963.
An autobiography filled with inside information on the workings of Broadway from 1913 to 1962. Valuable for Abbott's candid observations regarding homosexuality in the theatre and the hard-heartedness of theatre people in defense against being overcome by sympathy for one another's plight. As actor, director, producer, and "play doctor," Abbott saw the whole range of show business. He exposes it, along with his own imperfections, in readable style.

Aherne, Brian. *A Proper Job.* Boston: Houghton Mifflin, 1969.
British import Aherne made his New York debut as Robert Browning in *The Barretts of Wimpole Street* in 1931. He sets down in almost novelistic form his life in the theatre as part of his debt to American audiences for taking him into their arms. This reminiscence takes the reader up to his Broadway performance as Bernard Shaw in *Dear Liar*, but many "Yanks" saw him as Henry Higgins in the national company of *My Fair Lady* in the 1957-1958 season. His motto: "Per Ardua Surgo—Through Adversity I Rise." Brief curriculum vitae but no index. Good source for the flavor of the acting profession from the point of view of one who was not a superstar.

Allen, Fred. *Much Ado About Me.* Boston: Little, Brown, 1956.
From the modest title of this funnyman's biography to the last anecdotal pun ("I said good-by to June in January"), the story of Fred Allen's vaudeville days is told with wit and warmth. By concentrating on his earlier days rather than the radio personality that developed after a stage vaudeville career had declined, Allen gives readers a glimpse of theatre history from the inside. One chapter, "The Life and Death of Vaudeville," which the author inserts as a small obituary to vaudeville, is particularly insightful regarding the forces that moved theatre past this period into the next, soberer, decade: "For fifty years—from 1875 to 1925—vaudeville was the popular entertainment of the masses." Epilogue on Allen's death; index, and small photograph section.

Appelbaum, Stanley, and James Camner, eds. *Stars of the American Musical Theatre In Historic Photographs.* Mineola, N.Y.: Dover, 1981.
Contains 361 more or less formal portraits, from 1860 to 1950, of the beauties and beaus of the musical theatre stage. Captions provide basic biographical information tied to the celebrity's most famous roles and genres. Good for separating the stage work from the strictly musical work of some artists, such as Kate Smith (in *Honeymoon Lane* in 1926 and *Flying High* in 1930) and Buddy Ebsen, who danced in *Whoopee* in 1928. Real names, surnames, and married

names provided, and some information on radio, television, and film work. Index by photograph.

Atkinson, Brooks. *Broadway*. New York: Macmillan, 1970.
A very readable history of the professional New York theatre (not "the long thoroughfare," he assures the reader), broken into roughly twenty-year sections from 1900 to 1950. Atkinson's friendly coffee-table style is evident throughout; he was "there" even when he was not, and no one else would get away with the simple title. A comfortable, pleasantly organized way to absorb the history of this period. A postscript for the 1950-1970 period remarks: "Broadway is artistically and technically proficient, but no longer creative." Heavily illustrated; good index.

_____. *Broadway Scrapbook*. New York: Theatre Arts, 1947.
A very selective collection of Atkinson's "Sabbath encyclicals," Sunday *Times* articles, illustrated by Hirschfeld, covering the period 1935 to 1947. "What readers want is news of a good play. . . . Most of the articles salvaged for this book stand in praise of plays or actors or both." Perceptive about the current theatre and knowledgeable about the past, he takes time to compare and contrast the two as he moves easily from Broadway hit to classical background. Index.

Atkinson, Brooks, and Albert Hirschfeld. *The Lively Years: 1920-1973*. New York: Association Press, 1973.
This overview of Broadway theatre by one of its more responsible critics addresses many of the elements of theatrical history but concentrates on the playwright and the play. The Hirschfeld drawings are mostly new for this book, not reprints. Atkinson sees considerable dignity in much of the writing of the time, but he laments the more recent absence of hope for change: "A quality of hatred has crept into the plays about contemporary America. They despise contemporary America and they do not expect to change it." Index.

Baral, Robert. *Revue: The Great Broadway Period*. New York: Fleet Press, 1962.
Gone the way of minstrels, burlesques, and showboats, the revue featured "beauty, trust, glamour, soft-focus photography, simulated and then for-real nudity," according to Robert Landry's introduction to this *Variety*-style celebration of the revue form. Largely a picture book of beauties, and leaning heavily on the accomplishments of Flo Ziegfeld, it is a source of information for the Follies, The Passing Show at Winter Garden, the Greenwich Village Follies, George White's Scandals, Music Box Revues, and similar between-the-wars serial extravaganzas. Chronology in appendix; index.

Barrymore, Ethel. *Memories: An Autobiography*. New York: Harper, 1955. Reprint. Kraus Reprint, 1968.

A generously illustrated and gracefully expressed self-portrait by a true lady of the theatre who retired from the stage and film to write for fans and posterity alike. Excellent document for following the fortunes of the Barrymores from the feminine perspective, not always, despite her own talent, out of the shadow of John himself. Anecdotes about President Theodore Roosevelt and Somerset Maugham, and a marvelous portrait of Miss Barrymore as a nun in *The Kingdom of God*, opening the Ethel Barrymore Theatre in 1928. Index.

Barrymore, John. *Confessions of an Actor*. London: Robert Holden, 1926.

"Oh, my poor kids, what will ever become of them?" Barrymore's mother was said to have uttered on her deathbed. This autobiography "confesses" that one of them at least did fine, posing as Beau Brummell or Richard III from some thirty-three illustrations. Barrymore had made the transition from stage to film by this time, and he spends much time remembering the highlights of his stage career. Valuable as a document of changing autobiographical style. Bidding farewell to the reader, Barrymore ponders how to get a love interest into the film version of *Moby Dick*.

Barton, Lucy. *Historic Costume for the Stage*. Boston: Walter H. Baker, 1938.

Not exactly American theatre history, except that it informed the next three or four generations of American costume designers, especially academics, and became the single most reliable (and therefore much imitated) source of what the world looked like for the past three thousand years. Each chapter begins with a brief overview of the era—the "new century" of 1900-1915 featured dance crazes and armament accumulation—before describing men's and women's clothing habits. Valuable illustrations and a postscript on costume (as opposed to real clothing) construction. Index, strong bibliography.

Beckerman, Bernard, and Howard Siegman, eds. *On Stage: Selected Theater Reviews from "The New York Times" 1920-1970*. New York: Arno, 1973.

Taken from the multivolume collection of *Times* reviews. By carefully choosing plays that have subsequently become part of American theatre history (*Waiting for Lefty*, Orson Welles's *Macbeth*, *The Connection*), and combining those selections with the best of European and British imports, this collection serves as a first look at what has become theatre history. Full cast and designer credits, with a strong discussion of the first impressions of these plays, seen by such authoritative critics as Brooks Atkinson and Alexander Woollcott. Author and title indexes.

Bentley, Joanne. *Hallie Flanagan: A Life in the American Theatre*. New York: Alfred A. Knopf, 1988.

This comprehensive biography of the Federal Theatre's guiding genius uses old sources but corrects them as it fills in and comments with fresh insight. Flanagan's early start in writing short stories as well as for the theatre is particularly well covered here. "I want five regional theatres, each taking on the color of the region. That is my present dream," she wrote, and she got her wish fifty years later. Index, and good notes referring directly to specific pieces of information. Recommended reading—read this perhaps even before reading Flanagan's *Arena: The History of the Federal Theatre.*

Berg, Aubrey. *Collaborators: Arthur Hopkins, Robert Edmond Jones, and the Barrymores.* Ann Arbor, Mich.: University Microfilms, 1982 (Ph.D. dissertation, University of Illinois at Urbana-Champaign, 1979).
The years 1918-1923 saw an "uncluttering" of the American stage by means of a significant collaboration among producer-director, designer, and acting family. The inception, process, and results of this unique recipe for theatrical success are documented in surprisingly readable form, especially considering the absence of any extant promptbooks. Appendices include a chart of collaborations and production data. Bibliography.

Bernardi, Jack. *My Father, the Actor.* New York: W. W. Norton, 1971.
Jack and his famous brother Herschel had a not-so-famous but much-loved father, Berel, who played the Jewish theatre circuit during the first half of the century. He is lovingly remembered by young Jack, not by brother Herschel, "because I really don't [remember]. He was, at best, a hazy image" in the nine-year-old's mind, "sometimes a cough . . . a few times a grunt of pain; finally his death, which I remember very clearly." This biography fills a void for both brothers and submits to historians a deliciously detailed backstage vision of Jewish theatre during the period, cast with family members, "also actors, managers, relatives, neighbors, landlords, roaches, and rats." A few photographs, including a cast portrait from the Yiddish play *King Solomon* in Chicago in 1915.

Blum, Daniel. *Great Stars of the American Stage: A Pictorial Record.* New York: Greenberg, 1952.
A good source for publicity photographs and head shots of the famous and once-famous from the American stage, from Lillian Russell to Sarah Bernhardt (though French, Bernhardt made her American debut in 1880) to Charles Nolte (who was the best Billy Budd) to Joan McCracken. Brief bios circled by production stills, baby pictures, kitsch and curls, with full-page portraits of each star in his or her prime. An enjoyable reminder of the fleeting nature of fame: Joseph Santley, Mary Nash, Judith Evelyn. Also Marlon Brando, Lynne Fontanne, and Uta Hagen.

Bolin, John Seelye. *Samuel Hume: Artist and Exponent of American Art Theatre.* Ann Arbor, Mich.: University Microfilms, 1976 (Ph.D. dissertation, University of Michigan, 1970).
From 1885 to 1962, Hume's career carried over from the nineteenth century into the New Stagecraft and Art Theatre of the early twentieth century, and into the first serious academic theatre experimentation. Hume trained with Gordon Craig and George Pierce Baker and helped to set up the New Stagecraft Exhibition in 1914. He designed the "permanent set" that served as many as eleven different plays for the Arts and Crafts Theatre in 1917. "Ideally representative of a non-commercial theatre educator and Art Theatre director and designer," Hume (Bolin argues) should be more prominently placed in American theatre history texts.

Bordman, Gerald. *American Musical Comedy: From "Adonis" to "Dreamgirls."* New York: Oxford University Press, 1982.
The second work in Bordman's trilogy (operetta and revues are the subjects of the other entries) on American musical theatre, this short but informative study starts with the great burlesques, moving through Harrigan and Hart, the jazz era, up to *A Chorus Line*: "One can only wonder if something is not lacking" in current directors, lyricists, etc. First appendix lists "important" musical comedies with principals and credits; second appendix is the text of William Gill's *Adonis* (1884). Index.

_____. *American Musical Revue: From "The Passing Show" to "Sugar Babies."* New York: Oxford University Press, 1985.
"A brief look at what made revues develop, what made them tick, and, eventually, what caused them to die away." This study completes a trilogy, the others on operetta and musical comedy. Chapters on *The Passing Show*, Ziegfeld (misspelled in table of contents), the changes in the 1940's, and "What's Past Is Epilogue." Appendix is a selective list of revues; index.

Brenman-Gibson, Margaret. *Clifford Odets, American Playwright: The Years from 1906 to 1940.* New York: Atheneum, 1982.
A biography taking Odets's life through his successes with the Group Theatre, up to its disintegration and the failure of *Night Music*. Deeply psychological in its approach, the biography nevertheless provides information on theatre practices, especially the Group Theatre, during this period; for example, a good discussion of Harold Clurman. Best as theatre history when starting with the expanded index/digest; personal chronology, list of works, notes and comments, selected bibliography.

Bricker, Herschel L., ed. *Our Theatre Today: A Composite Handbook on the Art, Craft, and Management of the Contemporary Theatre.* New York: Samuel French, 1936.

By describing and discussing "theatre today" in the present tense of 1936, these thirteen practitioners provide valuable historical documentation of the attitudes and posturings of their time. No better documents of directing styles, for example, could be found for this pivotal period in American theatre history than the three chapters, all titled "My Method of Directing," by Melville Burke, Bertram Harrison, and Priestly Morrison. Finding this "how-to" collection of theatrical "rules" is like finding a medieval manual of monastic behavior—pontifical, self-righteous, admonishing and bolstered by unquestioned faith. "As long as our present economic system governs the theatre . . . any play which does not yield an appreciable profit must be withdrawn." Bibliography, index, and a valuable appendix of technical photographs and graphs, especially in lighting.

Bronner, Edwin J. *The Encyclopedia of the American Theatre: 1900-1975*. New York: A. S. Barnes, 1980.
Providing much information at the sacrifice of some style yet easily consulted, this straightforward reference covers Broadway and off-Broadway plays written by American or Anglo-American playwrights. Arranged alphabetically by play title, but supplemented with every kind of appendix: Theatre Calendar of Notable Premieres, actors' and playwrights' debuts, longest-running productions, statistical records, awards, and a massive index of every proper name. Sine qua non.

Brown, Jared. *The Fabulous Lunts: A Biography of Alfred Lunt and Lynn Fontanne*. New York: Atheneum, 1986.
An authoritative and profession study of the famous pair of dramatic actors, who held the stage (usually together) for almost four decades. Culled from hundreds of interviews of those who knew them well, this book covers the material neutrally but respectfully. The Lunts had not encouraged a biography, but after their deaths (he in 1977, she in 1983) Brown completed his long and thorough work; it will not have to be done again soon. Full notes and index.

Brown, John Mason. *Two on the Aisle: Ten Years of the American Theatre in Performance*. New York: W. W. Norton, 1938.
"Tallulah Bankhead barged down the Nile last night as Cleopatra—and sank." Mincing no words, and taking little time to digest the evening's fare, Brown covers the years of American theatre from 1928 to 1938 with candor and energy. Rearranged somewhat arbitrarily by topic ("Old Wine in New Bottles," "America Speaks," and so forth) and lacking some of the journalistic factual identification that helps the reader through the event, this collection serves admirably as an articulate and witty theatregoer's immediate response to, for example, the Theatre Guild's presentations, mid-career O'Neill, burlesque's dubious contributions (in the section entitled "For the Tired Business Man and Woman"), and subjective evaluations of fellow critics, notably Brooks Atkinson. Index.

_____. *Upstage: The American Theatre in Performance*. New York: W. W. Norton, 1930. Reprint. Port Washington, N.Y.: Kennikat Press, 1969. Remarkably modern in its approach, this study concentrates on the performance elements that generated, sometimes independent of experimental plays and playwrights, a new idea in the theatre. Especially insightful about acting styles, a part of performance difficult to describe and chronicle. Brown comes down hard on the managers of old, who demanded celebrities rather than true actors and thus fostered much of what was wrong, until the modern actor caught up with the universal trend toward honest artistic expression. A well-written, convincing admonishment from the master.

_____. *The Worlds of Robert E. Sherwood: Mirror to His Times, 1896-1939*. New York: Harper & Row, 1965. An almost sociological account of the life and times of the author of *Idiot's Delight* and *The Petrified Forest*. Readable and informative about the theatre of the time, and the sense of cynical helplessness the artist felt toward the problems of the country: "Although [Sherwood] participated happily in the fun [the Twenties] offered and enjoyed their frivolities, he was appalled by their excesses." Good descriptions of production events, relations with other theatre people, and more. Index.

Bryer, Jackson R., ed. *"The Theatre We Worked For": The Letters of Eugene O'Neill to Kenneth Macgowan*. New Haven, Conn.: Yale University Press, 1982. Some 164 letters (mostly O'Neill's) between "America's greatest playwright and an important director-producer-dramatic critic who shared his ideals and hopes for a truly 'new' and exciting American theatre." They came to know each other in 1921, seven years after Macgowan's seminal treatise, "The Theatre of Today," was published, and at the beginning of O'Neill's great work. For thirty years they shared ideas by correspondence. Good insights into O'Neill's working habits. Index.

Burke, Billie. *With a Feather on My Nose*. East Norwalk, Conn.: Appleton-Century-Crofts, 1948. The theatre career of Billie Burke (Mrs. Florenz Ziegfeld, Jr., for eighteen years), the "skitter-witted" lady of comedy, both on stage and screen, is chronicled in a pleasant autobiographical style. Named for her clown father, Billie found out early that her voice would not sustain an operatic career but discovered that her comic propensities could carry her far. From starring in her husband's Follies around World War I to her happiest role as a real grandmother (1948) of three children, "by all possible odds the finest Ziegfeld productions yet." Appendix of roles, and index.

Buttitta, Tony, and Barry Witham. *Uncle Sam Presents: A Memoir of the Federal Theatre, 1935-1939*. Philadelphia: University of Pennsylvania Press, 1982.

Sprinkled with wonderful drawings by Don Freeman, this warm-hearted reminiscence by a reporter for *The Federal Theatre Magazine* augments Hallie Flanagan's *Arena*, giving the humorous and whimsical side of the story. Personal day-to-day experiences, such as learning to "eat like a New Yorker" in the automat, give Buttitta's account a liveliness and honesty that both reduces the lofty project to human size and gives it a dignity beyond the bureaucracy that engendered it. Index and brief bibliography.

Cargill, Oscar, N. Bryllion Fagin, and William J. Fisher., eds. *O'Neill and His Plays: Four Decades of Criticism*. New York: New York University Press, 1961.
Indispensable collection of theatre reviews and dramatic criticism from now-famous reviewers, beginning with his own letter of application to George Pierce Baker's playwriting class at Harvard in 1914, and moving from Haywood Broun's review of *Bound East for Cardiff* to Joseph Wood Krutch's 1957 book review of *A Touch of the Poet*. Puts O'Neill's contributions into their contemporary theatrical contexts, by arranging critical observations in chronological order. Several of O'Neill's own "offstage" observations are included in the text, as well as extensive informational apparatus, including exhaustive alphabetical checklist of O'Neill's works, strong bibliography of O'Neill scholarship, and index.

Carson, William G. B. *Dear Josephine: The Theatrical Career of Josephine Hull*. Norman: University of Oklahoma Press, 1963.
You may not recognize the name, but her face is very familiar: Radcliffe graduate Josephine (Sherwood) went on to marry Shelley Hull and to star in *Arsenic and Old Lace* (on stage and in the film), *You Can't Take It With You*, and many other theatrical staples. "Josephine Hull is the nearest thing to a human plum pudding there is" was how she was described in her 1953 appearance in *The Solid Gold Cadillac*. Someone else said she had "the body of an old coal barge and the face of an ugly English pug." Show business. Bibliography and index.

Carter, Jean, and Jess Ogdon. *Everyman's Drama: A Study of the Noncommercial Theatre in the United States*. New York: American Association for Adult Education, 1938.
This pamphlet, part of a longer study "in the social significance of adult education in the United States," is audience oriented. A typical inquiry is: "Are participants primarily interested in the local theatre or dramatics group as a means to professional training, or are they seeking to express an avocational interest?" A chapter entitled "On Being an Audience" tries to list the reasons for going to the theatre, dividing them roughly between "emphasis on sociability" and "an intellectual as well as emotional reaction." Good short early study of audience psychology, especially in the regions and on the noncommercial level.

Carter, Randolph. *The World of Flo Ziegfeld*. New York: Praeger, 1974.
A stunning pictorial review of Ziegfeld with hundreds of photographs, many of Joseph Urban's designs for the Follies in full color. Born in 1868, "amply endowed with daring, daring bordering on the reckless, imagination, charm (when he cared to exert it), talent and an ability to head straight for a goal even by uncharted paths," Ziegfeld built an empire on his opinion that American girls were beautiful. The Ziegfeld Follies held the New York stage spellbound from 1907 (the 1915 Follies is considered by many to be the best) to the Crash (actually 1931); Hollywood welcomed him then. A good introduction to what all the excitement was about. Chronology and bibliography.

Charters, Ann. *Nobody: The Story of Bert Williams*. New York: Macmillan, 1970.
Readers may not know him by name, but that is because "Negro comedian Bert Williams" was "neatly trapped by the prejudice and intolerance of his times"—the vaudeville years from 1892 to 1922. He is known and loved for his theme song, however: Williams was the Ziegfeld Follies staple who, starting in 1905, sang "Who soothes my thumpin', bumpin' brain? Nobody." An all-too-brief look at his career, his still outrageously funny comic routines, and the world in which he learned to be "somebody." Many illustrations, musical scores of his hits, and index. Required reading for the flavor of vaudeville and how this great comedian smiled through a life "full of clouds and rain." Index, and discography (with list of cylinder records) of Williams' voice.

Cheney, Sheldon. *The Open-Air Theatre*. New York: Mitchell Kennerley, 1918. Reprint. Millwood, N.Y.: Kraus, 1971.
This book is interesting for the American applications of the theories it presents, including Vassar College, the Bohemian Grove in California, the University of Wisconsin theatre on Lake Mendota, College of the City of New York Stadium, Los Angeles Greek theatre, Macomb Nature theatre, Pomona Greek Theatre, Bar Harbor Nature Theatre, and dozens of others. A good early study acknowledging the contributions of Gordon Craig and Granville Barker. Excellent drawings and photographs of outdoor theatre architecture and its benefits to simple staging.

Churchill, Allen. *The Theatrical 20's*. New York: McGraw-Hill, 1975.
"We all have a girl friend and her name is Nostalgia," says Ernest Hemingway. Churchill remembers her birthday year by year in this pictorial revue of the decade of the flapper silhouette, the Follies, and the Marx Brothers. Rushed, often one-sentence sketches of the best (by which is meant flashiest, craziest, most outrageous) and worst. Each chapter ends with a "roundup," with play titles in boldface for quick reference. While the discussion is flippant and superficial in many respects, so was the age, and the student reader can get an accurate overview of a zany period in these pages. Brief bibliography; index.

Clurman, Harold. *The Fervent Years: The Story of the Group Theatre and the Thirties*. New York: Hill & Wang, 1957.

The definitive apology for the American theatre movement of the 1930's that brought such luminaries as Elia Kazan, Cheryl Crawford, Lee Strasberg, and Clifford Odets into stage history. Clurman updated this work from its first (1945) publication, revising at the same time some of his views regarding the public's response to this volatile and innovative theatre group from which all subsequent American theatre grew. Balances fact and opinion to offer the best portrait of the creative energies of the times. Index.

Conolly, L. W., ed. *Theatrical Touring and Founding in North America*. Westport, Conn.: Greenwood Press, 1982.

Contributions in Drama and Theatre Studies, Number 5. Though this collection is heavily weighted with Canadian studies (the conference was held in Toronto), several of these essays deal with touring histories in American cities as well, including a California tour in 1902-1903, and the formation of the Group Theatre. The theme of the papers is the transition of touring from a commercial to an artistic (that is, not-for-profit) enterprise. The editor provides a bibliographic survey of relevant material and an all-article index.

Cooper, Paul Reubin. *Eva Le Gallienne's Civic Repertory Theatre*. Ann Arbor, Mich.: University Microfilms, 1972 (Ph.D. dissertation, University of Illinois, 1967).

Among her many stage accomplishments, Miss Le Gallienne began the Civic Repertory Theatre in 1926 on the premise that "the great dramatic classics ought to be made available to the people, easily and permanently, and that a low priced, classical repertory theatre was the best means of doing this." Her own company was established in New York; other cities (Detroit, Indianapolis, Portland) also tried their versions. Cooper seeks to do for the Civic what Harold Clurman did for the Group Theatre in *The Fervent Years*: "to clarify the ideals out of which the Civic sprang, to define its aims, to describe and to evaluate its achievements." Drawing from Miss Le Gallienne's own prompt scripts, interviews with up to fourteen participants in the experiment, and other sources, Cooper follows the few seasons the Civic survived (the Depression finally closed it). Notes and bibliography and an appendix of the Civic Repertory record.

Courtney, Marguerite. *Laurette*. New York: Atheneum House, 1968. Reprint. Limelight Editions, 1984.

In his introduction to the life of Laurette Taylor, Brooks Atkinson says, "For her two decades of glory in the theatre led to that awful period when she touched the lowest depths of misery and helplessness—the luminous stage star fading into the darkness and torment of a sick woman." Taylor, an actress of the highest caliber during and following World War II (though her career blossomed in 1912), succumbed to alcoholism in her later years. Her daughter tells the story in intimate detail, sparing no reader the ordeal, yet honoring her mother in this tribute to what she once was, the quintessential Amanda in Tennessee Williams' *Glass Menagerie* (1945). Index.

Crawford, Cheryl. *One Naked Individual: My Fifty Years in the Theatre.* Indianapolis: Bobbs-Merrill, 1977.
With Harold Clurman and Lee Strasberg, Crawford founded the Group Theatre, the most creative force in 1930's American theatre. But her own life was much larger; she produced and directed scores of productions on and off Broadway, as part of several companies and independently. Two photograph sections divide her life into Group and non-Group productions and underscore her deep friendship with other artists such as Kurt Weill and Tennessee Williams. The title, taken from a misunderstanding of the Pledge of Allegiance, seemed to encapsulate Crawford's philosophy of the theatre artist. Chronology of "productions" (not separated by director or producer) and an index.

Crowley, Alice Lewisohn. *The Neighborhood Playhouse: Leaves from a Theatre Scrapbook.* New York: Theatre Arts, 1959.
"Memories . . . in no way thought of as an historical record" of the Neighborhood Playhouse. In 1915, the European experimental theatre came to New York and presented amateur, scaled-down versions of *Jephthah's Daughter*, *Petrouchka*, and other classic fare. Crowley was an early student of the Neighborhood's grand dame Sarah Cowell Le Moyne, working on Browning monologues. She remembers the hunger for artistic food, the feasts, the famines. Chronology, bibliography, index.

Davis, Owen. *My First Fifty Years in the Theatre.* Boston: Walter H. Baker, 1950.
Subtitled "The Plays, the Players, the Theatrical Managers and the Theatre itself as one man saw them in the fifty years between 1897 and 1947," this diarylike recollection of events is more name-dropping and afterthought than pure chronology. Davis was a modestly successful playwright (he won the Pulitzer Prize for *Icebound* in 1923) and first president of Dramatists Guild, but an immodestly fervent admirer of all things theatrical. His folksy style is best captured in his promise to write "My First One Hundred Years in the Theatre" in 1997. No critical apparatus.

Dressler, Marie. *My Own Story.* Boston: Little, Brown, 1934.
This autobiography, as told to Mildred Harrington, demonstrates how the energy and pure goodwill of the star came across on stage and screen over a fifty-year career that straddled the American popular entertainment revolution from stage to film. Good description as well of the formation of the American Woman's Association, for women in business and the professions, which Dressler founded

with her friend Anne Morgan. Dressler tells her story in humble but delightfully frank terms, revealing much about how the theatre worked at the same time and her love of it.

Eaton, Walter Prichard. *Plays and Players: Leaves from a Critic's Scrapbook.* Cincinnati: Steward & Kidd, 1916.
In some respects a continuation of his 1910 defense of "the New Theatre," this collection concentrates on dramatic criticism, first of American plays, then of foreign plays and Shakespearean revivals on the American stage. Because Eaton's interests lie in the survival of American theatre, these reviews are production oriented, especially when, as in his review of Granville Barker's *Androcles and the Lion* (1915), the "New Stage Craft" drives the production. Index.

_____. *The Theatre Guild: The First Ten Years.* 1929. Reprint. Freeport, N.Y.: Books for Libraries Press, 1970.
The administrative directors of the Theatre Guild—Theresa Helburn, Philip Moeller, Maurice Wertheim, Helen Westley, Lee Simonson, and Lawrence Langner—describe and discuss the achievements of the first decade, joined "by some 'spire of meaning'. . . some intellectual appeal, which makes their success the more surprising, and gives, of course to the Guild its chief banner of leadership." Eaton says it was begun "for the creation, as carefully and lovingly as lies within one's power, of the best drama of one's time, drama honestly reflecting the author's vision of life or sense of style and beauty." Full cast lists for subscription productions appended. The first source for study of the Guild.

Evans, Dina Rees. *Cain Park Theatre: The Halcyon Years.* Cleveland: Halcyon Printing, 1980.
"Halcyon" is not a word that springs to the lips to describe any theatre's history, but Evans argues (in the words of Sydney H. Spayde, a participant) that "In Cleveland Heights we taught each other every day that our work was the work of playing." Begun as a WPA project in 1934, and strolling through the war years to its eventual decline around 1950 (with numerous revivals through 1980), Cain Park Theatre was Dina "Doc" Evans's teaching tool: professional actors performing summer stock with local amateurs for high school audiences, and everyone else was invited. An appreciation.

Ewen, David. *Complete Book of the American Musical Theater.* Rev. New York: Henry Holt, 1959.
Starting from the quite valid premise that the musical is America's unique contribution to theatre history, Ewen offers here "a guide to more than 300 productions of the American musical theater." Starting with *The Black Crook* (1866) to the (1959) present, he lists plots, production histories, stars, songs, and more. The odd organizational principle—writers/producers/composers alphabeti-

cally—makes this collection valuable for students of creative voices during the period discussed, but see updated edition below. Two photograph sections.

_____. *New Complete Book of the American Musical Theater*. New York: Holt, Rinehart and Winston, 1970.
In addition to updating his earlier work, Ewen reorganizes the information into "a more functional, less cumbersome format" offering "a panorama of musical productions since 1866 to the present time [1970] alphabetically, the way an encyclopedia would." He then follows with biographies of composers, librettists, and lyricists. Discusses some five hundred musicals, with "more information about production history, plot, the stars, the songs." More comprehensive than the 1959 version but not as convenient for research by artist's name. Index and several photograph sections.

Farnsworth, Marjorie. *The Ziegfeld Follies*. New York: G. P. Putnam's Sons, 1956.
Billie Burke Ziegfeld provides the foreword to this fully illustrated overview of the Follies, from 1907 to 1931. The thrust of the book is the female stars and the human beings behind the candelabra headdresses; a "gallery of the glorified" is appended and gives the tone of the whole study. Beneath the text's rhetoric is a kind of resentment that so uncultured a man could become so famous exploiting whole generations of beautiful women. Index.

Flanagan, Hallie. *Arena: The History of the Federal Theatre*. New York: Duell, Sloan and Pearce, 1940. Reprint. New York: Benjamin Blom, 1965.
The classic description of the Federal Theatre Project, told by the dynamic woman who headed it until its sudden demise in 1939. "Danger: Men Not Working" describes the conditions for the formation of the FTP; "Men at Work," the most valuable section for American theatre historians, chronicles by geographic region the progress of the movement; "Blasting: Work Suspended" hurries through a rather complicated political history that resulted in the cutting off of the funding. A production record and financial statement are supplied in the appendix; bibliography selects "the most informative" of thousands of press exposures; index.

Fowler, Gene. *Good Night, Sweet Prince*. New York: Viking Press, 1944.
The official biography of John Barrymore by a personal friend who was there at his death in 1942. The tone of the book, in fact the entire editorial slant, is adulatory—"John Barrymore's favorite lines from Shakespeare," "John Barrymore's favorite photograph of himself," etc.—as though his life were a romance he acted out. Fowler's claims for a modest Barrymore ("It was so unlike Jack to be conceited about anything.") ring hollow. But this is also a portrait of a grand American theatre. Index and photographs.

France, Richard. *The Theatre of Orson Welles*. Cranbury, N.J.: Associated University Presses, 1977.

Welles may be best known for a radio play (*War of the Worlds*) and a movie (*Citizen Kane*), but both grew from his Mercury Theatre work and the plays he directed from 1931 to 1938. France discusses Welles as a man of the theatre, describing the mental processes that led to his aesthetic decisions in equally famous dramatic productions such as the "voodoo" *Macbeth*, *The Cradle Will Rock*, and *Danton's Death*. A bit short for the scope of the project, but informative and well written, this study includes many (unlisted) illustrations, notes, production lists, bibliography, and index.

Freedley, George. *The Lunts*. New York: Macmillan, 1958.

Number 10 in the Theatre World Monograph series, this is a small "appreciation" of Alfred Lunt and Lynn Fontanne, more than half photographs of production stills and portraits. Together, the Lunts toured the United States in dozens of "vehicle" plays such as Howard Lindsay and Russel Crouse's *The Great Sebastians*. The careers of Mr. and Mrs. Lunt are listed separately in appendices covering the years 1905 to 1957. A good introduction to the definitive couple of drawing-room drama in the twentieth century.

Frohman, Daniel. *Daniel Frohman Presents: An Autobiography*. New York: Lee Furman, 1935.

Briefly covering a wide range of theatrical experiences, this celebrity autobiography uses a theatrical metaphor throughout ("I made my first appearance on this stage of life" on August 22, 1851). Journalist, entrepreneur, real estate venturer, brother of the more famous Charles Frohman (the power behind the Syndicate), Daniel moved in theatrical circles without influencing them by his own personality. Chapters such as "Peeps at People" demonstrate Frohman's love of, but never full acceptance by, the world of theatre. Index and a marvelous gallery of photographic portraits, from Fannie Hurst to William Lyon Phelps. A companion piece, *Encore*, followed in 1937.

_____. *Encore*. New York: Lee Furman, 1937.

An "encore" to Frohman's first book of memoirs, *Daniel Frohman Presents*. Combining personal recollections with theatre gossip and historical reminiscences, Frohman treats American theatre (and British, in the later chapters) like a great party he threw, or at least helped to arrange. No discernible organizational principle gets in the way of Frohman's "rambles in anecdotia," not confined to theatrical events. Sepia illustrations of portraits and poses; bibliography and index.

Gargan, William. *Why Me? An Autobiography*. Garden City, N.Y.: Doubleday, 1969.

Gargan was a steady support actor on Broadway and in the movies (*The Bells of St. Mary's*) for thirty years, until throat cancer ended his career. This story, besides a warm-hearted and positive look at disability, is the saga of one-nighters, special friendships with critics (kinder than their legends), and the traveling shows of World War II, entertaining the troops behind (in theory) the front lines. Finally, a crusade for cancer research, but told between bottles of scotch.

Goldstein, Malcolm. *George S. Kaufman: His Life, His Theatre.* New York: Oxford University Press, 1979.
A much more scholarly and somehow less satisfying biography than Howard Teichmann's *George S. Kaufman: An Intimate Portrait*, this study offers details of Kaufman's life without clearly delineating the theatrical world where he thrived. The coauthor (with Moss Hart) of *The Man Who Came to Dinner* (1939) and the director of *Guys and Dolls* (1950) appears, in Goldstein's portrait, without his wit and charm. Notes and index, but no chronology.

Gottfried, Martin. *Jed Harris: The Curse of Genius.* Boston: Little, Brown, 1984.
"The golden boy of our theater's golden age," as Dick Cavett introduced him (taped just before Harris' death in obscurity in November, 1979), was a very talented theatrical producer and director who "invented Broadway" and presented all its great actors from 1925 to 1955. He was also the least-liked man in theatre, leaving behind a trail of hatred that included even Henry Fonda. This is a juicy, detailed, unglamorous way to see backstage Broadway, and a good balancer for other more antiseptic versions. Unfortunately, no critical apparatus, except an index.

Green, Stanley. *The Great Clowns of Broadway.* New York: Oxford University Press, 1984.
The short step from burlesque to legitimate theatre was first taken by the "clowns" of Broadway, whose broadly farcical styles fit comfortably into the plots of Broadway's early modern comedies. Included are Fanny Brice, Jimmy Durante, W. C. Fields, Bert Lahr, Ed Wynn, and a handful of others in brief, chapter-long biographical sketches and accompanying production photographs. A good introduction to each performer, with an index, and a valuable list of stage credits (lyricists, producers, cast, lengths of runs, and so forth) for the productions in which these comedians found their way to audiences' funnybones.

Hagen, Uta. *Sources: A Memoir.* New York: Performing Arts Journal Publications, 1983.
Dedicated to her granddaughter, this memoir of America's best-known acting coach (*Respect for Acting*) remembers the source of her training techniques, drawn from gardening metaphors and from her mother's words: "Breathe deeply, look hard, listen well. Touch gently. Taste all. Embrace, help, be thankful. And

when you *feel*, express it." More personal than professional remembrances, but good for tracing her progress through some great roles. Part 3 is most helpful theatrically, with details of the Le Gallienne company. Some personal photographs and a few production stills.

Hammond, Percy. *This Atom in the Audience*. New York: John C. Hammond, 1940.
Privately printed collection of reviews and comments originally appearing in the *Chicago Tribune* and the *New York Herald Tribune* from 1912 to 1933. A modest man and a witty writer, Hammond saw the theatre through the eyes of an iconoclast without choler. "In the capacity of quasi-adviser to the hesitant playgoer," Hammond offers opinions dipped in gentle humor, adroitly turned phrase, and quiet understanding of the way the theatre works. Part 2 contains random "vagrant" vignettes and often touching personal observations, sometimes about theatre. No critical apparatus.

Hardy, Michael Carrington. *The Theatre Art of Richard Boleslavsky*. Ann Arbor, Mich.: University Microfilms, 1977 (Ph.D. dissertation, University of Michigan, 1971).
The Russian contribution to modern American theatre may have begun with Chekhov and Stanislavsky, but Stanislavsky's student Boleslavsky, the founder of the First Studio, was to have virtually equal influence in this country. From the 1922 production of *Revue Russe* under Boleslavsky's direction, through his management of the American Laboratory Theatre, his gifts to American acting were legion, including his filming of *Les Miserables*. Good bibliography to continue the study of the Russian/American theatrical alliance.

Harris, Jed. *Watchman, What of the Night?* Garden City, N.Y.: Doubleday, 1963.
A late autobiography of sorts, titularly written by Harris but, according to Martin Gottfried, loosely dictated to a secretary who "cleaned it up." After learning of what others thought of this producer/director of Broadway, 1925-1955, it is interesting to read how he justifies his malice and plain mendacity: "What I read in the reviews seemed to bear no relationship to anything I had done." It is a sad comment on his entire life. A must-read for students of Broadway's golden age, but only along with soberer opinions such as Gottfried's.

Harrison, Gilbert A. *The Enthusiast: A Life of Thornton Wilder*. New York: Ticknor & Fields, 1983.
In passing through the personal details of Wilder's life, Harrison gives us glimpses of his relation to Alexander Woollcott, Gertrude Stein, Max Reinhardt, Lillian Gish, and dozens of other theatre lights of his era. Much information on the writing, casting, production, and criticism of *Our Town* and *Skin of Our Teeth*; central photograph section, mostly candid shots of Wilder and friends. Index.

Hayes, Helen. *On Reflection: An Autobiography.* New York: M. Evans, 1968.
A gracefully descriptive reminiscence by the "first lady of the (American) theater" that discusses her friendships with Alexander Woollcott, Robert Benchley, F. Scott Fitzgerald, Victor Mature, and many others. Written "with" Sanford Dody, the book combines backstage anecdotes with her ongoing struggle for spiritual faith. Virtually devoid of specific dates; no apparatus.

Henderson, Archibald, ed. *Pioneering a People's Theatre.* Chapel Hill: University of North Carolina Press, 1945.
At the height of World War II, during the sesquicentennial of the university, North Carolina put out this paean to The Carolina Playmakers, in part as a memorial to Frederick Henry Koch, its founder. The Playmakers had just completed its one-hundredth presentation (*A Winter's Tale*, 1944) and had established itself as a model for other noncommercial ventures throughout the United States. The history of the company, which was based on Koch's belief "that if the locality were interpreted faithfully, it might show us the way to the universal," is recorded here.

Higham, Charles. *Ziegfeld.* Chicago: Henry Regnery, 1972.
Ziegfeld's first discovery, in London, was Anna Held, and with his partner Charles Evans he spent a lifetime discovering and presenting stage beauties on both continents. Ziegfeld was garish, "utterly devoid of intellect," a womanizer of the first order, a theatre genius, his "personality" was often abrasive, and he was always ambitiously business-directed and occasionally gracious. This biography sorts out the highs and lows. Photograph section concentrates on cheesecake, portraits, and office candids, with some production stills.

Hild, Stephen Glenn. *United States Patents Pertaining to Theatre, 1916-1945.* Ann Arbor, Mich.: University Microfilms, 1973.
An index to all patents of the period linked recognizably to a specific theatrical application. Very valuable for studying the progress of, for example, the mechanics of moving stage scenes, the development of light-projecting techniques, or the invention and refinement of drum revolves, hydraulic lifts, light grids, circuit boards, and similar theatre "hardware." During this period, theatre moved toward representation but at the same time paid attention to special effects, eventually coming around to expressionistic theatre once again. The opening, "background" chapter succinctly summarizes the points of contact between theatrical innovation and American ingenuity in general. Drawings and specifications for selected inventions.

Hill, Charles R. *Brock Pemberton: Broadway Producer.* Emporia: Kansas State College, 1975.
A monograph (from Dr. Hill's dissertation) on one of the more successful

producers of dramas between the world wars. From 1920 to 1950, he was Broadway's "gentleman" producer of such standards as *Harvey* (1944) and *Strictly Dishonorable* (1929), but scoring only about a 40 percent success rate, according to Hill. A short but informative overview of Pemberton's career, with bibliography.

Hill, Errol, ed. *The Theater of Black Americans*. Vol. 1 in *Roots and Rituals*. Englewood Cliffs, N.J.: Prentice-Hall, 1980.
A collection of critical essays, some on drama rather than theatre, presented as part of the Twentieth Century Views series. Part 1 is particularly useful as the history of the transformation of African-American theatre from ritual enactments to artificial performance—or, as Kimberly W. Benston puts it in one essay, "from mimesis to methexis." The editor defines the theme in the introductory essay: drama is conflict, and African-American drama is the struggle for identity in a hostile, sometimes hopeless, environment.

Himelstein, Morgan Y. *Drama Was a Weapon: The Left-Wing Theatre in New York 1929-1941*. New Brunswick, N.J.: Rutgers University Press, 1963.
According to a substantial foreword by theatre anthologist John Gassner, the book's thesis is that "the communist movement of the nineteen-thirties endeavored, but failed, to win control of the American theatre." The title is actually a slogan of the Communist party, used to rally actors and audiences around a collective notion of public art as agitation propaganda. This study, a bit of anticommunist propaganda itself, nevertheless organizes the evidence supporting Gassner's conclusions about this important period in American theatre history. Scholarly but very readable; production stills, notes, bibliography, index.

Hinkel, Cecil Ellsworth. *An Analysis and Evaluation of the 47 Workshop of George Pierce Baker*. Ann Arbor, Mich.: University Microfilms, 1972 (Ph.D. dissertation, Ohio State University, 1959).
In two volumes (to 1919, and beyond into the Yale years), this analysis of Baker's methods and the structure of the classroom experience itself serves as a solidly informative document for examining to what degree the 47 Workshop actually formed (rather than simply discovered) the talents of its participants. It is also, however, a study of how American theatre worked on the experimental and educational level between the wars. According to Hinkel, "no person in America . . . had a richer background in theatre than did George Pierce Baker when he assumed the role of director of the now world famous 47 Workshop." A final chapter evaluates the workshop. Full critical apparatus.

Hinsdell, Oliver. *Making the Little Theater Pay*. New York: Samuel French, 1925.
"A practical handbook" not only for producing plays on an amateur basis but also for showing a modest profit. With no-nonsense enthusiasm for the practical,

beginning with a belief in the value of the product, Hinsdell goes step by step through the fund-raising, budgeting, marketing, and management of a typical little theatre of the time. Includes the time-blessed axioms, including "Balancing the Playbill," "Support of Business Clubs," and "Scenery Makeshifts That Save Money." A helpful guide through the unaesthetic and often unromantic stuff of amateur theatre production and promotion. Appendix on the by-laws of the Little Theater of Dallas—as good a model as any.

Hopper, Arthur B., Jr. *Sheldon Cheney: Spokesman for the New Movement in the American Theatre, 1914-1929.* Ann Arbor, Michigan: University Microfilms, 1970 (Ph.D. dissertation, Indiana University, 1969).
This study gives book-length attention to American theatre's delayed but precipitous entrance into the "New Theatre" movement of Europe during the first three decades of the century. The biographical details (many supplied by Cheney himself) lead to his establishing *Theatre Arts Magazine* in 1916, Cheney's major contribution to American theatre. A theorist, critic, and historian, Cheney had the ability to "synthesize trends and theories into principles," which gave him pride of place among early New Theatre advocates. Exhaustive bibliographies of works by and about Cheney.

Hopper, DeWolf. *Reminiscences of DeWolf Hopper: Once a Clown Always a Clown.* Garden City, N.Y.: Garden City Publishing Company, 1925.
Playing road shows from New Orleans to Montreal, Hopper made a life of comic acting on stage before films took vaudeville away. "Hundreds of actors of the first rank did not play New York at all. . . . The road was the theater and the theater the road until about 1910." Hopper never managed to be taken seriously as an actor outside of comic roles, and reconciles himself to the fact in this oddly humorless (despite the retelling of humorous anecdotes) recollection. Illustrations sprinkled throughout—not always of Hopper, however; one marvelous exception shows Hopper and Marshall P. Wilder in an outrageous balcony scene. A good history of the "working drudgery" of show business to 1925.

Houseman, John. *Run-Through.* New York: Simon & Schuster, 1972.
In the middle of a long stage and television career, Houseman begins his memoirs in this volume, moving quickly past his youth and slowing down for a closer look at "the apprentice years," 1931-1935. The Federal Theatre Project is dealt with next, then the forming of the Mercury Theatre with Orson Welles. "Act Three" gets through *Citizen Kane* to *The Voice of America* (1942). Excellent illustrations of sets, costume designs, character portraits, and much more. Essential reading for the modern theatre student. Index reads like a "who's who" of American theatre.

Hurlbut, Gladys. *Next Week: East Lynne!* New York: E. P. Dutton, 1950.
Theatrical stock companies—moving from town to town, showing their wares to the unsophisticated but highly critical audiences of urban America—take their lumps, as do their members. Never a great name in theatre history, Gladys Hurlbut recounts her touring days with a sense of humor and a flair for the anecdote that makes her book both a history of the type and a personal memoir. Covers years from her graduation from the American Academy of Dramatic Arts in 1918 to about 1940, when she once more encounters Guthrie McClintic, a director who once said of her, "She may be the most promising ingenue . . . she's certainly the most disagreeable one!"

Kazacoff, George. *Dangerous Theatre: The Federal Theatre Project as a Forum for New Plays*. New York: Peter Lang, 1989.
Taking his title from Hallie Flanagan's remark that good theatre is always dangerous, and making use of the George Mason University archives, Kazacoff concentrates on the playwriting aspect of the Project's innovations. As a forum for new plays, he says, the FTP invited "honest" plays "alive to the problems of today's world." By focusing on how the plays were written, evaluated, tested, and produced, he returns one of the FTP's main functions to the critical spotlight. Valuable for the details of play production decision making, and as a checklist, apparently exhaustive, of new play activity during this period.

Keegan, Marcia. *We Can Still Hear Them Clapping*. New York: Avon Books, 1975.
"We" are the stars of the Golden Age of Vaudeville, here defined as "the first quarter of the twentieth century." This photographic essay finds the near-stars of that era, aged and aging, presently residing in and near Broadway, and gives them a chance to remember their youth and the excitement of the stage. Holding old photographs against their present portraits, and telling their stories in the first person, these ladies are more beautiful and these men are more handsome now than they ever were. The text preserves, as a sort of oral tradition, some of their personal memories of the past. Touching and inspiring; one beauty, Vesta Wallace, pins it down: "People that had never done anything in their life and you even mention you've been in show business, they're mad, I don't know why. They're jealous, I guess."

Kinne, Wisner Payne. *George Pierce Baker and the American Theatre*. Cambridge, Mass.: Harvard University Press, 1954.
Few academics have influenced the arts, especially theatre, as has Baker, whose Harvard 47 Workshop (named for the course title, not the year of its inception, which was 1913) inspired a generation of playwrights, directors, and producers. That chapter is not covered until chapter number 23, however; Baker's theatre biography, entertainingly related by a theatre scholar and writer of some merit, begins much earlier, with his first impressions of English imports in the nine-

teenth century. All the names of American theatre—Gordon Craig (British but influential here), Eugene O'Neill, Max Reinhardt—pass through the book, whose best contribution is its defense of the sometimes shaky marriage of theatre and the university. Several valuable appendices, including a list of the published plays of Baker's students at Harvard, Radcliffe, and Yale. Index.

Kittle, Russell Dale. *Toby and Susie: The Show-Business Success Story of Neil and Caroline Schaffner, 1925-1962.* 2 vols. Ann Arbor, Mich.: University Microfilms, 1976 (Ph.D. dissertation, Ohio State University, 1969).
Tent theatre, especially the Tent-Repertoire-Toby Shows, thrived under the Schaffner Players' energies. One of the most successful of this kind of theatre featured country bumpkin character Toby, red-mopped and freckled. A comprehensive view of the type is offered, listing companies, lengths of operation, company size, equipment lists, and more. It then concentrates on the Schaffners from 1925 to their 1949 season (only sketched in from 1930-1939 because of the absence of account books), with a few looks forward to *In Bed with Grandpa* (1960). Definitive study for this brand of circus-cum-theatre phenomenon.

Klein, Elane Sylvia Small. *The Development of the Leading Feminine Character in Selected Librettos of American Musicals from 1900 to 1960.* Ann Arbor, Mich.: University Microfilms, 1972 (Ph.D. dissertation, Columbia University, 1962).
After describing the differences between operetta and musical comedy before the 1940's, this study focuses on the female characters as they took on different traits during the period of changing generic ground rules of early American musical theatre. Basically a literary study but full of information on the period's biases, predilections and expectations from actress and female character; covers the subject up to *West Side Story* and *My Fair Lady*. Bibliography.

Kobler, John. *Damned in Paradise: The Life of John Barrymore.* New York: Atheneum, 1977.
Taking a rather despondent view of the Drew/Barrymore dynasty, Kobler provides a dramatic biography of the central figure who bridged the gap from stage to film. Begins one chapter before his birth in 1882. "Popular" in style and occasionally sensationalistic without justification, this biography is nevertheless well researched and a good beginning to the study of the family and the period. Illustrations and index.

Kreizenbeck, Alan Dennis. *The Theatre Nobody Knows: Forgotten Productions of the Federal Theatre Project, 1935-1939.* Ann Arbor, Mich.: University Microfilms, 1982 (Ph.D. dissertation, New York University, 1979).
This scholarly study fills in the gaps between better-known productions of the Federal Theatre Project, such as *Spirochette* and *Power*. Taking advantage of the then-newly opened Research Center for the Federal Theatre Project at George

Mason University, Kreizenbeck quickly reviews known material, then moves on to such subjects as touring troupes, African-American theatre, foreign-language units, and puppet productions. Essential reading to get the true flavor of the size and ambition of Hallie Flanagan's vision. Large factual appendices.

Lang, William Aloysius II. *The Career of Alice Brady, Stage and Screen Actress.* Ann Arbor, Mich.: University Microfilms, 1975 (Ph.D. dissertation, University of Illinois at Urbana-Champaign, 1971).
Alice Brady's most famous role, Lavinia in the Theatre Guild's 1931 production of Eugene O'Neill's *Mourning Becomes Electra*, gets its own chapter in this short but interesting dissertation on one of the best actresses who made the transition from stage to film in the early part of the twentieth century. She received mixed reviews for her "repressed emotion" or "classic restraint" in the role, but all agreed it was the highlight of her career. The Great Depression finally drove her back to Hollywood. Good bibliography.

Langner, Lawrence. *The Magic Curtain: The Story of a Life in Two Fields, Theatre and Invention by the Founder of the Theatre Guild.* New York: E. P. Dutton, 1951.
The literally hundreds of photos, from Eva Le Gallienne to Katharine Hepburn to Armina Marshall (Mrs. Lawrence Langner), are themselves a history of America's progress from vaudeville to *A Touch of the Poet.* Langner invented the automobile self-starter, among other things, and here he describes how invention and the theatre come from one impulse, "living in an era which was one of the most turbulent in recorded history, yet the most creative in invention and one of the most creative in the theatre." Good source of information on the Theatre Guild's inception (in 1919) and policies, acting company, alternating repertory system, and more. Appendices on the Washington Square Players, the Lunts, Shaw letters, the Westport Country Playhouse (1931), and other details; index.

Laurent, Eugene Martin. *Walter Hampden: Actor-Manager.* Ann Arbor, Mich.: University Microfilms, 1975 (Ph.D. dissertation, University of Illinois, 1969). This study concentrates on Hampden as actor in major roles, but it also deals with his successes as "romantic theatre" manager of the Hampden Theatre in the last half of the 1920's. A section on his "partial retirement" from 1937 to 1955 is interesting for its depiction of small stock company life in Kansas, New York state, and New Jersey. His twilight film career, through the good offices of his friend Cecil B. DeMille, was modest but professional: "He learned his lines quickly, took direction humbly, and never was the cause of an extra take." Bibliography.

Le Gallienne, Eva. *At 33*. New York: Longmans, Green, 1934.
Not exactly an autobiography (a task she would undertake some twenty years later), but a review of a rich life at a turning point—her New York Civic Repertory Theatre had closed its doors after eight years. "If [it] proves to be the pioneer that has prepared the way" for better theatre conditions, she is happy. Well-written descriptions of her travels and backstage struggles to make her voice heard in a largely male, conservative theatre world. Good reading. List of Civic Theatre productions.

_____. *With a Quiet Heart: An Autobiography*. New York: Viking Press, 1953.
"Here is Eva Le Gallienne off stage as well as on," but, more important to theatre history, here are three generations of famous stage figures seen through the shrewd but eminently humanitarian eyes of one of the great actresses of the twentieth century. Once she said no to David Belasco; another time, she turned her back on Broadway itself to organize a repertory theatre (the Civic Repertory from 1926 to 1934). Her international travels and exciting stage life are recalled in sprightly, even feisty paragraphs. She had a considerable career after this autobiography was written, and in this respect it is out of date. Index.

Lee, Lawrence, and Barry Gifford. *Saroyan: A Biography*. New York: Harper & Row, 1984.
Saroyan's *The Time of Your Life* assured his place in American theatre history, but his subsequent efforts were less successful (though *The Cave Dwellers* is a great lost play). Lee and Gifford report his fall from grace through interviews and a strong narrative style, soft-pedaling Saroyan's snarly temper and erratic behavior and exposing the viciousness and unforgivingly selective memory of the postwar theatre world. Much of Saroyan's output was in short-story form. Chronology, notes, and index.

Leonard, William Torbert. *Once Was Enough*. Metuchen, N.J.: Scarecrow Press, 1986.
In a pure example of complementary selling, Leonard has written a book about the flops of Broadway, the one-night stands that got "brodied" by the critics. His substantive research is frosted with brisk comments and snipings (the word is not too strong) from typical reviews. Contains the facts, the poignant regret, the candor, and the honest smile of admission. Could Roger Stevens really produce five clinkers and still keep going? Good indexes provided on every manner of culprit: playwright, designer, producer, and others; and a general index. Introductory essay offers information on an early practice in theatre: trying out plays in single-performance matinees.

Levine, Ira A. *Left-Wing Dramatic Theory in the American Theatre*. Ann Arbor, Mich.: UMI Research Press, 1985.
Levine revised his 1980 dissertation for this study of the politically dangerous theatre of John Howard Lawson, Paul Sifton, and others during the 1920's and into the period (1929-1939) from the Crash to the establishment of the Popular Front and its eventual aesthetic manifestation in the Living Newspapers. Equally comfortable in the theatre world and the complex political arenas of this volatile time, Levine describes how the bourgeois critics gradually diluted the effectiveness of agitprop theatre, leaving it to succumb to the wartime and postwar flush of status quo patriotism. Strong bibliography and index.

Lewis, Emory. *Stages: The Fifty-Year Childhood of the American Theatre*. Englewood Cliffs, N.J.: Prentice-Hall, 1969.
Beginning with the premise that "one cannot separate theatre from man's other activities," Lewis finds a thread running through a diverse half-century as he corrects the "unsound" practices of other critics, who separate theatre from its sociocultural context. Total theatre is his point of view, by which he means a humanism that incorporates—even embraces—theatre arts and social science. He is, however, more comfortable with dramatic literature than with production and performance, and treats the period (1910-1960) from a distance. Index.

McArthur, Benjamin. *Actors and American Culture, 1880-1920*. Philadelphia: Temple University Press, 1984.
A larger and more thematically difficult study than one simply looking at economic considerations, this is an examination of the actor's place in the "classless" but strictly layered society of turn-of-the-century America, to which "the honorable profession" turned for approbation but which excluded or patronized the actor. What cultural bonds, if any, did actors as a group enjoy? To what constraints were they subjected when such powerful, selfish interpreters of the free enterprise system as the Syndicate began to tell them their place? Strong study of a fairly short period; a cross between theatre history and sociology. Notes and index.

McCabe, John. *George M. Cohan: The Man Who Owned Broadway*. New York: Doubleday, 1973.
By titling the book this way, McCabe is demonstrating his interest in the megalomaniacal side of Cohan; one chapter is called "The Man Who Had to Own Broadway." Good, readable account of the life, with several telling anecdotes (an 1889 Mirth Makers' program announced "10 minute intermission during which Master Cohan will offer for sale Autographed Photographs of this fun-creating family"). Good illustrations, including his last appearance in *Return of the Vagabond* in 1940. Tabular appendix of Cohan's plays; index.

McCleery, Albert, and Carl Glick. *Curtains Going Up*. New York: Pitman, 1939.
In many ways a continuation of Clarence Stratton's illustrated record of amateur theatre, this long and valuable update includes more than fifty photographs, mostly production stills, of where regional theatre has gone since the heyday of the mid 1920's. Lighthearted text ("The Revolt of the Dowagers," "The Menfolk Declare Their Independence," and so on) gets the reader through a series of "here's how we did it in Hutchinson, Kansas," chapters. Altogether a valuable history of a movement too widespread to follow in the *New York Times* alone. Several helpful appendices follow the last chapter, "Declaration of a National Policy."

McClintic, Guthrie. *Me and Kit*. Boston: Little, Brown, 1955.
Kit is Katharine Cornell, and McClintic tells their story, along with his own career anecdotes, in a readable and friendly style that belies his often acerbic nature in theatrical circles. Full of photographs, personal and professional, of himself and his wife. A good introduction to the working Broadway world (1920-1960) through the eyes of the producer, director, and husband of a famous actress. His theories of doing the classics were well known: "The actors must be made to forget they are doing Shakespeare." List of plays; index.

McDermott, Douglas. *The Living Newspaper as a Dramatic Form*. Ann Arbor, Mich.: University Microfilms, 1972 (Ph.D. dissertation, State University of Iowa, 1963).
While several studies examine the theatricality, production histories, and sociopolitical events depicted in the Living Newspapers, this work looks at the pieces as literature. Designed quickly and journalistically around the newspaper events of the week, these scripts, now preserved in the Federal Theatre archives at George Mason University, deserve some attention for their structure and for the rhetorical devices the compilers used to get their point across. Since the time of this study, however, newly discovered photographs, promptbooks, and costume swatches in the archives have added a great deal to what is known about the mechanics of the form. In that light, McDermott's work, relying too heavily on the text (were they, in fact, "written" exactly?), seems a little thin and literary, given the immediacy of the pieces' genesis. Recent re-creations of Living Newspapers, notably at the First Amendment Theatre, could refer to this study for some guidance. Full bibliography, but out of date.

Macgowan, Kenneth. *Footlights Across America: Towards a National Theater*. New York: Harcourt, Brace, 1929.
Possibly the first prospectus and call to arms of the noncommercial theater in America, and still referred to by all subsequent idealists, Macgowan's book moved a generation of theatre artists to look beyond the limitations of Broadway. A travelogue in a sense (he covered 14,000 miles in 1928-1929), it records his

visits to many of the more than one thousand community theatres, university theatres, and neighborhood playhouses that, in his eyes, spelled the birth of a national theatre. Macgowan had started *Theatre Arts* a decade earlier and written "The Theatre of Today" in 1914, the first American manifesto for the "New Theatre." Maps, photographs, diagrams of the best—the Goodman, the Carolina Playmakers, the Lisbon, North Dakota, stage, and a hundred others of the same promise and hope. Several appendices, including a fascinating survey; index.

McNamara, Brooks. *The Shuberts of Broadway: A History Drawn from the Collections of the Shubert Archive.* New York: Oxford University Press, 1990.
The first substantial product of the newly opened Shubert archives, some fifteen years in the organizing, since McNamara was asked to "look over some papers" in the Shubert offices. The massive archive will never be fully explored, but McNamara offers an excellent and heavily illustrated introduction to the task. Not so much a study as an overview of the subject, it is nevertheless the first place to stop in researching the brothers Shubert, who broke the Syndicate's stranglehold and started a century-long monopoly of their own. Index and selected bibliography.

Malvern, Gladys. *Curtain Going Up! The Story of Katharine Cornell.* New York: Julian Messner, 1943.
Following Cornell's story of her life (*I Wanted to Be an Actress*, 1939), this biography expands on the personal and theatrical details, but reads almost like a teenager's gushbook: "Kit's Career Begins," "Kit Learns a Lesson," "Kit Goes to London," and, finally, "Katharine Cornell Goes to the White House." Readable, without enough critical stock-taking, but good about how theatre changed around her from 1916 to World War II. Thirty pages of amazing pictures; she was mercilessly beautiful in 1921 as Sydney Fairfield in *The Bill of Divorcement.* Index.

Mason, Hamilton. *French Theatre in New York: A List of Plays, 1899-1939.* New York: Columbia University Press, 1940.
"Exhaustive" is the intention of this listing of first-run and second-run French plays, both in French and in English, "in Manhattan." This is a reference book, a starting point for continued scholarship in related fields, arranged numerically (other than its introductory chapter) like a checklist of theatrical events (1443 by Mason's count). A plot summary for each play is very helpful, since play titles shift from language to language (*Le Fils surnaturel* becomes *Papa's Darling*, for instance). Index and bibliography.

Massey, Raymond. *A Hundred Different Lives.* Boston: Little, Brown, 1979.
Massey had a full stage life before finding fame in the movies, and this autobiography covers that career in well-written style. As a Broadway and West End

star and as a producer, Massey tells of the Golden Age of New York theatre and his own gradual decline; in one of his last roles, Tennessee Williams' *The Night of the Iguana*, Massey forgot his lines. He tells of the nightmare in straightforward, honest tones, a sign of his whole character. This is the story of a man of the stage. Index.

Mathews, Jane de Hart. *The Federal Theatre, 1935-1939: Plays, Relief, and Politics*. Princeton, N.J.: Princeton University Press, 1967.
"Writing from a different perspective and with a different purpose" from Hallie Flanagan's, Mathews plumbs the National Archives to discuss the Federal Theatre Project, this time "as a national institution—its origins and administration, the personalities, ideas, and circumstances which shaped it, the problems it faced, and the contributions it made." The study is as much a document of social science as of theatre, and its value lies in the combination. Bibliography and index.

Matlaw, Myron, ed. *American Popular Entertainment: Papers and Proceedings of the Conference on the History of American Popular Entertainment*. Westport, Conn.: Greenwood Press, 1979.
The Lincoln Center conference held in 1977 generated dozens of valuable papers, gathered (as number one in the series Contributions in Drama and Theatre Studies) around the major subheadings of minstrel shows, vaudeville, burlesque, tent repertoire shows, circus, Wild West shows, medicine shows, dance, and "environmental entertainment" (a term embracing amusement and theme parks). The best of these marry information with opinion, avoiding the squabbles over fine points that mar some collections of this nature. Very valuable "historical perspective bibliography" by Don B. Wilmeth (which had been distributed at the conference), and an all-article index.

Meserve, Walter J. *Robert E. Sherwood: Reluctant Moralist*. New York: Pegasus, 1970.
A strong biographical overview of Sherwood's contributions to American drama, including a fairly detailed account of the formation of the Playwrights' Company in 1938. Admired by his fellow playwrights (including John Howard Lawson, the expressionist playwright) and considered a clear voice of left-wing politics, Sherwood was an idealist who renounced the theatre to serve in World War II as a civilian war propagandist. Brief selected index.

Mielziner, Jo. *The Shapes of Our Theatre*. New York: Crown, 1970.
The master of stage design sets down the major principles of theatre architecture in this much-cited and well-illustrated (with his drawings showing abstract audience and playing space) primer. The development of open-thrust stages, proscenium stages, and "multi-choice in a single theatre" are discussed, with a

seminal chapter on the "program" for theatre facilities. Appendix of Mielziner designs and consulting projects; index.

Mordden, Ethan. *The American Theatre*. New York: Oxford University Press, 1981. Mordden asks some standard and some unusual questions—"How has the native culture informed the material?"—toward an inquiry into "what is American in American theatre." After a nod to pre-World War I drama, the study concentrates on reporting "on the evolving purpose of theatre in America." Mordden's most important question is, "Can elitist experimentalism coexist with mass-cult conventionalism?" Modern theatre "is useful in enlarging our awareness, in countering the culture" rather than affirming middle-class homilies. "For further reading" conclusion, and index.

_____. *Better Foot Forward: The History of American Musical Theatre.* New York: Grossman, 1976.
The first half of this friendly study, which covers musical theatre, the operetta, and related stage forms up to the 1940's, is a good source of information for revues, comic opera, Cohan and Herbert and Ziegfeld, up to *Porgy and Bess*. The second section is moodier, less enthusiastic, remarking on the "decline" of the 1960's and the "fall" of the 1970's. The last chapter, on *Follies* and *A Little Night Music*, is more upbeat. A preface on the nature of theatre history gives some insight into the process of recapturing the essence of an era gone by: "Photographs . . . recollections . . . contemporary reviews, for starters." Index.

_____. *Broadway Babies: The People Who Made the American Musical.* New York: Oxford University Press, 1983.
Watching the transfer of power from the producer (beginning around 1900) to the writers, Mordden concentrates on the creative people who collectively brought American musical theatre to its present (1983) excellence. This is the history of the musical as a tribute to the individuals—Victor Herbert, Gertrude Lawrence, George Balanchine, Michael Bennett—who brought it life, moved it from the safety of the status quo to the exhilarating heights of risking the new. Index and selective discography.

Morehouse, Ward. *George M. Cohan: Prince of the American Theater.* 1934. Reprint. Westport, Conn.: Greenwood Press, 1972.
"The man who owned Broadway" gets a friendly biographical treatment (one year after Cohan's death), organized in rough chronological order by turning-point events: divorce and remarriage, "Over There," Cohan versus Actors Equity, and so forth. Illustrations show Cohan's gradual aging, especially with Sam Harris (partner since 1904 in the Cohan & Harris Minstrels). Not a scholarly biography, lacking an index (and exasperatingly devoid of first names and important dates in the text itself), but adding a chronology.

_____. *Matinee Tomorrow: Fifty Years of Our Theater*. New York: Mc-
Graw-Hill, 1949.
An "informal history of the New York theater," from Lillian Russell to Mary
Martin, from Clyde Fitch to Tennessee Williams—in short, the first half of the
century. Morehouse's recollections (he was quite active in theatre management
and production, but fails to give himself a biography or index entry), are filtered
through a thorough knowledge of what makes theatre good and bad. Excellent
illustrations, including group cameos of the best actors, actresses, playwrights,
critics, producers, and others of the period. The index, much more comprehensive than a mere list of proper names, helps turn this personal tribute into a
viable source of theatre history.

Moussinac, Leon. *The New Movement in the Theatre: A Survey of Recent Developments in Europe and America*. 1932. Reprint. New York: Benjamin Blom,
1967.
In 1932, the "new movement" meant Gordon Craig, Loie Fuller, Jean Cocteau,
Leopold Jessner, Lee Simonson, and other movers and shakers who combined
modern art, new technology, and a period of socioeconomic chaos to create the
scripts of expressionism, Dada, surrealism, and agitprop. This source's best
feature is its pictorial record of Simonson, Norman Bel Geddes, and Robert
Edmond Jones in America and Vsevolod Meyerhold, Karl Kapek, Pablo Picasso,
and Erwin Piscator in Europe. Exciting visual display of genius caught between
the wars. Introductory essays by Gordon Craig and R. H. Packman.

Nadel, Norman. *A Pictorial History of the Theatre Guild*. New York: Crown, 1969.
Black-and-white glossy photographs of the Guild's productions and stars (if that
word can be applied to the experiment), with an informative text and "special
material" by Lawrence Langner and Armina Marshall, cofounders of the Guild.
A good visual introduction to what the Guild accomplished—alternating repertory,
unit sets on standard flats in neutral colors, the Lunts—with a final chapter on
where it seemed to be going as of 1969. List of productions, but no cast lists;
Theatre Guild radio productions discussed and listed as well. Index.

Nathan, George Jean. *The Theatre, the Drama, the Girls*. New York: Alfred A.
Knopf, 1921.
Nathan can cut his theatre experiences in any direction, but here he is at his most
cynical and subjective. By paying attention to femininity on the stage ("I have
never seen a really pretty girl on either the French or German stage, and I have
looked"), he finds an artificial focus for yet another collection of theatre opinions. Valuable, however, because he deals with much stage material that is not
generally reviewed seriously. He finds, for example, Zoe Akins "one of the few
interesting young women writing for the native stage," and notes that "there may
be less imaginative music show librettists than Miss Anne Caldwell, but I am not
privy to their names." At least he mentions them, which is a rarity.

_____. *The World in Falseface*. New York: Alfred A. Knopf, 1923.
The continuing saga of Nathan's penetration of his obsession, the theatre, this time in the form of brief, even pithy, observations, not always about the theatre. A taste: "Art states what we know in terms of what we hope." From a longer entry he takes his own advice: "When criticism becomes snobbish it becomes imbecile." Valuable only to students of interwar theatrical rhapsodizing and phrase-making, and to Nathan devotees.

New York Times Theater Reviews, 1920-1970. New York: New York Times/Arno Press, 1971.
Eight volumes of reprinted (photographic) reviews, with two volumes of indexes. A veritable history of Broadway (and occasionally off-Broadway) theatre, as seen through the critical gaze of such notable reviewers as Alexander Woollcott, John Corbin, Arthur Hopkins, Brooks Atkinson, and Anonymous. The immediacy of the reaction, the journalistic writing style, the awesome commercial power of the newspaper, and the reviewers' multiple motives to be honest, fair, witty, and right at the same time make this collection a work of art. Indexed (in volume 9) by awards and prizes, summaries of productions and runs, season titles and production companies; volume 10 is a personal-name index.

O'Connor, John, and Lorraine Brown, eds. *Free, Adult, Uncensored: The Living History of the Federal Theatre Project*. Washington, D.C.: New Republic Books, 1978.
A large, well-illustrated, well-written book full of insight. Organized (after introductory chapters) by major productions—*It Can't Happen Here*, *Big Blow*, *Haiti*, *One-Third of a Nation*, and so on—it draws on the then-newly discovered archives of the FTP, which had been lost in a warehouse for decades. Posters, production stills, stage designs, and costume sketches bring the history to life as promised in the subtitle; chronology and index.

Odets, Clifford. *The Time Is Ripe: The 1940 Journal of Clifford Odets*. New York: Grove Press, 1988.
Prefaced by his son Walt, who found the diary among trunks full of Odets's papers after his death in 1963, this internal record of Odets's single year tells a lot about how theatre worked in his time and about his relation to it as he saw it. The year followed his successes of the 1930's with the Group Theatre and saw the failure of *Night Music*. It was a turning point, according to William Gibson (introduction): "A play has failed, the Group is disintegrating, the world of the thirties is being blown apart by Nazi dive bombers." Index and brief biographies of Odets's associates mentioned in the diary.

Palmieri, Anthony F. R. *Elmer Rice: A Playwright's Vision of America*. London: Associated University Presses, 1980.

Beginning with *On Trial* (1914), Elmer Rice contributed a considerable body of work to American theatre, analyzed in this study for literary and theatrical merit. A history of his progress, especially valuable for study of the Playwright's Company, established in 1938 with Maxwell Anderson, S. N. Behrman, Sidney Howard, and Robert E. Sherwood. Many of his plays were produced by the Theatre Guild, and his relation to that organization is well documented. Index and bibliographical note.

Parola, Gene Joseph. *Walter Hampden's Career as Actor-Manager.* Ann Arbor, Mich.: University Microfilms, 1976 (Ph.D. dissertation, Indiana University, 1970).
Hampden is not among the actor-managers of the great nineteenth century tradition; rather, he is a twentieth century phenomenon specializing in romantic plays, "a style of play that in those sophisticated times was thought to have been dead and known to spell ruin." He plied his trade from 1919 to 1930, at his own Hampden Theatre in New York from 1925. Only briefly mentioned in other theatre histories, he is given full treatment as actor, director, and manager, and his success is measured "in terms of his goals." Five appendices of play lists, casts, and a list of short biographies of members of his company.

Patterson, Lindsay, ed. *Anthology of the American Negro in the Theatre.* New York: Publishers Company, 1967.
One volume of the International Library of Negro Life and History, this "critical approach" does what no other study has done. As Arna Bontemps puts it in the essay on the Karamu Theatre of Cleveland, it tells "the story of a good deed shining in a naughty world." By collecting these records of African-American theatre in America, the editor celebrates the contributions of a whole culture, rather than simply pointing to isolated phenomena, as though each African-American actor, playwright and producer were working without cultural nourishment. Among the inevitable diatribes against past injustices, and the aberrations of history (Bill Cosby cited as "the first Negro to be starred in a weekly dramatic series—*I Spy*"), the voices of future promise speak out here. Heavily illustrated; bibliography and index.

Phelps, William Lyon. *The Twentieth Century Theatre: Observations on the Contemporary English and American Stage.* New York: Macmillan, 1918.
Covers the first eighteen years of the twentieth century, with the interesting observation: "The Modern Drama is so much greater than the Modern Theatre that we are confronted with a huge problem." Phelps recognizes that American theatre experiment lags behind European advances, and calls for support of the "sixty Little Theatres in the United States" as of June, 1918. Index.

Plotkins, Marilyn Jane. *Irving Berlin, George Gershwin, Cole Porter, and the Spectacular Revue: The Theatrical Context of Revue Songs from 1910 to 1937.* Ann Arbor, Mich.: University Microfilms, 1984 (Ph.D. dissertation, Tufts University, 1982).
Flo Ziegfeld and his imitators plundered Tin Pan Alley at will during these decades; the benefits were mutual. It is generally acknowledged that the songs and the usually very thin "theatrical context—the theatrical situation created from characters, settings, costumes, and action" were not matched with much care; Plotkins takes the opposite view and supports her contention well. Illustrations of musical scores, and some lyrics. Bibliography.

Poggi, Jack. *Theater in America: The Impact of Economic Forces, 1870-1967.* Ithaca, N.Y.: Cornell University Press, 1968.
Comparing theatre with General Motors (both "social and economic institutions"), Poggi notes that theatre has become centralized but has also become smaller. This study marks a low point in the economic importance of theatre because his observations were made before regional theatre exploded in all American cities of size and before the financial base of stage life changed. Although final chapters deal with regional theatre, the economics had not yet been stabilized when Poggi published this study. Despite this sense of being out of date, his study is excellent for summarizing the marriage of money and art during the last century of American theatre. Particularly strong on discussions of the Syndicate and the economies of the Group Theatre. Good bibliography.

Raider, Roberta Ann. *A Descriptive Study of the Acting of Marie Dressler.* Ann Arbor, Mich.: University Microfilms, 1976 (Ph.D. dissertation, University of Michigan, 1970).
Although best known for her film career (Best Screen Actress of 1931), Dressler survived the transformation from stage to screen and changes from touring stock companies to packaged shows from New York, working in "over a hundred roles in stock and light opera companies, fifteen years as a Broadway star, ten years as one of the most popular vaudeville attractions," before her film career. The story of that transformation is told in this scholarly but readable biography, which draws on Dressler's own biography. Chapter 6, "Summary and Conclusions," is a good focused overview of Dressler's techniques and methods.

Rice, Elmer. *The Living Theatre.* New York: Harper & Brothers, 1959.
As a playwright, Rice is well known for his expressionistic play *The Adding Machine.* During a stint as professor and scholar at New York University, he gathered his ideas into lecture form, and this informative and little-studied treatise was "written from scratch" after his teaching experience. Includes a fascinating student study of the "unbridgeable gulf between art and commercialism in the theatre," citing the long-run comedies never studied as literature. One of the

earliest Broadway voices to call for "the establishment of decentralized permanent repertory theatres" in America. Index.

Ridge, Patricia Lin. *The Contributions of Hallie Flanagan to the American Theatre.* Ann Arbor, Mich.: University Microfilms, 1976 (Ph.D. dissertation, University of Colorado, 1971).
A fairly brief study of the force behind the Federal Theatre Project. Adds something to other, better-known studies, including Flanagan's, especially her contributions to the experimental theatre of the colleges where she served: Grinnell, Vassar, and Smith. As the first woman to be awarded a Guggenheim grant, Flanagan is important to any study of American theatre in the 1930's. This piece uses only the Lincoln Theatre collection; the George Mason University archives had not been discovered and made available in 1971. List of plays produced; bibliography.

Rigdon, Walter, ed. *The Biographical Encyclopaedia & Who's Who of the American Theatre.* New York: James H. Heineman, 1966.
The first book, according to George Freedley (introduction), "that has comprehensively and definitively recorded the history, sociology, personalities, organizations and relationships of the [American] theatre." In addition to the body of the work (biographies), this reference includes an alphabetical listing of New York productions from 1900 to 1964; playbills from 1959-1964 (by date, with play title index) not only of New York but also Actor's Workshop, Alley Theatre (Houston), Arena Stage (Washington, D.C.), Cleveland Playhouse, and about ten other regional theatres, early in their histories. Includes a valuable section of "biographies" of theatre groups such as Circle in the Square, American Repertory Theatre, and Pasadena Playhouse (and a good source for brief histories of such organizations as Actors Equity Association, Association of Theatrical Press Agents and Managers, and Committee on Theatre Architecture of the American Institute of Architects). Much more. Worth investigating.

Roberts, J. W. *Richard Boleslavsky: His Life and Work in the Theatre.* Ann Arbor, Mich.: UMI Research Press, 1981.
This series of theatre and dramatic studies (this book is number 7) is valuable as thoroughly researched and well-organized scholarship. Roberts spends two chapters on Boleslavsky's Russian and European experiences, then discusses in great detail the Laboratory Theatre (established in 1923) on which his American reputation is based; students of Boleslavsky formed the Group Theatre. Particularly articulate regarding "the system" and its American manifestation. Illustrations are unfortunately absent, except a frontispiece; a filmography appendix, notes, bibliography, and index.

Robertson, Roderick. *The Friendship of Eugene O'Neill and George Jean Nathan.* Ann Arbor, Mich.: University Microfilms, 1976.
The critic Nathan and the playwright O'Neill enjoyed a long personal friendship "in spite of the obvious threats to them by the very nature of the critic's profession." Nathan was "helpful to the creative work of the dramatist." How the relationship was fruitful for both is the topic of this study, which, in the course of examining the records of the period, offers much to the theatre historian regarding the working habits of both men. Notes and bibliography.

Ross, Theophil Walter, Jr. *Conflicting Concepts of the Federal Theatre Project: A Critical History.* Ann Arbor, Mich.: University Microfilms, 1982.
Examines the conflicts inherent in the many facets of FTP's dynamics—social, political, artistic, cultural—for an explanation of what went wrong with the noble experiment. Did the program "faithfully retain and pursue a clearly defined hierarchy of goals"? "The aspirations and accomplishments of the Federal Theatre Project in all four areas created damaging and eventually fatal weaknesses in the program." Selected bibliography.

Sarlos, Robert Karoly. *Jig Cook and the Provincetown Players: Theatre in Ferment.* Boston: University of Massachusetts Press, 1982.
In 1915, George Cram ("Jig") Cook and a few other vacationing New Englanders took over a little wharf in Provincetown, "a small building for plays given in an intimate way," as Thomas Dickinson described "little theatres." From it grew the first important "new theatre," imitating at its core the European impulses of chamber theatre, but bringing to it American vitality, especially in the form of new playwrights such as Eugene O'Neill and Susan Glaspell. By 1916, they had established themselves in New York's Macdougal Street, producing *Bound East for Cardiff.* Sarlos captures the excitement, and recounts the progress, of the young experimenters who gave birth to modern American theatre. Chronology, excellent rare photographs, notes, bibliography, description of physical structure (the Wharf, the 139 Macdougal playhouse, the 133 Macdougal playhouse, and the famous "dome" scenic device) and index.

Sayler, Oliver M. *Our American Theatre.* New York: Brentano's, 1923.
An early, optimistic look at American theatre about to explode into its identity. Start here to witness the birth of a theatre impulse ready for Eugene O'Neill, Eva Le Gallienne, and Robert Edmond Jones. Lucie R. Sayler supplies about thirty simple but effective silhouette illustrations, as the book describes "the period of awakening" from Vera Kommissarzhevskaya's 1908 European smorgasbord, to George Bernard Shaw's *Devil's Disciple* at the Garrick in 1923. Excellent appendices of award winners, seasons, little, experimental, and community theatres, and so forth, by state. Index.

Seldes, Gilbert. *The Seven Lively Arts*. 1924. Rev. 1957. Reprint. New York: A. S. Barnes, 1962.
A first appreciation of popular entertainments, this mistitled book collects Seldes' writings and thoughts from *The Dial*, *Vanity Fair*, and other publications during his life as a columnist and reviewer. "Lively" for Seldes means not stuffy, not "fine," accessible and enjoyable without pretensions. Valuable for comments on vaudeville, jazz, American musicals, and the advent of film. No critical apparatus, and not organized for factual reference.

Seller, Maxine Schwartz, ed. *Ethnic Theatre in the United States*. Westport, Conn.: Greenwood Press, 1983.
Twenty essays summarizing the histories of the combination of American and ethnic theatre traditions imported along with the immigrants of the past two centuries. Highly informative overviews, containing tables and chronologies of ethnic theatre among diverse cultures; particularly valuable are studies of Eastern European theatre in America, such as that of Latvia, Lithuania, Poland, and Hungary. Fifteen illustrations, mostly production stills. Each article is followed by notes and bibliography; an all-article index ties the essays together.

Sexton, R. W., and B. F. Betts. *American Theatres of Today*. New York: Architectural Book Publishing Co., 1927. Reprint. Vestal Press, 1977.
A major source of information on "living" theatres (some converted to movie houses and some specifically designed for film) in major American cities in 1927. Heavily illustrated "with plans, sections, and photographs of exterior and interior details." Volume 1 contains most of the illustrations; volume 2 contains short essays on such topics as design, planning, decoration, electrical installation, acoustics, heating and ventilating. Another plate section follows this volume. Highly recommended.

Shay, Frank. *The Practical Theatre*. New York: Appleton, 1926.
An early community theatre how-to book, "a manual for little theatres, community players, amateur dramatic clubs and other independent producing groups." Inspiring photographs of Wharf Theatre of the Provincetown Players, the Lobero Theatre, Santa Barbara, and others. Tables and charts of how things get done. Although some material is out of date and appears naïve ("Medium: see gelatines"), after a half-century the manual is still full of usable tips on making theatre happen. Bibliography for a basic theatre library is appended.

Sheridan, Phil. *Those Wonderful Old Downtown Theatres*. Columbus, Ohio: Private printing, 1978.
Sheridan's interest in old Columbus (Ohio) theatres began when the Ohio Theatre was threatened and saved in 1969. Combining old photographs of exteriors (buildings and burlesque queens) with a colorful text in the journalistic style of

a true fan (but occasionally descending to lists of famous names passing through), Sheridan marks the passing and the preservation of an era, reflected in the architecture but more vividly in the memories of the twilight generation. Some interesting reproductions of signatures and dedications by celebrities—Mae West is shown in 1938 thanking the producers for helping to break box office records.

Shivers, Alfred S. *The Life of Maxwell Anderson*. Briarcliff Manor, N.Y.: Stein & Day, 1983.
A sensitive biography of the author of *What Price Glory? High Tor*, and *Elizabeth the Queen*. Covers his professional and private life, his successes on Broadway, his friendship with Kurt Weill, his contributions to the founding of the Playwrights' Company, the "golden years" of the 1930's that included *Winterset*, *The Wingless Victory*, and *Knickerbocker Holiday*, and his reasons for adopting a poetic writing style for the stage. Center photograph section; index.

Smith, Wendy. *Real Life Drama: The Group Theatre and America, 1931-1940*. New York: Alfred A. Knopf, 1990.
A strong study of the cultural-economic conditions of the 1930's as the backdrop against which the accomplishments of the Group Theatre are silhouetted. Chapters divide this chronicle-cum-sociology by struggles: hard times, conflict, organization, falling apart, regrouping, new agendas are the signposts for Smith's arrangement of the story. A major history of both the theatre and the times, this massive and ambitious work serves as the Group's biography fifty years after it lived and died. Full chronology, index, and notes; selected bibliography.

Sothern, E. H. *Julia Marlowe's Story*. Edited by Fairfax Downey. New York: Rinehart & Company, 1954.
An odd "autobiography" told to her husband and edited by a fan who saw her in her heyday (1890-1924). Her Juliet was famous, as was her portrait painted by Irving R. Wiles and reproduced here. An unassuming self-study of a woman who has been called the "foremost living actress in tragic and romantic roles, greatest interpreter of the Immortal Bard of Avon" in 1921. She died in 1950.

Stickney, Dorothy. *Openings and Closings*. Garden City, N.Y.: Doubleday, 1979.
Stickney and her husband, Howard Lindsay, lived through the best years of Broadway, often (as in *Life with Father* in 1939) on stage together. This autobiography follows her progress throughout her career but is best when describing private moments, such as the burglary that cost her favorite ring and the storm that blew down the tree outside her window. It is difficult to follow the theatre history because of the scarcity of dates and the absence of a chronology, but there is an index. Two sections of photographs—some candid, some character portraits.

Stone, Fred. *Rolling Stone*. New York: McGraw-Hill, 1945.
"I've outlived a dozen towns I used to know," begins this autobiography of a
"covered wagon" actor, circus performer, tightrope walker, minstrel man, and
all-round vaudeville star. Stone became president of the National Vaudeville
Artists in 1922. He was a friend of Will Rogers, Jim Corbett, Annie Oakley, and
Alfred E. Smith. His autobiography, vague on dates ("During the riotous days
of prohibition" is a typical notation) and facts ("I got to seeing more and more
of Will Rogers"), reads like the happy reminiscences of a clown who made an
easy transition to the movies. No critical apparatus.

Stratton, Clarence. *Producing in Little Theaters*. New York: Henry Holt, 1921.
Books such as this are theatre history because they reveal how theatre used to
be thought of. At the time, however, they were textbooks, guides for the amateur
and university theatres that Stratton spent his life encouraging and recording. The
lighting instruments and even costume technology are out of date, but some of
the observations are timeless: "There are some attempts in certain amateur groups
to try to dispose of a director." Not recommended here, though the impulse is
acknowledged as a human one. One hundred illustrations (mainly production stills
and stage sets) and index.

_____. *Theatron: An Illustrated Record*. New York: Henry Holt, 1928.
If only for the more than two hundred photographs of very early regional theatre
productions, this book, named for the Greek word meaning "the seeing place,"
belongs on every theatre historian's bookshelf. The articulate accompanying text,
dedicated to the physical realization of the plays in the various stage venues
(many more elaborate than Broadway), describes in some detail the designers'
solutions to specific play scripts. No volume can do better at transforming the
theories of the textbooks into the magic of theatrical technology while at the same
time celebrating the nationwide love of theatre. Unfortunately, no index.

Taylor, Karen Malpede. *People's Theatre in Amerika*. New York: Drama Book
Specialists, 1972.
The "communistic" spelling of America is deliberate. An early and strong
chronicle/manifesto of left-wing experimental theatre, this document collection
and study suffers nevertheless from inflamed rhetoric. Compares the collapse of
the Federal Theatre in 1939 with Madrid's fall to the Fascists and Stalin's nonag-
gression pact with Hitler. Alternating her introductory essays with documents and
agitprop sketches otherwise inaccessible to the average reader, Malpede (in
current biographies) marches through a considerable body of material by the
angriest and unhappiest writers of the period (roughly the entire twentieth
century), from Paul Sifton's *The Belt* (1924) to El Teatro Campesino (1971).
Indispensable, nevertheless, for all further study of theatre and politics.

Teichmann, Howard. *George S. Kaufman: An Intimate Portrait*. New York: Dell Books, 1972.
Teichmann interviewed almost two hundred of Kaufman's friends and associates to fill his book with witty anecdotes about this most prolific collaborator of American stage comedy in the 1920's and 1930's. Part memoir, part biography, part reportage, part tribute, from Kaufman's collaborator on *The Solid Gold Cadillac*; good reading and a vivid portrait of a tough business. The touching conclusion, however, is all Teichmann's. Bibliography and index.

Tillinghast, John K. *Guthrie McClintic, Director*. Ann Arbor, Mich.: University Microfilms, 1973 (Ph.D. dissertation, Indiana University, 1964).
Sometimes dealt with in the shadow of his famous wife, Katharine Cornell, McClintic was a successful director in his own right, working for forty years on Broadway. McClintic debuted in 1921 and directed his wife in at least twenty-five of his more than one hundred plays. Known for his beneficence as well as his "self-absorption," McClintic wrote his own story, *Kit and Me*, in 1955. After losing interest in the producing end of theatre around 1961, he retreated from the complexities of Broadway, though he never officially retired. Tillinghast interviewed McClintic for this dissertation. Bibliography and list of plays directed and/or produced.

Urban, Joseph. *Theatres*. New York: Theatre Arts, 1929.
Flo Ziegfeld and Max Reinhardt were the theatre men, but Urban was the premiere theatre architect of his day. Collected here are his drawings, perspectives, and interior layouts for theatres (both realized and conjectural): the Ziegfeld (built in 1926), the Paramount (in Palm Beach), "a metropolitan opera house" originally designed for a specific site, the Reinhardt (which brings the actor "in immediate harmony with his audience"), the Jewish Art Theatre, and the Music Centre. Also a portfolio of Urban's designs for murals, foyers, hypothetical sites, and reliefs.

Wainscott, Ronald H. *Staging O'Neill: The Experimental Years, 1920-1934*. New Haven, Conn.: Yale University Press, 1988.
Eugene O'Neill considered stage directions as an opportunity for literary prose, and they were not always followed faithfully by his designers and directors, such as James Light, George Cram Cook, and Kenneth Macgowan. Taking a Greek drama motif for his organizing device through the masking, expressionism, and other theatrical experimentation, Wainscott moves from "Harnessing Furies" to "Eumenides" in twelve chapters on the "historical survey of the stage direction of the O'Neill dramatic canon." An interesting way into the theatre of the period. Bibliography and index; one photograph section of staging illustrations.

Waldau, Roy S. *Vintage Years of the Theatre Guild*. Cleveland: Case Western Reserve Press, 1972.

The years 1928-1939 are examined as the best the Theatre Guild offered. A producing company made of theatre artists rather than business persons, the Guild was responsible for upgrading the quality of Broadway fare after the Crash, when the Follies and vaudeville were bowing out. Appendices list productions (from *The Bonds of Interest* in 1911) through *Oklahoma!* in 1943, with full cast lists from 1928 on. Index, and Lee Simonson's famous letter to the Board of Managers in 1937 ("Dear Bored:" he begins). Good reading; packed with information.

Waldo, Paul Robert. *Production Concepts Exemplified in Selected Presentations Directed by Robert Edmond Jones*. Ann Arbor, Mich.: University Microfilms, 1976 (Ph.D. dissertation, University of Oregon, 1970).
Jones is in all the theatre history texts as a member of the Provincetown Players from 1923, as a stage designer who (according to Waldo) studied the European designers such as Adolphe Appia and brought those ideas to the American stage. There is some dispute on the matter, but this study supports the theory with details from several productions, especially *Desire Under the Elms*. Added are exasperatingly poor reproductions of dozens of interesting production stills. Strong bibliography.

Wallace, Irving. *The Fabulous Showman: The Life and Times of P. T. Barnum*. New York: Alfred A. Knopf, 1959.
The relation of circus clowning to legitimate theatre is complex. Wallace follows the master, one-half of Barnum and Bailey Circuses, as he brings audiences Chang and Eng, the Swedish Nightingale (Jenny Lind), and Jumbo. Important bibliography for scholarship and research in Western popular entertainments; index.

Wharton, John F. *Life Among the Playwrights: Being Mostly the Story of the Playwrights Producing Company, Inc.* New York: Quadrangle, 1974.
In 1938, five successful playwrights, rebelling against their "serfdom" under producers of Broadway fare, joined together to produce themselves. Led by Robert E. Sherwood, they formed the Playwrights Producing Company. Opening chapters provide the background for the rebellion and the formation of the experiment. Heavily illustrated with publicity and production shots of all the best Broadway actors of the period, the text celebrates the success of the experiment and laments current (1974) failures: "Clarity of theme is no longer regarded by critics as a necessity . . . praise may be heaped on an abstruse play which the author defiantly refuses to explain." Index; full chronology of productions from 1938 to 1960.

Williams, Anne St. Clair. *Robert Porterfield's Barter Theatre of Abingdon: Virginia; The State Theatre of Virginia*. Ann Arbor, Mich.: University Microfilms, 1976 (Ph.D. dissertation, University of Illinois at Urbana-Champaign, 1970).
Conceived in 1932 by Robert Porterfield as a response to New York-based

theatre of the depression era, the Barter opened in 1933 with *After Tomorrow* by John Golden. Porterfield lured actors from the big city with his slogan: "At least you'll eat!" Drawing largely from the Barter's own archives, Williams details the company's progress season by season, dwelling on financial and political problems and painting an interesting portrait of Porterfield himself, who was still alive when this study was done. Most valuable is the brief but informative state-of-the-economy chapter that begins the study. Appendices chronicle all details, including awards; bibliography.

Wilmeth, Don B. *The Language of American Popular Entertainment: A Glossary of Argot, Slang, and Terminology.* Westport, Conn.: Greenwood Press, 1981.
When researchers of circuses, vaudeville, medicine shows, burlesque, tent shows, and other popular entertainments run up against odd terms, this is the place to go for an explanation. Jim Crow, Joe Miller, and George Spelvin are included, doing Marinelli bends, plinging, and triple-taking for the load of hay. Good source for the derivations and gradual transformations of stage lingo into a more widely accepted vernacular. Everyone wings it once in a while.

Wise, Claude Merton. *Dramatics for School and Community.* Cincinnati, Ohio: Stewart Kidd, 1923.
Almost a primary document of noncommercial, amateur American theatre history, this text sets out in simple terms the elements for good theatre technique, as practiced in the continent-long shadow of Broadway. From "Sets and Poses from the Little Theatre, State Teachers' College, Kirksville, Missouri" (featuring "gloom," "hilarity," "conviviality," and "devotion") to outdoor pageants (and the inevitable Squaw Costume), here can be found the earnest effort of every community theatre before the Depression. Massive bibliographies and lists of plays in contemporary anthologies.

Wodehouse, P. G., and Guy Bolton. *Bring on the Girls! The Improbable Story of Our Life in Musical Comedy, with Pictures to Prove It.* 1953. Reprint. New York: Limelight Editions, 1984.
"Plum" Wodehouse was one of the funniest writers in New York (he wrote the words to "Bill" for *Show Boat*), and he is at his best when lampooning himself and friends, as here. Bracketed by a photograph section and a good index is the almost novelistic recounting of Wodehouse and Bolton's "contribution" to American theatre history: "It is the view of competent critics that—with the possible exception of *Abie's Irish Rose* and *Grandma's Diary—East is West* is the ghastliest mess ever put on the American stage, but this is an opinion held only by those who did not see *The Rose of China.* . . . It was the sort of piece where the eyes of the audience keep wandering to that cheering notice at the top of the program: 'This theater can be emptied in three minutes.'"

Worsley, Ronald Craig. *Margaret Webster: A Study of Her Contributions to the American Theatre*. Ann Arbor, Mich.: University Microfilms, 1977 (Ph.D. dissertation, Wayne State University, 1972).
"Actress, director, author, lecturer, and woman of the theatre," Margaret Webster died in 1972 after a long career as an actress and "the most influential female director the American theatre has thus far produced." From *King Richard II* on Broadway in 1937 to *Carving a Statue* in 1968, some twenty-eight Broadway productions later, Webster made her mark as the director of Shakespearean revivals and new plays. A good, if sometimes overrespectful, study. Chronologies and bibliography.

Young, Stark. *Immortal Shadows: A Book of Dramatic Criticism*. New York: Charles Scribner's Sons, 1948.
The value of this book to theatre history, aside from Young's place in creating the art of dramatic criticism, is that Young saw the American theatre as it was formed, at the theatre houses and in the productions that make theatre history today—*The Great God Brown* in 1926 at the Greenwich Village Theatre, *Street Scene* at the Playhouse in 1929, and *Glass Menagerie* there in 1945. The combination of great American plays and the comments of America's greatest critic make the publication a part of theatre history itself. Brief index of proper names.

_____. *The Theatre*. New York: Hill & Wang, 1954.
From 1921 to 1947, Stark Young was a thoughtful, almost philosophical voice of American theatre. As drama critic for the New Republic, he advised playwrights and directors, as well as audiences, on the balance of words versus spectacle, on the place of the actor in the theatrical mix, and on the relation of the director to the performance (the same that "the orchestra conductor has to music"). This small book holds the best of his advice and recommendations for "lofty and significant" theatre.

Young, William C. *Famous American Playhouses, 1900-1971*. Vol. 2 in *Documents of American Theater History*. Chicago: American Library Association, 1973.
A continuation of volume 1 (1716-1900), offering a double-column overview with many illustrations of the architecture of American theatre. Young divides his work by location, giving the first chapter to New York but the next to regional playhouses, then college and university playhouses (whose importance to theatre history increased considerably during this period), and summer playhouses. Bibliography, alphabetical and geographical index of theatres, and a separate index of "personal names and theatrical specialties." As with volume 1, well illustrated and usable; a primary source of information for twentieth century architectural innovations in theatre spaces: Dallas Theatre Center, Alley Theatre, Cincinnati Playhouse in the Park, and others. A valuable source for student and scholar and an interesting browsing book for the layperson.

Yurka, Blanche. *Bohemian Girl: Blanche Yurka's Theatrical Life.* Athens: Ohio
University Press, 1970.
For sixty years, from her first appearance in *The Bohemian Girl* to her outstanding portrayal of the Madwoman of Chaillot, Yurka loved and lived the
theatre. From 1901 to the time of this autobiography, she played major roles on
and off Broadway, after David Belasco discovered her (she compares her beginnings with modern university programs and other training methods), and fought
for Actors Equity Association. Famous names in the index indicate the kind of
company she kept for sixty years: Sarah Bernhardt, Edith Hamilton, John
Gielgud, Tyrone Guthrie, and Ian Keith (her husband).

Zabel, Morton Dauwen. *The Art of Ruth Draper: Her Dramas and Characters.* New
York: Doubleday, 1960.
Zabel's memoir of this remarkable solo actress is accompanied by a definitive
edition of thirty-five of her monologues, which she refined shortly before her
death in 1956. For some fifty years, Ruth Draper toured the United States,
Europe, and the rest of the world, performing and lecturing in hundreds of
characters, "the creation of a single person, a single voice and body, and of the
fewest aids to illusion [one] was likely to witness in a lifetime of theatre-going."
The accompanying photographs are testimony to her variety and depth of human
understanding. Highly recommended to all aspiring solo actors. An appendix lists
the stage requirements for Draper's appearances.

NEW YORK: 1945 TO THE PRESENT

Anderson, Maxwell. *Off Broadway*. New York: William Sloane, 1947.
A series of postwar essays on noncommercial theatre by Broadway's most successful poetic dramatist of the 1930's (*Elizabeth the Queen*, *Winterset*, and others). Among the best essays are a defense of poetic diction on the stage, a repair of Anderson's earlier criticism of Bernard Shaw, and the title essay, in which he outlines eight essential elements of all good playwriting, remarking, "In brief, I have found my religion in the theater."

Bain, Reginald Frank. *The Federal Government and Theatre*. Ann Arbor, Mich.: University Microfilms, 1977 (Ph.D. dissertation, University of Minnesota, 1972).
This thesis examines "a history of Federal involvement in theatre from the end of the Federal Theatre Project in 1939 to the establishment of the National Foundation on the Arts and Humanities in 1965." An interesting study of how government and the arts work, usually against each other, and usually focused on the visible evidence that art exists—buildings, theatres, exhibits—rather than the human element. Excellent documentation on projects such as the National Capital Center of the Performing Arts, and on the political considerations for and against federal support of the arts. Although the study ends at 1965, appendices provide figures for 1966-1971 NEH and other funding for regional theatre. Good selected bibliography, especially of federal documents.

Bentley, Eric. *The Dramatic Event: An American Chronicle*. New York: Horizon Press, 1954.
A fairly compressed period of time allows Bentley to offer some fifty reviews and more protracted essays. He saw the plays after their opening nights and often chose which plays to see only after reading the more immediate reviews of his colleagues. Combined with first impressions of opening-night critics, these views can inform the theatre historian who takes the time to compare and contrast both impressions. Bentley's remarks are clever and informed but not always instructive, as he often rushes to judgment without taking calm logic along for the trip. List of plays criticized added as appendix.

_____. *What Is Theatre?* New York: Atheneum, 1968.
This title is misleading, considering that this volume includes reviews from as far back as 1944 and as far forward as 1967; it incorporates the earlier "What is Theatre?" (reviews from 1954-1956) and "The Dramatic Event" (1952-1953), along with a few others, an essay, and a preface. When Bentley reviewed for *The New Republic*, he had the luxury of time to shape his views into essays, but this collection contains only honest reviews of more or less single productions. His resignation, announced in the off-Broadway *Showbill* (1957), proposes that all critics do likewise, ensuring off-Broadway's rejuvenation as "a place for experi-

mental productions of plays that either are literally or virtually new." "After-thoughts" and index.

_____. *What is Theatre? A Query in Chronicle Form.* Boston: Beacon Press, 1956.
The second half (with *The Dramatic Event*) of Bentley's reviews for *The New Republic* from 1952 to 1956, but thematically connected with a larger idea of the sense of theatre as meaningful play. Addressing the playwright's themes but at the same time dealing with the theatrical realization of those plays on the American stage, these reviews demonstrate the theatrical richness of this period, in which innovative style and realistic tradition intermix. In the title chapter, originally a lecture at the University of Virginia, Bentley states his thesis: "Theatricality is, by definition, audacious."

Blum, Daniel. *A Pictorial History of the American Theatre, 1890-1956.* New York: Greenberg, 1956.
Updated in subsequent editions to 1970, a rather different approach from Blum's other pictorial, this one is arranged chronologically. It concentrates on the great productions rather than the stars, though they are well represented in the hundreds of photographs and snapshots. Blum treats each season with enthusiasm, highlighting not only the entertainment hits (*Blossom Time* in 1921) but the serious drama that moved American theatre forward as well (*The Great God Brown* in 1926). Facts, too, on subjects such as these: Washington Square Players, Actors Equity Association, Pulitzer Prize-winners, and graceful retirements. Several pages per year; an excellent quick reference to costume styles and set design, though most stills feature the actors. Great trivia book.

Bragg, Bernard. *Lessons in Laughter: The Autobiography of a Deaf Actor.* Washington, D.C.: Gallaudet University Press, 1989.
Printed at the university for the deaf, and "signed to Eugene Bergman," this account of a deaf actor's life is the story of the gradual awakening of both the individual and the theatre business itself from the 1950's to the present. Full of anecdotes both discouraging and elated, the book owes much to the signed editor's style and sense of theatre. A good source of information on the limitations of and opportunities for deaf actors in a hearing theatre world, as well as a picture of deaf theatre's special gifts. As Bragg says to a friend, "You just signed a handful."

Brown, John Mason. *Dramatis Personae: A Retrospective Show.* New York: Viking Press, 1963.
Yet another collection of journalistic essays by the great packager of previously published material. Emphasis is on the drama as literature, though plenty of theatrical experience informs the rhetoric. Sections titled "The Changing Scene"

and "Off Stage, and On" are most theatrical; some sections ("Headmaster to the Universe—G.B.S.") are not strictly American theatre history. Index, and an epilogue on absurdist theatre, about which Brown hasn't a clue.

Chekhov, Michael. *To the Actor*. New York: Harper & Row, 1953.
Like Harold Clurman's *On Directing*, this acting text is also a statement of principle, by America's most influential acting teacher. Trained in Moscow, Chekhov opened an acting school in England and later transferred it to the United States, where it became the training ground for several generations of famous American stage actors. The improvisational exercises, the section on psychological gesture, and the chapter on how to approach the part are classics. No critical apparatus.

Chinoy, Helen Krich, and Linda Walsh Jenkins. *Women in American Theatre: Careers, Images, and Movements: An illustrated Anthology and Sourcebook*. New York: Crown, 1981.
The best kind of feminist publication because it draws attention to the massive but generally unacknowledged contributions of women to the American stage without resorting to polemics. Six chapters of strong essays are followed by a sourcebook (up to 1980) and a reference and resource section unique to literary scholarship. Text notes and index.

Clurman, Harold. *On Directing*. New York: Macmillan, 1972.
The definitive directing student's textbook, but much more: This treatise on directing reveals Clurman's work in a way that no outside observation can. Included are his own director's notes to several famous productions, including Clifford Odets's *Rocket to the Moon* and Eugene O'Neill's *A Touch of the Poet*. Included are his explanation of "The System" and "Method Acting," and eight pages of the great director in action. Index.

Conditions and Needs of the Professional American Theatre. Washington: National Endowment for the Arts, 1981.
From time to time, the National Endowment for the Humanities examines the American theatre and issues reports on what is right and wrong. This "history" is the discussion of "conditions"—financial, aesthetic, managerial—that prevailed during the ten- to fifteen-year period of this study, 1964-1980 on some charts, 1972-1980 on others. Bureaucratic rhetoric ties together the dismal facts.

Cullman, Marguerite. *Occupation: Angel*. New York: W. W. Norton, 1963.
A sort of happy-go-lucky novelistic account of a husband-and-wife team investing in Broadway shows during (at a guess) the 1940's and 1950's. Real names are used (Maxwell Anderson, Charlie Driscoll) and real plays are financed (*Mr. Roberts, Harvey*), but so few dates and places are provided ("A couple of years

slipped by," the author contributes at one point) that the book can lay no claim to theatre history. An appendix of financial statements and a few caveats about theatre investing help the book make sense, but in the absence of biographical facts, it is best treated as a theoretical history of a fictive enterprise.

Dandridge, Dorothy, and Earl Conrad. *Everything and Nothing: The Dorothy Dandridge Tragedy.* New York: Abelard-Schuman, 1970.
Dandridge is best known for her 1950's movie roles in *Carmen Jones* and *Island in the Sun.* In her own words, this is the story of her career in the theatre, her relations with white men, living through the agony of having a brain-damaged child, and trying to make a Las Vegas comeback with dignity and honor. It is really a story about sexual abuse and the invidious slavery of sex and race. Slightly to one side of theatre history, but Dandridge studied at the Actors' Laboratory even during her movie days.

Downer, Alan S., ed. *The American Theater Today.* New York: Basic Books, 1967.
A collection of essays by theatre practitioners and university scholars, especially clear-headed when the scholars discuss the practitioners. Background section gets the reader to World War II; "The Big Time" discusses postwar drama, mainly by playwright; the third section is present-tense interviews and views of modern (1967) theatre; the final section, "Off-Broadway," includes some decent discussion of university and educational theatre. The editor supplies an epilogue on theatre's future. All-article index.

Downs, Harold, ed. *Theatre and Stage: An Encyclopedic Guide to the Performance of All Amateur, Dramatic, Operatic, and Theatrical Work.* 2 vols. New Era Publishing, 1951. Reprint. Westport, Conn.: Greenwood Press, 1978.
A full-bodied guide to the way things were done in 1951, and theatre history in that sense. Not American in origin—most contributors are British, and many examples are drawn from British theatre—but widely adopted by American community and regional theatres from its first publication. A "how-to" book full of charts and schedules, as well as production stills and such borderline nonsense as a photograph of a dressing-room table and mirror. Spared many companies from reinventing the wheel. Two volumes divided alphabetically by subject.

Engel, Lehman. *The American Musical Theater: A Consideration.* New York: Macmillan, 1967.
An elegant but reservedly opinionated review of the musical form, larded with photos and stressing the not always healthy relation of Tin Pan Alley to the musical theatre. Brooks Atkinson provides a foreword, and the author supplies a preface calling for "standards" and decrying those who ignore the "precise skill involved in the creation of a fine show." Index, discography (out of date, but valuable for early recordings), and list of published librettos (also valuable).

Falk, Robert Frank. *A Critical Analysis of the History and Development of the Association of Producing Artists (APA) and the Phoenix Theatre (APA-Phoenix), 1960-1969.* Ann Arbor, Mich.: University Microfilms, 1976 (Ph.D. dissertation, Wayne State University, 1970).
An unusual configuration and merger between APA (essentially a touring company of actors under Ellis Rabb's direction beginning in 1960) and Phoenix Theatre, a New York company with a slightly longer (since 1953) history. The origins of APA and the association of the two from 1966 to 1969 are examined here in evaluative, "critical" rhetoric that asks questions, explores possible answers, and gathers the record for posterity. Chronological list in appendix. Bibliography, but no sorely needed index.

Farber, Donald C. *From Option to Opening: A Guide for the Off-Broadway Producer.* 2d ed., rev. New York: Drama Book Specialists, 1970.
This how-to book for theatre producers, written twenty years ago, acts as a history of off-Broadway ("outside a certain geographical area in the City of New York having more than 299 seats") expectations and ambitions at the time of its blurring the distinction between itself and Broadway, with off-off-Broadway taking up much of the experimental duties that off-Broadway thrived on since the 1950's. It is "a business," as the introduction points out, and is discussed as a money-making (and spending) proposition, with little attention to aesthetics.

_____. *Producing on Broadway: A Comprehensive Guide.* New York: Drama Book Specialists, 1969.
More a how-to or why-not-to guide than pure history, this large book of large ambitions has become a primary source to study how theatre used to work in the 1950's and 1960's. Its main fault is that it treats all theatre as organized negotiated contractual agreements, leaving little room for the volatile and contradictory personalities that actually make the theatre work. By comparing these "rules" with modern methods, the student can see how far the theatre has or has not come. Much good definition here; treated as an encyclopedia of terms, it is still very valuable.

Feibleman, Peter. *Lilly: Reminiscences of Lillian Hellman.* New York: William Morrow, 1988.
Augmenting and revising in some interesting ways Hellman's autobiographies, this look at American theatre's best-known woman playwright gives the reader a glimpse into her private friendships. Feibleman, who was a close friend of Hellman's for some forty years, writes freshly and clearly about the woman who wrote *The Little Foxes*, *The Children's Hour*, and *The Autumn Garden*. Playful but revealing dialogues in one-act play form give the sense of their conversations. No index, but a collection of tributes by friends after her death.

Fox, Ted. *Showtime at the Apollo*. New York: Holt, Rinehart and Winston, 1983.
From his opening anecdote (Elvis Presley visiting the Apollo in 1951), Fox
makes the Apollo seem like a magical musical black hole, where every name
African-American star got a start and came back to bail it out in hard times. The
phenomenon of a theatre building ensuring its own history by the stars on its
stage is far from unique to the Apollo, but Fox makes a case for preserving the
building simply for the memories it brings back to the actors and audiences who
witnessed its zenith. Full of photographs of stars and audiences; the fate of the
Apollo is in the balance as Fox closes his book. Index, but no chronology or list
of famous players.

Garfield, David. *A Player's Place: The Story of the Actors Studio*. New York:
Macmillan, 1980.
"Biography" of an acting company and chronicle of an aesthetic historical
moment in American theatre history. From its heritage in the Group Theatre
around 1947 to its 1980 roster of members (Marlon Brando, James Dean, Kim
Stanley) alive and deceased, this full-length portrait pays homage to a great
artistic organization. Photographs of classes, productions, parties, and awards
banquets, plus some famous publicity shots. Notes, selected bibliography, index.

Golden, Joseph. *The Death of Tinker Bell: The American Theatre in the Twentieth
Century*. Syracuse, New York: Syracuse University Press, 1967.
An "informal, yet serious . . . primer on the imperatives of theatrical life," this
essay collection is biased, even acerbic, in announcing (prematurely, it turns out)
the end of entertainment drama. Broadway-bashing mixed with unwarranted
admiration for what Joseph Golden calls "the modern medievalists"—allegorists,
moralists—gives this subjective, often tongue-in-cheek treatment a negative tone.
Very brief bibliography and no index.

Goldman, William. *The Season: A Candid Look at Broadway*. New York: Harcourt,
Brace & World, 1969.
A highly subjective and creatively expressed examination of the 1967-1968
Broadway season, but really a social study of the world of professional theatre
frozen in a season's moment. To understand how an abstraction, an institution,
can take on a life of its own, with its own anatomy, circulation, digestion,
elimination, procreation, and death, read this book as the biography of the animal
known as Broadway. Accurate? "Alas, not very." But the truth from first page
to last. Index.

Gordon, Albert Claude. *A Critical Study of the History and Development of the
Playwrights' Producing Company*. Ann Arbor, Mich.: University Microfilms,
1972 (Ph.D. dissertation, Tulane University, 1965).
The Playwrights' Producing Company was incorporated in 1938 in New York

by five of the great names in American drama: Maxwell Anderson, S. N. Behrman, Sidney Howard, Elmer Rice, and Robert E. Sherwood. This study details their agreement, their differences, and the twenty-two seasons of the company's existence from 1938 to 1960, which include sixty-four plays, three of which were Pulitzer Prize winners. Helpful appendices outline the "main events" in the company's history and reproduce the basic agreement and other memoranda of the relationship. Good chronology of the New York productions.

Gottfried, Martin. *A Theater Divided: The Postwar American Stage.* Boston: Little, Brown, 1967.
Gottfried is a little abrupt, if incisive, as he divides postwar theatre into the liberal forces of change and the conservative forces of tradition. The absence of any serious communication between the two extremes has resulted, according to Gottfried, in the current (1945-1965) unhappy "stultification of stage development." In central chapters, repertory and regional theatre are defined, praised, and prayed to as saviors of American theatre. On humor, Gottfried defines the sides by citing Jonathan Winters and Bob Hope. Good index.

Green, Stanley. *The World of Musical Comedy.* 4th ed. San Diego, Calif.: A. S. Barnes & Company, 1980.
Musical theatre history "as told through the careers of its foremost composers and lyricists." A large, double-columned reference edition with copious illustrations, organized around the biographies of the greats, chapter by chapter. Famous pairs and teams get chapters together: Rodgers and Hart (chapter 10) and Rodgers and Hammerstein (chapter 17), for example. "Musical comedy" is a suspect term, however. Especially interesting when discussing present-day working composers and teams such as Marvin Hamlisch, Edward Kleban, and Carole Bayer Sager. Stephen Sondheim is not paired with James Lapine, however. Appendix of musical production and discography; index.

Greenberger, Howard. *The Off-Broadway Experience.* Englewood Cliffs, N.J.: Prentice-Hall, 1971.
OB's biography begins with American rumblings about the European "new theatre," which found their first voice perhaps in the Washington Square Players in 1917. From there to Circle in the Square (1951) to off-off-Cafe Cino, Greenberger fondly remembers by asking "outstanding artists in every aspect of theater" to tell their part of the story in this collection of personal accounts of OB's highlights. Readable and well illustrated.

Guernsey, Otis L., Jr. *Curtain Times: The New York Theater, 1965-1987.* New York: Applause, 1987.
A comprehensive history of New York theater seasons, 1964-1987, with evaluative opinion and a lively recapitulation of the flavor and personality of each

season, "its hits and misses onstage and off, its aesthetic innards," culled from the series of *Best Plays* (published since the 1919-1920 season). Martha Swope provides the production stills and Hirschfeld the drawings, from *Fantasticks* to *Aunt Dan and Lemon*, on Broadway and off. As a reference encyclopedia, this collection is invaluable; begin with the appendix and end with the laments for better theatre, voiced every season by everybody who continues to make a living criticizing it.

Hobbs, Robert Louis. *Off-Broadway: The Early Years 1944-1952*. Ann Arbor, Mich.: University Microfilms, 1972 (Ph.D. dissertation, Northwestern University, 1964).
An interesting overview of the first impulses away from Broadway, and how quickly the theatre world accepted and acknowledged the off-Broadway movement. The Equity Library Theatre, begun in 1944, "possessed many off-Broadway characteristics" and left the question whether off-Broadway would furnish "new directions in American drama" or simply "help to find plays and players for Broadway." Good study of beginnings, but not quite as ambitious a bibliography as one might hope for.

Hoffman, Herbert H., comp. *Recorded Plays: Indexes to Dramatists, Plays, and Actors*. Chicago: American Library Association, 1985.
Designed "to guide people to performances and readings of plays that have been recorded" on phonodiscs, audio cassettes or tapes, videocassettes, and 16mm film. Lists 1,844 entries for 700 works by 284 authors, 127 of them writing in English. Author index, in which plays are numbered and described bibliographically, along with actors' names where available. Anthology entries listed in separate section (270 entries); title and actor indexes, and a directory of recording companies are added.

Houseman, John. *Final Dress*. New York: Simon & Schuster, 1983.
Houseman picks up where his first two memoirs leave off—at the American Shakespeare Festival, where he directed many works until 1964; then off to Paris and back to Julliard School of Music, where he served on the faculty from 1966 through 1972. "Over the years I have found these excavations of my past an occasionally painful but a consistently exhilarating experience." He is eighty years old at the end of this volume. Good index; illustrated with publicity shots, candid photographs, and production stills.

_____. *Front and Center: 1942-1955*. New York: Simon & Schuster, 1979.
The companion volume to *Run-Through* (covering 1902 to Pearl Harbor), this is John Houseman's memoir of one of the most exciting and creative times in American theatre history. Houseman's stage directing, screenwriting, and producing successes are described. As with his first autobiography, Houseman's motives

are to record for posterity his friends and associates through "the timid but irrepressible egotist known as 'I.'" This volume takes his career from "Voice of America" (after a brief review) through "the miraculous year" of 1947, to the MGM years (1954). As director and actor, Houseman was one of a kind. Graciously written and accompanied by important illustrations of documents, excellent photographic stills, and production shots; a little heavy on the film side of his career. Index.

Hughes, Catharine, ed. *New York Theatre Annual: 1976-1977 and 1977-1978*. 2 vols. Detroit: Gale Research, 1978.
Containing production information, a brief plot outline, cast lists, one production still (none for *Oh, Calcutta*, however), and a critical overview culled from reviews "to provide a balanced cross section of opinion on the various aspects of each production" for each play that opened "on and off Broadway" during the season, along with selected off-off-Broadway fare. Four sections. Indexes of plays and individuals or organizations.

Hughes, Langston, and Milton Meltzer. *Black Magic: A Pictorial History of the Negro in American Entertainment*. Englewood Cliffs, N.J.: Prentice-Hall, 1967.
Published shortly after Hughes's death in 1967, this very popular pictorial has become a primary source of portraiture for African-American artists, an excellent starting point for student research into this rich heritage. Page after page of stunning publicity photographs, production stills, and posters of African-American entertainments, energetic even in the reproductions. To choose only one among a hundred: Miriam Makeba, the Xhosa "click" singer from South Africa. Index.

Ilson, Carol. *Harold Prince: From "Pajama Game" to "Phantom of the Opera."* Ann Arbor, Mich.: UMI Research Press, 1989.
An accurate and colorful account of this leading producer-director (sixteen Tonys) of American (by which Ilson means Broadway) musicals. Lyricist Sheldon Harnick, in a brief foreword, says, "Ms. Ilson manages to give us the sense that we are actually onstage with Hal, smack in the middle of a rehearsal, complete with illuminating (and sometimes surprising) descriptions of his directorial rehearsal techniques." Organized by musical, the chapters move through Prince's career with vigor and dramatic intensity. Packed with insider information and drawing a full portrait of the way the Broadway musical has worked under Prince's creative genius for almost forty years. A must for students of contemporary Broadway theatre. Notes, illustrations, bibliography, index.

Kaplan, Mike, ed. *Variety International Showbusiness Reference*. New York: Garland, 1981.
"A distillation of key information" from *Variety*, the single most frequently read periodical of the performing arts. *Variety* gets thousands of phone calls daily for

show business information, and, judging from the nature of those calls, the editor has selected the kind of reference information most needed: biographies, necrology, Broadway play credits, 1976 through 1980 (production personnel and opening date, actors, and musical numbers), and Tonys from 1947. Full list of awards, by year. Film and television credits also, but mercifully in their own sections. The abbreviated, nonsentence style takes a little getting used to, but this volume is packed with facts.

Kernan, Alvin B., ed. *The Modern American Theater: A Collection of Critical Essays.* Englewood Cliffs, N.J.: Prentice-Hall, 1967.
A misleading title, since most of the essays deal with American drama. This collection tacitly defines "modern" as Arthur Miller to Edward Albee, with only a nod to the "Happenings" of Allan Kaprow. Part 3 ("The Theatres") deals with Broadway, off-Broadway, and what Elenore Lester calls "The Pass-the-Hat Theater Circuit," an unflattering reference to off-off-Broadway. The entire collection is out of date and unreliable, but it might point in some interesting directions. Brief bibliography.

Kerr, Walter. *The Theater in Spite of Itself.* New York: Simon & Schuster, 1963.
Pieces written from 1957 to 1962, not exactly retrospectives of plays, but rather quick sketches of Broadway and off-Broadway theatre's oddments. Drawn in large swipes of metaphor, dangled from thin thesis statements, swaying in the breeze of Kerr's own linguistic imagination (the style is catching). To what degree his observations are accurate or even fair cannot be assessed, but they are readable, witty, often nasty, sometimes incisive. They do not inform the history of American theatre so much as stand witness to the art of the subjective theatrical opinion. No critical apparatus.

Kislan, Richard. *The Musical: A Look at the American Musical Theater.* Englewood Cliffs, N.J.: Prentice-Hall, 1980.
A fundamental book for the beginner that provides simple information on the historical evolution, ideas, practices, and contributions of "mature" artists, and the major elements of musical shows. Could serve as a textbook or supplement to theatre history or introduction to theatre courses. Four "mature artists" are discussed: Jerome Kern, Rodgers and Hammerstein (as a team), and Stephen Sondheim. Farthest from theatre history but closest to unique is the section on the elements of musical theater, a guide through the creation and collaboration process. Highly recommended.

Langley, Stephen. *Theatre Management in America: Principle and Practice.* New York: Drama Book Publishers, 1974. Revised 1980.
This is theatre history in the sense that the principles of "producing for the commercial, stock, resident, college and community theatre" outlined here have

been culled from the history of American theatre. Also historical because two generations (a theatre generation is ten years) of theatre practitioners have been brought up on Langley's textbook for "the third century manager." Part 2 ("Methods of Theatrical Producing") contains historical background information on commercial, stock, and other company structures; from logo title layouts to appendices of box office figures to the index, this book explains how theatre has worked and can work. Highly recommended.

Laufe, Abe. *Broadway's Greatest Musicals*. New York: Funk & Wagnalls, 1973. This "illustrated edition" of Laufe's semischolarly, semipopular study splits its focus: some chapters deal directly with a single musical (*Show Boat*, *Oklahoma!*, *South Pacific*, *My Fair Lady*, each get their own chapter), whereas others take general periods ("The Mid 1940's," "The Late 1950's"). No clearly articulated thematic approach in the introduction, but the criteria for inclusion and the emphasis of the rhetoric are on box office receipts, length of runs, and similar unromantic data. Great, for Laufe, means "a run of at least 500 consecutive performances on Broadway." Bibliography, indexes of titles and names, and an appendix of long-running musicals.

Leiter, Samuel L. *Ten Seasons: New York Theatre in the Seventies*. Westport, Conn.: Greenwood Press, 1986.
A clear-headed, comprehensive account of every aspect of New York theatre during this audacious decade, or as much as Leiter could get into the first volume of what promises to be an encyclopedia. Excellent descriptions of off-off-Broadway events, often too fleeting and uncommercial to have left much of a trail behind for historians. This work might be the best starting place for study of more specific phenomena such as the Performance Group, Mabou Mines, Robert Wilson, and the Ontological-Hysteric Theatre because the flavor of the whole decade is here. Strong index.

Little, Stuart W. *Off-Broadway: The Prophetic Theater*. New York: Dell Books, 1972.
Said to have begun with Jose Quintero's production of Tennessee Williams' *Summer and Smoke* at Circle in the Square in 1952, "off Broadway" was more than a geographical observation. It was a declaration of independence from the profit-driven, commercial uptown theatre—professional, serious, but dedicated to artistic excellence rather than the demands of commodity. Little describes the younger, more idealistic years of the movement, stopping at the much more complex arrangement between the late Joseph Papp's Public Theater and commercial Broadway. A sound and thoughtful history of the era, with valuable lists of Obie winners to 1971 and an index that reads like a "who's who" of the off-Broadway phenomenon.

Little, Stuart W., and Arthur Cantor. *The Playmakers*. New York: W. W. Norton, 1970.

An insider's view of how Broadway works—its producers, directors, actors, stagehands, night watchmen, and make-up artists. Interviewing hundreds of theatre "professionals," Little and Cantor have assembled both a psychiatric casebook and a collage portrait of the Broadway beast on a typical day. One photograph section follows an actress through a typical day; another puts faces to famous behind-the-scenes names such as Clive Barnes and Audrey Wood. Index.

Logan, Joshua. *Josh: My Up and Down, In and Out Life*. New York: Delacorte Press, 1976.

Showing the "bare bones" of American Broadway, along with private admissions regarding his manic-depressive personality, Logan covers his busy career as director, author, and producer, from his first success (*To See Ourselves*, 1935) to *Rip Van Winkle*, a snoozer at the Kennedy Center in 1976. Logan ends his own story with his direction of the film version of *Picnic*, the culmination of his genius. Chronology, index, and about fifty snapshots and production stills.

Loney, Glenn, ed. *Musical Theatre in America: Papers and Proceedings of the Conference on the Musical Theatre in America*. Westport Conn.: Greenwood Press, 1984.

The conference, held in 1981 at the C. W. Post Center of Long Island University, generated these papers—some historical, some futuristic—on the state of the American musical. Arranged in rough chronological order, by century, with a final section on "Preserving the Heritage." Sixty-four illustrations have been added for this publication. Refer to the table of contents for specific areas of inquiry. Selected bibliography; cross-article index.

McCarthy, Mary. *Mary McCarthy's Theatre Chronicles 1937-1962*. New York: Farrar, Straus, 1963. Expanded from *Sights and Spectacles*, New York: Meridian, 1956).

Written with charm and insight by "an insufferable little-magazine reviewer" (*Partisan Review*), clearly cognizant of her earlier voice, that "of a young, earnest, pedantic, pontificating critic, being cocksure and condescending." McCarthy covers the most important new plays of her time, selected from twenty-five years of reviewing, not as arid literary products but as theatrical experiences ("The main actors in *Look Back in Anger* appear to be three newspapers and an ironing-board"). Gives a decidedly socialistic, if not Bolshevik, slant to her criticism, all the while denying any such bias. Valuable because of her magnificent writing style—thus Eugene O'Neill's *The Iceman Cometh*: "The play is like some stern piece of hardware in one of those dusty old-fashioned stores into which no Pyrex dish or herb shelf or French provincial earthenware had yet penetrated, which dealt in iron-colored enamel, galvanized tin, lengths of pipe and wrenches, staples, saws, and nails, and knew nothing more sophisticated than the double boiler." If her judgment is suspect, her enthusiasm for the stage is not. No critical apparatus.

McClave, Nancy R. *The American Repertory Theatre, Inc.: A Case Study*. Ann Arbor, Mich.: University Microfilms, 1985 (Ph.D. dissertation, Kent State University, 1982).
Repertory is a difficult kind of theatrical arrangement, often idealized but seldom accomplished among the practicalities of theatre compromise. This group (not to be confused with the current ART at Harvard University) lasted one year (1946-1947), despite the impressive credentials of its three founders: Cheryl Crawford, Eva Le Gallienne, and Margaret Webster. McClave cites "lack of funds" as the main root of the three artists' troubles, but more specifically it was the difficulties of the classic fare seeking and finding a Broadway audience. Good documentation and good source of brief biographies of some of the actors, including Victor Jory. Financial tables; bibliography.

McGill, Raymond D., ed. *Notable Names in the American Theatre*. Clifton, N.J.: James T. White, 1976.
An updated, revised version of *The Biographical Encyclopaedia and Who's Who of the American Theatre* (1966). Headings (before the body of the work, which is "Notable Names in the American Theatre") for New York productions, premieres in America, premieres of American plays abroad, theatre group biographies (particularly valuable for research in regional theatre), theatre building biographies, awards, biographical bibliography, and necrology.

Mapp, Edward. *Directory of Blacks in the Performing Arts*. 2d ed. Metuchen, N.J.: Scarecrow Press, 1990. 1st ed. 1978.
Valuable single-volume source for information on African-American performing artists, "a compendium of biographical and career facts on more than 850 African-American individuals, living and deceased, who have earned a degree of recognition for their work in the performing arts." From John Hewlett, star of the 1821 African Company, to Bert Williams ("Nobody"), the little theatre groups in Harlem ("the proving grounds for Ossie Davis, Ruby Dee . . . Sidney Poitier, Harry Belafonte, Alice Childress and on and on"), to Esther Rolle's Lady Macbeth off-Broadway in 1977 (the end of the first edition) and Ntozake Shange (but ten years out of date on this entry, added in the second edition). One category is perhaps unique: relationships (Altovise Gore, who studied with Lee Strasberg, is the wife of Sammy Davis, Jr.). Adds a very good bibliography and directory of organizations. Highly recommended, but some entries are not entirely current.

Miller, Arthur. *Timebends*. New York: Grove Press, 1987.
The long-awaited autobiography of a very complex man, this is a primary source
for Miller's reactions and reportage of his several Broadway successes (*All My
Sons*, *Death of a Salesman*, *The Crucible*) and his marriages to Inge Morath and
Marilyn Monroe. Tells stories well; for example, the story of his takeover as
director of *The Price* in Washington. Index helps readers find theatre information
among the personal anecdotes.

Mitchell, Loften. *Voices of the Black Theatre*. Clifton, N.J.: James T. White, 1975.
Seven theatre people—Ruby Dee, Abram Hill, Eddie Hunter, Dick Campbell,
Vinnette Carroll, Frederick O'Neal, and Regina M. Andrews—are first introduced, then speak in their own voices about their careers as pioneers of black
theatre, though (as Ruby Dee points out) the history of black theatre began long
ago and far away. As a history of the universal struggle to succeed in the theatre
world, which is at the same time both hostile toward and indifferent to color, this
collection of brief autobiographies works very well. An interlude on Paul Robe-
son is also given; portraits and index.

Moody, Richard. *Lillian Hellman: Playwright*. New York: Pegasus, 1972.
A study of her life and plays, with considerable theatrical information embedded
in the text: opening-night activities, critical responses, relations with fellow
theatre professionals. Written some years before her death. Stills of six plays.
Notes on sources, selected bibliography, and index.

Moore, Thomas Gale. *The Economics of the American Theater*. Durham, N.C.:
Duke University Press, 1968.
The invisible side of theatre, money management, is discussed in a partly how-to
and partly descriptive study. Out of date as to figures but not in terms of the
forces driving theatre forward. Charts, graphs, tables of all kinds; audience
surveys and statistics, box office procedures, production tallies—the fuel and fire
of theatre reduced to numbers. As much an economics sourcebook as theatre
history, but it does chronicle the development of federal funding, state arts
councils and commissions. Bibliography (selected) and an elaborate index.

Mostel, Kate, and Madeline Gilford, with Jack Gilford and Zero Mostel. *170 Years
of Show Business*. New York: Random House, 1978.
The title adds up the years that the four authors have logged in "that crazy world
called show business." Husband-and-wife teams, the Mostels and Gilfords were
the funnymen and funnywomen of Broadway during the 1960' and 1970's, though
photographs (mostly snapshots of everyone mugging for the camera) go back to
about 1930. The text is chatty and informal, full of anecdote but a little sparse
in biographical skills. Worth exploring if one is seeking a warm-hearted backstage view of the comic life.

Nathan, George Jean. *The Theatre Book of the Year, 1942-1947*. New York: Alfred
A. Knopf, 1942-1947.
A series of review collections by this most intellectual and acerbic of reviewers.
"A Record and an Interpretation" more than first-night reviews per se, this series
is more valuable for the "record" than the "interpretation," in that Nathan never
quite avoids making the mistake he attributes to Noel Coward (in the 1946 review
of *Present Laughter*), "which consists in blowing soap bubbles through an
upturned nose." Emblematic of the pomposity of the entire project is Nathan's
"honor list" of the "best new" categories, and his appendix of "Especially
Interesting Performances." Nevertheless, as theatre document, this series can lead
to fruitful inquiry.

Nelson, Benjamin. *Arthur Miller: Portrait of a Playwright*. London: Peter Owen,
1970.
Perhaps too much a dissection of Miller's writing to be pure theatre history, but
enough discussion of the methods that Miller used to accommodate the theatre
producers and directors waiting for his next work, the "genesis" of the texts, to
warrant inclusion in a theatre history bibliography. Discusses autobiographical
elements in several of his plays. Mentions of William Saroyan, Jo Meilziner, Elia
Kazan (interesting material on the withdrawal from Lincoln Center Repertory
Theater), and other theatre acquaintances; index.

New York Cultural Consumer. New York: New York Foundation for the Arts, 1976.
An odd bit of statistical gossip about who attends "cultural" events (museums
included) and why. Revealing of the compilers because the questions asked are
full of fear and predilections. "Attitudes Toward Theatre," one category, gives
a vote of confidence to the volatile 1970's: "Seven in ten audience members
disagreed . . . that 'there is very little new in theatre; most modern plays are just
rehashes of what has been better done before.'" Compared with opera audiences,
theatre audiences "are more heavily female, somewhat younger, but still well
educated and affluent."

Nugent, Elliott. *Events Leading Up to the Comedy*. New York: Trident Press, 1965.
A valuable lesson in stage collaboration from James Thurber's coauthor of *The
Male Animal*, this autobiography of a little-known actor, producer, and director
chronicles the transitional years between Hollywood and Broadway. Nugent, a
man "who was perhaps better able to cope with defeat than victory," describes
his own alcohol problems and Thurber's near-misses candidly and honestly.

O'Donnol, Shirley Miles. *American Costume, 1915-1970: A Source Book for the
Stage Costumer*. Bloomington: Indiana University Press, 1982.
From "a fine figger of a woman" to vinyl rainwear ensembles, the American
silhouette through the twentieth century is drawn, photographed, and discussed

in a valuable sourcebook by one of Lucy Barton's protéges and colleagues. Not strictly stage history, but a way into production stills; social habits, accessories, even ways of standing are discussed. Fully illustrated, with bibliography.

Perry, Jeb H. *Variety Obits: An Index to Obituaries in 'Variety,' 1905-1978.* Metuchen, N.J.: Scarecrow Press, 1980.
One of the fastest ways to get information on theatre history because everyone alive is automatically out of the running. Gives professional name, real name, age at death, date of death, principal professional title, and location of obituary in *Variety*, date and page. List includes legitimate stage, minstrelsy, and vaude-ville (as well as movies, television, and radio), but excludes burlesque, cabaret, circus, night clubs, and outdoor amusements. Borderline: knife throwers, fire-eaters, mind readers, headless horsemen, and animal acts. Indexes such as this one save a lot of thumbing through back issues.

Preminger, Erik Lee. *Gypsy and Me: At Home and on the Road with Gypsy Rose Lee.* Boston: Little, Brown, 1984.
Written by her son by Otto Preminger, this intimate account of the life of an "exotic dancer" tells the real story behind the glamorized musical version, *Gypsy*. A non-scholarly but convincing description of a distinctly American stage form, and an unromantic view of life on the road for someone desired by all but loved by few. No critical apparatus except an index.

Redfield, William. *Letters from an Actor.* New York: Viking Press, 1967.
In 1964, John Gielgud directed and Richard Burton performed the title role in *Hamlet*, trying out in Toronto and Boston and opening in New York in April. One of the cast members (he played Guildenstern) wrote letters regularly and colorfully during the process to a friend and "literary man who is curious about the inner workings of the theatre." Edited for publication, these are insightful, immediate observations from an actor's view of one of the great productions of modern theatre. Campy and catty and good reading.

Robbins, Jhan. *Yul Brynner: The Inscrutable King.* New York: Dodd, Mead, 1987.
Written by a journalist who knew Brynner since the 1950's, this study deals with the whole man: photographer, television director, furniture designer, "America's new sex symbol," and, perhaps down the line, actor. While his film career is dealt with extensively here (along with a filmography), his stage work, especially in *The King and I*, is well documented and identifies the star qualities that Brynner brought to the part. "A typical Mongolian boy," Brynner revived his role in 1985, the year of his death by lung cancer. Robbins asks the question, was his career wasted? He answers yes.

Roberts, Kenneth Harris. *The Lincoln Center Repertory Theatre, 1958-1965*. Ann Arbor, Mich.: University Microfilms, 1976 (Ph.D. dissertation, Ohio State University, 1966).
Conceived as the center of a new age in American theatre, the Lincoln Center experience has been far from Utopian to the several producers and artistic directors attempting the metaphorical "long cross." After describing the elements that brought the company and the theatre building into existence and chronicling the Whitehead-Kazan failures, Roberts ironically titles the final chapter "The Future: Blau and Irving." He knowingly hints of troubles even as he closes his dissertation. A good, neutral recap of the socioeconomic, architectural, and aesthetic complexities of the project. Bibliography but no index.

Rodgers, Richard. *Musical Stages: An Autobiography*. New York: Random House, 1975.
The American musical is unique to theatre history, and Richard Rodgers' contribution to that phenomenon is unassailably first-rate. With Lorenz Hart (their first success was in 1925) and then with Oscar Hammerstein II, Rodgers supplied some of the best-loved music of the stage, including *Oklahoma!* (1943), *The King and I* (1952), and *The Sound of Music* (1959). His pre-Hammerstein days are well recalled, but photographs concentrate on postwar successes. Index but no chronology.

Ross, Lillian, and Hellen Ross. *The Player: A Profile of an Art*. New York: Simon & Schuster, 1962.
An interesting stylistic device—"autobiographies" based on long interviews with the actors—separates this collection from other "portraits of the artist." Twenty-one of the fifty-five pieces appeared in *New Yorker Magazine* between 1958 and 1962; taken together, they constitute an historical record of the acting industry during that volatile period. Photographs by the author. Useful index.

Rumley, Jerry Bruce. *An Analysis of the Adaptation of Selected Plays into the Musical Form from 1943 to 1963*. Ann Arbor, Mich.: University Microfilms, 1975 (Ph.D. dissertation, University of Minnesota, 1969).
A study of how the American musical transforms the often mediocre prose plays of its source into the musical book of such greats as *Oklahoma!* (from Lynn Riggs's *Green Grow the Lilacs*) and the sometimes great plays into mediocre musicals (*The Rainmaker* into *110 in the Shade*). Rumley outlines the problem and the history of the practice for almost half the book, then treats four adaptations (including *Street Scene* and *Wonderful Town*, after *My Sister Eileen*). Appendices include a list of musicals adalpted from plays or film scripts that appeared in New York on or off Broadway from 1943 to 1963. Bibliography.

Schneider, Alan. *Entrances: An American Director's Journey.* New York: Viking Press, 1986. Reprint. New York: Limelight, 1987.

The autobiography of a talented director and articulate advocate of new plays from World War II to his death in 1984, nine days after delivering this manuscript to the publisher. His is the story of the discovery and production of the plays of Edward Albee, Samuel Beckett, and dozens of other contemporary playwrights, and the story of how new talent finds its way to the stage. Most important, it is the story of genius recognizing the genius in others. Excellent photograph sections of cornerstone productions and Schneider in action, his famous cap in evidence. Index, and an immense production-direction list covering forty years, tragically cut short at James Duff's *The Home Front*.

Shelton, Lewis Edward. *Alan Schneider's Direction of Four Plays by Edward Albee: A Study in Form.* Ann Arbor, Mich.: University Microfilms, 1976 (Ph.D. dissertation, University of Wisconsin, 1971).

An insightful look at Schneider's "directorial intention in terms of his use of four elements of form," concentrated on four Albee plays: *Who's Afraid of Virginia Woolf?*, *The American Dream*, *Tiny Alice*, and *A Delicate Balance*. Works toward supporting the hypothesis that "Schneider sought to preserve each text's presentation of reality through its appropriate theatrical form." Benefits from complete access to Schneider's personal production files and an interview with the director. Full production data for all Albee plays under Schneider's direction. Bibliography. Good for comparing with Schneider's autobiographical discussion of the same works.

Simon, John. *Uneasy Stages: A Chronicle of the New York Theater, 1963-1973.* New York: Random House, 1976.

A collection of Simon's reviews and retrospectives from *New York Magazine* and *The Hudson Review*, slightly revised. Simon is known for his learned, "elitist" style, as he himself points out in the introduction. Arranged by the four seasons and moving through a fairly arbitrary ten-year period, beginning with *Beyond the Fringe* and ending with *That Championship Season*, these essays cannot be accused of even-handedness or tact. Occasionally, however, they say something telling about actors, directors, or theatre in general. Long index.

Smith, Harry Willard. *Mielziner and Williams: A Concept of Style.* Ann Arbor, Mich.: University Microfilms, 1973 (Ph.D. dissertation, Tulane University, 1965).

Mielziner designed the sets for seven of Williams' plays; this study assumes "the sound bases in aesthetic and dramatic values common to the work of the two men" revealing "a fundamental similarity of stylistic approach." Following the method of the designer himself in analyzing the plays, Smith determines and defines the fundamental concepts of the plays, then turns (in an entire chapter) to "the development of Jo Mielziner's design style . . . structured on forty years in the main stream of American professional theatre." Excellent approach, revealing of both men's work. Appendix lists eleven Broadway productions with directors and designers. Bibliography.

Spoonberg, Arvid F. *Broadway Talks: What Professionals Think About Commercial Theater in America.* Westport, Conn.: Greenwood Press, 1991.
The views, in interview format, of those who are under-represented in theatre print: producers, designers, labor and management spokespersons, and, finally, playwrights. Forty-seven interviews from 1983 to 1989, but only twenty (and those excerpted) are given here. A brief biography begins each interview; bibliography and index help the researcher through the information, which is sometimes chatty and informal but adds considerably to what is known about how the theatre works as part of the free enterprise system. Especially informative on the Broadway/regional theatre partnership.

Spurrier, James Joseph. *The Integration of Music and Lyrics with the Book in the American Musical.* Ann Arbor, Mich.: University Microfilms, 1982 (Ph.D. dissertation, Southern Illinois University, 1979).
This examination of the lyric/music integration starts with early ballad opera, minstrel shows, burlesque, and comic opera and works its way through *Show Boat, Pal Joey,* and *Oklahoma!* up to *Hair* and Stephen Sondheim. Analyzes "the techniques by which and the degree to which the musical elements, the music and lyrics, of American musicals have been integral to the advancement of the plot." Appendixed are scores from representative musical pieces; bibliography.

Stevenson, Isabelle, ed. *The Tony Award: A Complete Listing with a History of the American Theatre Wing.* New York: Arno Press, 1975.
Antoinette Perry chaired the American Theatre Wing, originally a ladies' war relief effort in 1917, during its World War II years. The Tony Awards, Broadway's most prestigious honors, are named after her. An official list of the winners in some twenty-seven categories (plus special awards) over the 1947-1974 period. An introduction gives a brief history of the society, and an appendix offers the exact wording of the Tony Award criteria.

Suskin, Steven. *Opening Night on Broadway: A Critical Quotebook of the Golden Era of the Musical Theatre, "Oklahoma!" (1943) to "Fiddler on the Roof" (1964).* New York: Schirmer Books, 1990.
Arranged alphabetically, not chronologically, these entries give the usual information: cast, writers, and so on (along with a photofacsimile of the poster). They go further, however, answering other questions: "What were the shows really like for the audiences sitting in the theatres? What was it about the classic musicals that set them apart?" Suskin goes back to the reviews for a sense of

immediacy, writing in anecdotal but enthusiastic style and inserting review quotations to back up his impressions. The opening chapter gives an overview of musical theatre before *Oklahoma!*, which "expanded, advanced, and exploded the parameters of the musical theatre." Chronology, notable careers, and a good appendix of critics' biographies; index.

Swain, Joseph P. *The Broadway Musical: A Critical and Musical Survey.* New York: Oxford University Press, 1990.
An unusual and very effective study of the American musical form, this time concentrating on the ability of the music to inform the themes and structure of book and lyric. Requires a basic understanding of musical terminology and an ability to read music. Swain's thesis—that music and song "establish characters, move the plot, intensify conflicts, and constitute other events that would be expected of a spoken play"—is well argued and demonstrated with examples, mostly from post-*Oklahoma!* selections. Provides "a musical analysis . . . [to connect] the songs in their detail with the dramatic elements of plot, character, and action." Notes and index.

Webster, Margaret. *Don't Put Your Daughter on the Stage.* New York: Alfred A. Knopf, 1972.
Collecting "never before told" stories of thirty-five years of theatre (from 1937), this lovable lady of the stage, a contemporary of Eva Le Galliene and Helen Hayes, offers her warm-hearted memoirs to the long list. Something of her directorial spirit prevails as well; photographs of her demonstrations of "dying," "stabbing," "dancing," and "being a villain" grace her own generous text.

Weiss, David William. *Jo Mielziner's Contribution to the American Theatre.* Ann Arbor, Mich.: University Microfilms, 1973 (Ph.D. dissertation, Indiana University, 1965).
Volume 1 of this examination of the famous designer, "one who appeared at the peak of the new wave of design theory early in this century to carry on and expand that theory in a fresh and continually exciting manner," is Weiss's text. Volume 2 reproduces, with only partial success, the plates Weiss uses to illustrate his points. Weiss looks backward at Gordon Craig and Adolphe Appia before examining "ten of Mielziner's most successful designs" which "represent not only some of Mielziner's best work but the full extent of the variety of plays for which he has designed scenery, including classics, poetic drama, realistic serious drama, and musical plays." Weiss himself went on to a successful career in designing for academic theatre. Bibliography.

Who's Who in Entertainment. Wilmette, Ill.: Marquis Who's Who, Macmillan Directory Division, 1988.
Anyone who was making a living in 1988 doing anything that "diverts, amuses,

stimulates, or engages one's imagination and attention," is listed here. Many serious artists are not listed. "Not intended as an homage to those who entertain us; rather, it is a valuable reference source for users both inside and outside the entertainment industry." Interesting fact: 25 percent reside in either Los Angeles or New York City. Those listed reviewed proofs for accuracy, and "individuals of high reference interest" were researched independently (denoted by asterisk).

Wilk, Max. *Every Day's a Matinee: Memoirs Scribbled on a Dressing Room Door.* New York: W. W. Norton, 1975.
Six years old in 1926, scared under his seat at a movie, Wilk begins his memoirs, "born thirty years too late" and in love with the dying art of vaudeville. Not exactly theatre history, this humorous look at the transition from stage to film of vaudeville's unwritten rules serves to raise the bridge (or lower the river) for safe passage from theatre to the silver screen. Wilk's last anecdote (1970) finds Leland Hayward and two turtle-necked FBI men at the Mark Taper's production of *The Trial of the Catonsville Nine*—"eventually," says Wilk in a serious moment, "a tortured self-examination for all of us." Good index.

Williams, Tennessee. *Memoirs.* New York: Doubleday, 1975.
Among the dozens of biographies and personal remembrances of Williams, this one gives a good sense of how the theatre worked around him. Protracted discussion of his agent Audry Wood, especially when their relationship soured. A candid self-appraisal of his personal and professional life. "How can I honestly say, 'Je ne regrette rien'?" Good description of the disastrous first reading of *Sweet Bird of Youth* in "that great barn, the Martin Beck." Several photograph sections; index.

Woll, Allen. *Dictionary of the Black Theatre: Broadway, Off-Broadway, and Selected Harlem Theatre.* Westport, Conn.: Greenwood Press, 1983.
An unusual but effective treatment of theatre history: an alphabetical review of people and events in black theatre history. Arranged in two parts, by shows and by personalities and organizations, the book adds appendices of chronologies and discographies. Selected bibliography, name index, play and film index, song index, and notes on contributors. Especially valuable are the off-Broadway summaries, the references to the Negro Ensemble Company, the New Federal Theatre, and the Public Theatre, and Woll's opening essay, a brief history of the black theatre, full of facts and free of rhetoric.

Wood, Audrey. *Represented by Audrey Wood.* Garden City, N.Y.: Doubleday, 1981.
The most famous theatrical agent in America, Wood "discovered" Tennessee Williams, Robert Anderson, Preston Jones, Arthur Kopit, Carson McCullers, and Brian Friel, to name a few. This self-portrait, aided by theatre man Max Wilk,

gives a different view on the world of theatre, from the desk of the diminutive but all-important go-between for the playwright and producer. Along with inside information on the playwright-script relationship are many personal glimpses of Audrey herself as a wife, friend, and inveterate humanist. Well written and entertaining, even when grim; she died in 1981, and Wilk provides an affectionate postscript. Index.

REGIONAL THEATRE

Alexander, Darrel Eugene. *A History of the Mummers Theatre Oklahoma City, Oklahoma, 1949-1972*. Ann Arbor, Mich.: University Microfilms, 1978 (Ph.D. dissertation, Louisiana State University, 1974).
Begun as "Mayde Mack's Summer Mummers" in a summer tent theatre well before the American play explosion of the 1960's and moving to an "indescribable" new facility in 1970, Mummers mounted popular productions of comedies and musicals, with "name" guest actors filling out a more or less permanent local company. The company did not survive the financial burdens of its new facilities, though the buildings did win architectural acclaim. Much information came from interviews with Mack Scism, the group's creative center. Volume 2 contains all documents and appendices. Poor reproduction of photographic material.

Bergin, Ron. *Sponsorship and the Arts: A Practical Guide to Corporate Sponsorship of the Performing and Visual Arts*. Evanston, Ill.: Entertainment Resource Group, 1990.
A small booklet for businesses seeking their first venture into "an arrangement between a corporation or business and a fine arts or entertainment organization through which the sponsor promotes a product or itself." Although using rock group sponsorships as models, the book concentrates on fine arts sponsorships, including the Old Globe Theatre arrangement with Montgomery Ward (but not other, better examples in the theatre world). A glossary of terms ("product placement," "psychographics," and other grim representatives of the business world), and sample contractual letters.

Bigsby, C. W. E. *Beyond Broadway*. Vol. 3 in *A Critical Introduction to Twentieth-Century American Drama*. Cambridge, England: Cambridge University Press, 1985.
This third volume of Bigsby's important work necessarily converts his study from dramatic literature to theatre history, given that the theatre companies in his purview do not rely on prescriptive texts to generate their performances. The introduction summarizes the advance of non-Broadway theatre to prominence; the text singles out five playwrights, six performance companies, and four special interests (Native American, African-American, gay, and women's theatre). Strong bibliography and index, and Theatre Communication Group's outline of the growth of nonprofit professional theatre.

Brustein, Robert. *Making Scenes: A Personal History of the Turbulent Years at Yale 1966-1979*. New York: Random House, 1981.
Brustein did more than design Yale Repertory into a top-notch regional theatre; he transformed the volatile director-playwright relationship and made the aca-

demic acting company concept work out of the shadow of academic bureaucracy. The Yale Repertory Theatre and the Yale School of Drama both owe their notoriety to the energies of Brustein, who, disenchanted with the university's inability to take artistic chances, removed himself to Harvard in 1979 to establish the American Repertory Theatre company. This record of the events, both aesthetic and political, of his tenure in New Haven reads like an adventure, and it was. Taking his experiences year by year, season by season, he discusses the infighting, the aesthetic compromises, and the grinding, ever-present conflict between aesthetic vision and financial reality. List of Yale Rep productions 1966-1979; index. Highly recommended to students of contemporary play development and classic revival dramaturgy.

Charles, Jill, ed. *Regional Theatre Directory*. New York: Theatre Communications Group, 1991.
An annual project (since the mid-1980's) of TCG, the center for regional theatre communications. Contains handy and valuable fact sheets on theatres, including names of artistic and producing directors, size of house, season dates, hiring policies and salary ranges, internship opportunities, and more. Essentially a sourcebook for theatre artists, but also a historical document for regional theatre through periods of growth and change of management. It is a mistake for libraries to discard old volumes when new ones are issued.

Clark, William Benjamin, Jr. *A History of the Cleveland Play House 1936-1958*. Ann Arbor, Mich.: University Microfilms, 1981 (Ph.D. dissertation, Tulane University, 1968).
Studies of this kind fall into the trap of emphasizing ticket sales figures, union disputes, economic booms and busts, and similar financial matters, as though the play company's history is the history of its pocketbook. Clark is slightly better than most, dealing with, for example, the artistic reasoning behind the children's wing of the theatre. His season by season summaries dwell once again on the almighty dollar, however, not on aesthetics, as the core of theatrical success. Myriad appendices, documents, bibliographies.

Coe, Linda C., comp. *Funding Sources for Cultural Facilities: Private and Federal Support for Capital Projects*. Washington, D.C.: National Endowment for the Arts, 1980.
Briefly describes 135 foundations as sources for capital improvement support to the arts (performing and visual). Bricks-and-mortar construction, renovation and improvements, land or building acquisitions, and more. Three types—private foundations, community foundations (public charities), and company-sponsored foundations. Arranged by state, with asterisks denoting national funders. Each entry provides addresses, contact names, restrictions, priorities, amounts of 1977 awards, and examples. Also describes twenty-one major federal programs

providing funds for culturally-related capital projects. Adds a good bibliography for private funding source information.

Cohen, Edward M. *Working on a New Play: A Play Development Handbook for Actors, Directors, Designers, and Playwrights.* Englewood Cliffs, N.J.: Prentice-Hall, 1988.
In the process of describing for the first time the process by which modern playwrights bring their stage work to final form, Cohen gives an overview of the new play activities of the Jewish Repertory Theatre (where he serves as associate artistic director), as well as anecdotal evidence that the process occurs all over New York and in major theatre cities such as Minneapolis and Chicago. Indispensable for understanding how creative stage work is born, grows, and matures.

Cooper, Roberta Krensky. *The American Shakespeare Theatre: Stratford, 1955-1985.* Washington, D.C.: Folger Books, 1986.
Stratford, Connecticut, was the home of this thirty-year American love affair with the Bard, one that ended in divorce and Chapter 11. The "third party" in the suit was the almighty dollar, but the villains were a board of trustees sending mixed messages to an artistic staff that tried to ride the two horses of aesthetic excellence and popular appeal. What started as a company of resident actors ended as a "star system" fiasco (a 1980 production of *Richard III* embodied all that was wrong with the project). Cooper tells the story well, with details in the appendix, but it is a tragedy, or at least a melodrama.

Coyne, Bernard Ambrose. *A History of Arena Stage, Washington, D.C.* Ann Arbor, Mich.: University Microfilms, 1978 (Ph.D. dissertation, Tulane University, 1964).
"In the vanguard of [the regional theatre movement] was Arena Stage . . . founded in reaction to the commercialism of the Broadway theatre." Its first building, the Hippodrome (1950 to 1955), and its second home, "the Old Vat" (1956 to 1961), saw Zelda Fichandler's most creative productions; she opened the archives to Coyne for this thorough study, which includes architectural notes by Harry Weese, architect of the present building, dimensions, fact sheets, and a good bibliography.

Emmes, David Michael. *South Coast Repertory, 1963-1972: A Case Study.* Ann Arbor, Mich.: University Microfilms, 1978 (Ph.D. dissertation, University of Southern California, 1973).
The theatre's aesthetic intentions, articulated by Emmes (one of the group's directors since 1965), put new play production fairly far down on the list of goals, but it subsequently expanded that part of its activities, when classic production ran into problems. After working in borrowed spaces in Orange County until 1968, the company found its first home in the tiny Second Step

Theatre, then moved to the Third Step Theatre. Appendices give production histories and financial figures; bibliography includes many seminal books from the period.

Epstein, Lawrence, comp. and ed. *A Guide to Theatre in America*. New York: Macmillan, 1985.
Valuable collection of names and addresses of agents, colleges, directors, festivals, foundations, libraries, producers, suppliers, unions, and dozens of other categories, with a contact index. Unfortunately, much has been left out; many colleges with solid programs are not represented, for example. Nevertheless, this is a good source book for research into the present-day theatre world via letters of inquiry, as well as information on founding dates, budget sources, and so on. Good for dramaturgical help with regional theatre histories; the contact personnel listed could be most helpful, if this work is updated periodically (lists affiliation with American Theatre Association, now defunct). The list of acronyms is especially worthwhile.

Faust, Richard, and Charles Kadushin. *Shakespeare in the Neighborhood: Audience reaction to "A Midsummer-Night's Dream" as Produced by Joseph Papp for the Delacorte Mobile Theater*. New York: The Twentieth Century Fund, 1965.
In the summer of 1964, Joseph Papp brought Shakespeare to the poor neighborhoods of New York's five boroughs, a monumental task calling for considerable dedication to a principle. The Bureau of Applied Social Research of Columbia University funded this booklet study of audience response, and the results speak to the mixed success of the experiment. Some chapter titles tell the downside: "What Was Done About Rock Throwing"; "Characteristics of Gangs"; "Ineffectiveness of the Police." "Within the context of our empirical framework," however, the experiment was a success.

FEDAPT Box Office Guidelines. New York: FEDAPT, 1977.
The Foundation for the Extension and Development of the American Professional Theatre (FEDAPT) put out this box office how-to in several editions, before the computerized box office became the standard. Using the Mark Taper Forum as a model, the booklet explains front-office protocol, ticketing, designing and implementing a box office statement, advance reporting, and auditing, with the full text of the International Alliance of Theatrical Stage Employees (IATSE) treasurers' and ticket sellers' contract. Should be required reading for theatre students.

Flory, Julia McCune. *The Cleveland Play House: How It Began*. Cleveland: Press of Western Reserve University, 1965.
From the personal collection of programs, newspaper clippings, and memorabilia by this very active member and supporter. Raymond O'Neil, the first director

of the Play House, was "profoundly influenced by The Moscow Art Theatre" and built the Cleveland amateur stage and repertory on the same experimental principles. Flory is especially florid in describing the funding fights among the "pure" artists and the "brick and mortar" proponents (she is one of the latter), but adds quickly, "I do not complain of these members." Readable and well illustrated, this account "No Ends" at the theatre's move to East 86th Street in 1926.

Fogelberg, Donald Dewey. *The Impact of the Architecture of the Tyrone Guthrie Theater on the Process of Play Production.* Ann Arbor, Mich.: University Microfilms, 1982 (Ph.D. dissertation, University of Minnesota, 1979).
The Guthrie theatre structure, with its thrust stage available to a steeply raked, 200-degree audience and its magnificent lobbies, offers challenges to every stage designer who walks in its doors. This fascinating study, however, deals with the headaches of its production facilities and the woes of production preparation and running. Essential reading for all theatre designers, technicians, and stage managers, and good reading for anyone who has ever marveled at what can be done in this simultaneously awkward and creatively alive space. The poor illustration reproduction in the microfilm series is really disturbing to those who want to see details of the physical plant.

Gard, Robert E., Marston Balch, and Pauline B. Temkin. *Theater in America: Appraisal and Challenge.* New York: Theatre Arts Books, 1968.
Compiled for the National Theatre Conference over a six-year period, this summary of the state of American theatre, particularly not-for-profit theatre, serves as a descriptive catalog to the kinds and levels of theatrical activity in every part of the country. Valuable for sorting out the differences among community, not-for-profit professional, amateur, educational, and commercial theatre. Bibliography, index, and concluding recommendations for improvements.

Gunn, Donald Lynn. *Moral Censorship of the Los Angeles Stage, 1966-1968: Two Case Studies.* Ann Arbor, Mich.: University Microfilms, 1974 (Ph.D. dissertation, University of California at Los Angeles, 1970).
Studies of the controversy over John Whiting's *The Devils* and Michael McClure's *The Beard*, representative of the radical theatre of this period and society's overreaction to them. Interviews, public statements, university lectures, correspondence, and official records, as well as inductive argument, form the study, as much a social document as one of theatre history. Gunn's point: "the social function of stage plays was largely misunderstood, and . . . the potential of theater as a meliorative influence in a culturally fragmented community was not recognized." Bibliography.

Guthrie, Tyrone. *A New Theatre*. New York: McGraw-Hill, 1964.
After four and a half years of planning and work, Sir Guthrie opened his theatre on May 5, 1963, in Minneapolis. It was unique at the time, a response and reaction to the commercial theatre and its artistic limitations, and it triggered a massive regional theatre movement that even today looks to the Guthrie Theatre for guidance and inspiration. Told in his own words, this is the story of the theatre company's formation and incipient season. Production stills of *Hamlet*, *The Miser*, *Death of a Salesman*, and *Three Sisters*. A must read for students of regional theatre history.

James, S. Walker. *Paul Baker's Concept of Theatre: Space and the Creative Artist*. Ann Arbor, Mich.: University Microfilms, 1973 (Ph.D. dissertation, University of Denver, 1968).
The theatre department of Baylor University was the main home of Paul Baker during the late 1950's and early 1960's, but he was director of the Dallas Theater Center when this dissertation was written (1968). Describes "his methodology of theatre education and . . . his theatre practice." It was to accommodate his theatrical ideas that Frank Lloyd Wright built the Dallas Theater, which still is the landmark for the company. More than seven doctoral dissertations were written on this subject by Baker's students, but this one summarizes much of what the others have to say.

Laming, Dorothy Wise. *Ellis Rabb: A Man of Repertory*. Ann Arbor, Mich.: University Microfilms, 1975 (Ph.D. dissertation, Ohio State University, 1972).
The founder and artistic director of the Association of Producing Artists (APA), Rabb advocated the repertory company idea of theatre for years (APA survived from 1960 to 1970) and, in collaboration with the Phoenix Theatre, attempted to realize his concept. The experiment was not entirely successful (the company and its leader are often depicted as "tired"), as is here related in both scholarly form and in an appendix of personal reminiscences by colleagues of Rabb during the APA years (perhaps the most valuable part of this study). Long cast lists, appendices of prospectuses, legal structure, and so on. Bibliography.

Langley, Stephen, ed. *Producers on Producing*. New York: Drama Book Specialists, 1976.
A series of interviews with theatrical producers, organized around the kinds of theatre they generally produce: educational, resident, off-off-Broadway, Broadway, and more. Interesting chapter on government, business, and the foundations as producers, and a strong opening discussion of grassroots theatre. As theatre history, these pieces often give firsthand accounts of the origins and development of successful creative visions, such as the Arena Stage (Zelda Fichandler), Circle in the Square (Theodore Mann), and La Mama Experimental Theatre Club (Ellen Stewart); photographs of the contributors, but no index.

Larsen, June Bennett. *Margo Jones: A Life in the Theatre.* Ann Arbor, Mich.:
University Microfilms, 1984 (Ph.D. dissertation, University of New York, 1982).
Margo Jones began Texas regional theatre, first as a director of Houston's
Federal Theatre (1935-1936), then at Austin at the University of Texas, then at
the Dallas Theater Center after some Broadway work. Her biography, here
treated as a scholarly exercise, includes the premieres of fifty-eight plays and
close professional ties with Tennessee Williams, William Inge, and many others.
A feminist tone overtakes Larsen's style occasionally, as when she cites the chain
of inspiration from Jones: "Nina Vance was the first bearer of Margo Jones'
torch. . . . Like an Olympic runner, Zelda Fichandler was the next to take the
flame." Good inside information of Jones's struggles and accomplishments.

Leacroft, Richard, and Helen Leacroft. *Theatre and Playhouse: An Illustrated
Survey of Theatre Building from Ancient Greece to the Present Day.* London:
Methuen, 1984.
As the Leacrofts move through the history and development of theatrical spaces,
they illustrate several historically important American contributions, notably the
Auditorium Building (Chicago), the Ziegfeld Theatre (New York), the Shakespearean Festival Theatre (Ashland, Oregon), the Guthrie Theatre (Minneapolis),
and the Loeb Drama Center (Midland, Texas). Their placement in twentieth
century theatre history is based on the uniqueness of these documents. Stunning
isometric drawings are included among more than three hundred illustrations.
Very strong bibliography and index.

Little, Stuart W. *After the FACT: Conflict and Consensus.* New York: Arno, 1975.
A report on the First American Congress of Theatre (FACT), held in Princeton,
New Jersey, in 1974. Opens with a statement of purpose directed not at the
aesthetic considerations of good theatre art but at the economic and financial
problems besetting the entire discipline (avoiding the word "business"). About
two hundred theatre practitioners (list appended) were there; what they discussed
and what they decided constitute a historic review of the indigenous conflict
between not-for-profit artistic theatre and the free enterprise system. This little
book sums up their findings and recommendations. Depressing reading.

_____. *Enter Joseph Papp: In Search of a New American Theater.* New
York: Coward, McCann & Geoghegan, 1974.
In some respects, a continuation of Little's first book, on off-Broadway, but
concentrating on one of the most outstanding theatre figures in the new movement. Papp organized and ran the New York Shakespeare Festival (NYSF) from
the mid-1950's, meeting each new obstacle with another creative solution. Little
examines Papp's relationship with Lincoln Center and his bitter association with
CBS, especially his attempts to get *Sticks & Bones* onto television. More discussion of money, contracts, and negotiations than theatre production; good accounts
of how NYSF and Papp went about funding their projects. Index.

London, Todd. *The Artistic Home: Discussions with Artistic Directors of America's Institutional Theatres.* New York: Theatre Communications Group, 1988.
London, a staff member at TCG, reports on the National Artistic Agenda Project, which, "conceived as an exploration and a dialogue. . . aimed to develop a tool for each theatre to address its specific artistic needs in its own way." This small but packed booklet attempts "to convey in writing the essence of discussions that took place over a total of 17 days, to reveal the process behind those deliberations, and to synthesize the major themes, issues and examples gleaned." Essential reading for anyone wishing to learn about theatre in the 1980's or planning to join the theatre in the 1990's.

Lowry, W. McNeil, ed. *The Performing Arts and American Society.* Englewood Cliffs, N.J.: Prentice-Hall, 1978.
Though not dealing exclusively with theatre and its social history, this collection of essays enlightens the reader on all questions of performing arts, where they seek dignity and acceptance among the diverse and fickle American public. The term "egregious elite," coined by Lincoln Kirstein in one of the essays, sums up the dangers of imagination, which (Kirstein quoting Sir James Fraser) "may kill . . . as certainly as a dose of prussic acid." By contrasting the treatment of the Apollonian to the Dionysian arts, Kirstein speaks for all: "Artists are . . . a condign threat to the body-politic." Index.

McDonough, Patrick Dennis. *A Comparative, Descriptive Study of Management Planning Practices in the Tyrone Guthrie Theater and the Milwaukee Repertory Theater.* Ann Arbor, Mich.: University Microfilms, 1977 (Ph.D. dissertation, University of Minnesota, 1972).
An unusual and valuable comparative study of two management styles, both of regional theatres with considerable reputation and from the northern Midwest. Some of the most fruitful employment opportunities in theatre reside where the money meets the artist, and this study reveals the tough business side of even not-for-profit ventures such as these capital-heavy enterprises. Insightful regarding money matters, whether economic comparisons are history or speculation.

Marder, Carl John III. *A History of the Development and Growth of the Dallas Theater Center.* Ann Arbor, Mich.: University Microfilms, 1977 (Ph.D. dissertation, University of Kansas, 1972).
Frank Lloyd Wright designed this complex, and nothing says more about the quality of the aesthetic efforts that have come from it since its inception in 1954. Originally planned as "a place in which the drama major graduating from college would work and prepare for a life in professional theater," the project grew into the most successful "of twenty-six theaters in twenty-five cities in twenty states considered to be regional theaters" by 1968. Interesting documents appended, including form letters for season ticket sales, curricula for graduate students and

guidelines for cast parties. Some diagrams of the building's structure and layout; bibliography.

Morison, Bradley G., and Kay Fliehr. *In Search of an Audience: How an Audience Was Found for the Tyrone Guthrie Theatre*. New York: Pitman, 1968.
In one of the oddest births the theatre world has known, the Guthrie Theatre was formed in Minneapolis, not solely from some organic desire on the part of Minnesotans to found a theatre but from the need for Sir Tyrone Guthrie to find "an appropriately small pond in which to be a big fish." This book explains, entirely after the fact and with the benefit of hindsight (as the authors admit), how such a company happened upon such a place. The years 1963 to 1966 are examined closely, but in an entertaining, readable style. A nice study in audience demographics, with maps and charts.

Morrow, Lee Alan, and Frank Pike. *Creating Theater: The Professionals' Approach to New Plays*. New York: Vintage Books, 1986.
As the history of the new play development system, as practiced in the regional theatres, playwrights' labs, and New York showcase houses, is gradually recorded, this series of interviews will emerge as an important document, especially as regards the attitudes of the participants toward the process itself. By shuffling the responses of several artists underneath a single question, the editors have managed to articulate a collective response to important points of contention. Playwrights, actors, directors, designers, and critics are consulted. The consensus: Creating theater is and will always be a cooperative effort of the entire theatre community.

Novick, Julius. *Beyond Broadway: The Quest for Permanent Theatres*. New York: Hill & Wang, 1968.
The idea of a resident professional theatre in every major U.S. city was born with Margo Jones's efforts in Dallas in 1947, Nina Vance's Alley Theatre in Houston, Zelda Fichandler's Arena Stage in Washington, D.C., and Actor's Workshop of San Francisco, which was founded in 1952 by Herbert Blau and Jules Irving. By 1966 there was enough theatrical activity to warrant a transcontinental tour by Novick to review and evaluate the movement as a whole. This book contains a record of his observations and serves as the first history of the healthily continuing regional theatre circuit. The index serves as a cast list of early contributors to the movement.

Oldenburg, Chloe Warner. *Leaps of Faith: History of the Cleveland Play House, 1915-85*. Cleveland, Ohio: Private printing, 1985.
Paeans of this kind are necessary to preserve the history of the first attempts at ensemble approaches to regional production. Underneath the rhetoric and self-advertisement are the facts of Cleveland Play House's growth: from the American

version of "new theatre" imported after Raymond O'Neil's European tour of theatre in 1914, through his subsequent organization of the Cleveland Play House as its director, its constitutional amendments of 1919, the closing of the old Cedar Avenue theatre in 1927 ("its noisy ventilator, its leaky roof, its backstage mice"), to its 1984-1985 season, still experimental, still daring, this affectionate recounting delights and informs. Lists of artistic and support staff, trustees, and foundation presidents up to Richard Hahn. Playbills, posters, and illustrations.

Payne, Ben Iden. *A Life in a Wooden O: Memoirs of the Theatre.* New Haven, Conn.: Yale University Press, 1977.
Payne was a great advocate of "the modified Elizabethan staging" for Shakespeare's plays in America. This memoir was written after fifty years of solid theatre activity, much of it at Carnegie Institute of Technology, where, in the 1930's, he taught on the faculty. At the San Diego National Theatre Festival (The Old Globe) in 1949 he directed *Twelfth Night* and worked at the University of Texas up to 1969. Exasperatingly few dates and other references, but a good description of Payne's ideas and their Shakespearean justifications. Bibliography.

Quintero, Jose. *If You Don't Dance They Beat You.* Boston: Little, Brown, 1974.
Quintero, whose Circle in the Square productions of *Summer and Smoke* and *The Iceman Cometh* are considered to be the benchmark productions of off-Broadway theatre, writes in a subjective style that omits dates and other objective data in favor of a sometimes painful stripping away of barriers to get at himself. His thoughts, his emotions as his life and his theatre take form are depicted here—not the superficial, witty, anecdotal style of so many theatre autobiographies. Unfortunately, there is no appendix or index to help the reader, but the man's soul is here, and that will do. Along the way, Geraldine Page and the rest of his company are exposed as well. Required reading for any student of off-Broadway theatre.

Rickert, William, and Jane Bloomquist. *Resources in Theatre and Disability.* Lanham, Md.: University Press of America, 1988.
Combining several data banks begun under the auspices of the late American Theatre Association, this sourcebook provides addresses and bibliographies for information on the interface between theatre and handicapped and disabled programs. A little difficult to use because it gathers so much disparate material, but internal indexes help somewhat. Tries also to be a polemic on proper focus—theatre or therapy—of future projects involving disabled participants.

Robinson, Alice M., Vera Mowry Roberts, and Milly S. Barranger, eds. *Notable Women in the American Theatre: A Biographical Dictionary.* Westport, Conn.: Greenwood Press, 1989.
A solid and valuable addition to theatre reference, though compiled with a chip

on the shoulder: "Intellectuality and creativity were not ascribed to any of the generally acknowledged roles for women: wife/mother, virgin/nun, and whore/outcast. . . . Over the decades, professional actresses struggled to prove that they were respectable working women, not seductive sex symbols who were unfit company for wives and children." This said, the work moves forward with strong essays on often neglected figures deserving of respect and biographical acknowledgment. It is selective biography, however, choosing to mention only what the feminist sensibility allows: Karen Malpede is Karen Malpede Taylor in some citations, but no explanation can be found; the reader does learn, however, that "she now lives with Burl Hash" and has a daughter by him. Best on contemporary figures such as Tina Howe, Elaine May, Twyla Tharp, Adele Edling Shank, Emily Mann, and Ntozake Shange.

Ryzuk, Mary S. *The Circle Repertory Company: The First Fifteen Years*. Ames: Iowa State University Press, 1989.
A relative latecomer to experimental theatre in New York, but quickly becoming a driving force in new play production, especially the "lyric realism" of Landford Wilson and the direction of Marshall W. Mason. From 1969 to 1984, the Circle made a circle of its own, "from a free-spirited ensemble . . . to a major developer of new plays and new playwrights, and back to a revolving repertory ensemble." Mason, who left in 1987, provides an afterword explaining his coproduction with South Coast Rep of Jim Leonard's *V&V Only*. Production stills and candid shots; chronology of season, bibliography, and index.

Schaffner, Neil E. *The Fabulous Toby and Me*. Englewood Cliffs, N.J.: Prentice-Hall, 1968.
Tent repertory history told by a grand participant: "All around the country, traveling companies of actors came to town once a year, erected a huge tent on a vacant lot somewhere and presented 'a new and different play each and every night.'" Melodramas, musicals, moral comedies (*Why Girls Walk Home*) thrived for the Paul English Players, the Horace Murphy shows, and Harley Sadler's tent (with a fly loft and a proscenium arch a hundred feet long), as "legitimate" theater scorned these itinerant thespians. Schaffner, active from about 1900 to 1967, and from 1929 head of The Schaffner Players, makes the life sound exciting and varied, even spiritually profitable. Good index.

Selby, David Lynn. *A History of the American Place Theatre, 1963-1968*. Ann Arbor, Mich.: University Microfilms, 1976 (Ph.D. dissertation, Southern Illinois University, 1970).
St. Clement's Church in New York was remodeled to house this interesting and successful company, dedicated to becoming "a theatre that concerns itself with the crucial themes of contemporary life," as Selby quotes the prospectus. Wynn Handman served as artistic director during the period covered in this study. Four

seasons are dissected, with recaps of aesthetic choices, critical reviews, and financial outcome. Appendix reproduces playbills.

Sheehy, Helen. *Margo: The Life and Theatre of Margo Jones*. Dallas: Southern Methodist University Press, 1989.
A modern biography of "the patron saint of playwrights" (Jerome Lawrence), "a fighter, builder, explorer, and mixer of truth and magic" (Thornton Wilder), "the Texas Tornado" (Tennessee Williams), who made Houston, Austin, and Dallas the theatre center of America during her lifetime (1911-1955) and helped to pioneer the resident regional theatre. A strong descriptive biography, the chronicle of regional theatre's beginnings told along with the story of Margo Jones's struggles and triumphs. Highly recommended. Index, source notes, and list of Margo Jones Award recipients.

Spearman, Walter. *The Carolina Playmakers: The First Fifty Years*. Chapel Hill: University of North Carolina Press, 1970.
Begun in 1918 as an educational theatre experiment in Chapel Hill, the Play-makers set the precedents for the subsequent explosion in university theatre departments and productions, especially those marrying the professional theatre to the academic curriculum. It produced Paul Green, Thomas Wolfe, and other dramatists who wrote and produced about one thousand plays. Early chapters trace the advent of theatre and Frederick H. Koch's arrival from North Dakota; Wolfe was one of his first students. Many photographs (to 1969) and a look forward; index of names.

Stevens, David H., ed. *Ten Talents in the American Theatre*. Norman: University of Oklahoma Press, 1957.
A collection of ten essays by working theatre people, including Alan Schneider, director of Edward Albee's work in America, contrasting New York theatre with several regional experiments; Paul Baker, Baylor University's artistic director at that time, discussing Yale Theatre in the 1930's; and Margo Jones, the wizard of Dallas theatre, describing how Theatre '50 came to Texas. All are united in desiring "a nationwide interest in artists and in the arts of the drama, which can discover and create under favoring circumstances on a nationwide scale." A very good source for identifying the earliest impulses that brought regional American theatre to its present fruition. Index.

Sweet, Jeffrey. *Something Wonderful Right Away*. 1978. Reprint. New York: Limelight Editions, 1986.
"An Oral History of the Second City & The Compass Players" in interview form. Much interesting information on Viola Spolin's influence on the companies' formation and aesthetics and on the strange energies of the University of Chicago during the period. Anecdotes recall some of the best moments, and Sweet's

introductory remarks to each interview help sort out the cast of "characters."
Photograph section, but no index.

Theatre Facts 1982. New York: Theatre Communications Group, 1982.
This booklet, distributed by the TCG staff and its president, Peter Zeisler,
assesses the state of regional not-for-profit theatre—especially the theatres of the
League of Resident Theatres—for their effectiveness as instruments of art (para-
phrasing Eva Le Gallienne) rather than machines of financial generation. It is a
call for permanent constructive solutions: "One can't build a house without a
hammer and nails, and the American theatre is trying to use rubber cement."
Survey samples 22 of 123 theatres over a nine-year period for earned income,
contributed income, expenses, effects of inflation, and "the bottom line." A
strong source for facts to support the righteous "anger" that "turns things
around."

Transition in the Not-for-Profit Theatre. New York: FEDAPT, 1980.
Two monographs bound together from material discussed at FEDAPT's 1976
conference on theatre administration. Hartford Stage Company and Indiana
Repertory Theatre are examined in detail, each "a chronicle of the problems and
difficulties encountered by these theatre organizations while establishing, develop-
ing, and sustaining a professional theatre." Excellent how-to book, if theatre
learns from its mistakes. Interview format for much of each section; a chronology
of the theatres' conception, development, and realization is particularly valuable
to the history of regional theatre. A Long Wharf addition is sometimes bound
with this volume.

Treser, Robert Morris. *Houston's Alley Theatre*. Ann Arbor, Mich.: University
Microfilms, 1973 (Ph.D. dissertation, Tulane University, 1967).
Nina Vance's Alley Theatre, a model for many regional theatres, is examined
in an attempt to discover the magic formula that makes it work. Calls for a
regional theatre, sent out as early as 1949 by Samuel Seldon in the *New York
Times*, were answered by Margo Jones (in Dallas in 1947) and her colleagues
and students, who found Houston an amenable and understanding community.
With donations, support, and enthusiasm, the Alley flourished; Treser spends
much of time chronicling the financial history dime by dime.

Vaughan, Stuart. *A Possible Theatre: The Experiences of a Pioneer Director in
America's Resident Theatre*. New York: McGraw-Hill, 1969.
Founder and/or artistic director of several regional theatres—Phoenix (which
Norris Houghton began in 1953) and Seattle Repertory (1963) among
them—Vaughan earned his reputation directing Shakespeare for the New York
Shakespeare Festival. His story, highly readable, even enchanting ("One night
over beers at McSorley's, Hal Holbrook and I were talking about . . ."), is really

the story of the impulse toward regional theatre and the first modern pioneers who ventured "west of the Hudson." Vaughan, a creative and inspiring man, is gracious toward new playwrights. Highly recommended.

Volz, Jim. *Shakespeare Never Slept Here: The Making of a Regional Theatre.* Atlanta, Ga.: Cherokee Publishing, 1986.
A history of the Alabama Shakespeare Festival, originally in Anniston (1971) but lodged in magnificent digs in Montgomery only a year before this commemorative volume was published. Volz, managing director and largely responsible (with artistic director Martin Platt) for ASF's health, pays tribute to the theatre's beginnings while promising much for the future. ASF is, in many respects, the epitome of Southern Theatre in its gradual insistence on cultural excellence, even in the permanent shadow of "the recent unpleasantness," as southerners refer to the Civil War. Optimistic rhetoric throughout this coffee-table history. Fully photographed, with chronologies and documentation.

Warye, Richard Johathan. *A Descriptive Study of Community Theatres in the Metropolitan Areas of the United States.* Ann Arbor, Mich.: University Microfilms, 1973.
A 1967 dissertation full of statistics, covering mostly the 1962-1963 seasons, on attendance, performance figures, costs, sources of subsidy, play selection, and similar quantifiable data on the community theatre world of major cities. The data were compiled from questionnaires mailed to one hundred large metropolitan areas; the resulting thirty-two tables, along with several appendices and a bibliography, make heavy reading but could inspire generalizations and extrapolations both backward and forward in theatre history.

Wilk, John R. *The American Conservatory Theatre: The Creation of an Ensemble.* Ann Arbor, Mich.: University Microfilms, 1984 (Ph.D. dissertation, Wayne State University, 1982).
Administrative assistant and casting coordinator for ACT during the time of this writing, Wilk had access to William Ball's personal recollections (one interview on February 2, 1982, is included) as well as the full archival material of ACT to write this study, which concentrates on the idea and the implementation of Ball's ensemble acting aesthetic. Thorough and readable, with a long bibliography, financial figures, cast lists, and other data in appendices.

_____. *The Creation of an Ensemble: The First Years of the American Conservatory Theatre.* Carbondale: Southern Illinois University Press, 1968.
Although ensemble, "no-star" acting has a respectable history, it never flourished in America until William Ball succeeded at Lincoln Center with *Tartuffe* and established his company. Wilk details its beginnings (1965-1968) only one year after William Ball found a home for it in San Francisco, comparing the theoreti-

cal structure with its realization. Ball, who died in 1991, is referred to as "a regisseur," and the acting school from which the company emerges is given considerable space in this early but solid study of the birth of an important theatre company. Strong photograph section, notes, bibliography, and index; appendices include the ACT statement of purpose.

Zeigler, Joseph Wesley. *Regional Theatre: The Revolutionary Stage.* Minneapolis: University of Minnesota Press, 1973.
"Revolutionary" would not be the word to describe contemporary regional theatre, but in 1973 many of the best impulses toward a nontraditional theatricality were coming from Minneapolis, where such thinkers as Arthur Ballet were finding and publishing new plays that took chances. Follows the fortunes of regional theatre by following the careers of its first visionaries—Zelda Fichandler, Margo Jones, Sir Tyrone Guthrie, for example—through the next generation of long-lasting successes (Mark Taper Forum, APA-Phoenix, American Conservatory Theatre) fed on the energies of Jules Irving, Herbert Blau, William Ball, Adrian Hall, and others. Essential reading for the history of not-for-profit professional theatre history, especially the most idealistic and future-driven days. Notes and index.

EXPERIMENTAL, ETHNIC, COMMUNITY, ACADEMIC, AND CHILDREN'S THEATRE

Beck, Julian. *The Life of the Theatre: The Relation of the Artist to the Struggle of the People*. San Francisco: City Lights Books, 1972.
Contains 123 expressionistic, fragmented, energized, and energizing notes, in no immediately discernible order, from the founder (with Judith Malina) of the Living Theatre. A diary, manifesto, travelogue, and notebook of one of the brightest and most radical of avant-garde theatre people. Beck, Judith Malina, and the Living Theatre set the pace for experimental theatre, both in New York and across America, from their first "meditations" through the 1970's. Beck collects, Zen-like, in short bursts of verbal celerity, the impressions of his personal, political, and aesthetic journey further and further from conventional notions of theatre. A true primary document of the energies that fed, and still feed, contemporary American theatre, this disjointed salvo of large ideas contains the core of Beck's aesthetic, along with observations global in range (Brazilian prisons included) and paranoiac in tenor: "Buckminster Fuller builds for the Army. Watch out."

Bernhard, Randall Lee. *Contemporary Musical Theatre: History and Development in the Major Colleges and Universities of Utah*. Ann Arbor, Mich.: University Microfilms, 1982 (Ph.D. dissertation, Brigham Young University, 1979).
A study of "how musical theatre began in the four major colleges and universities of Utah," but at the same time the history of academic interest in the form. Often beginning as an extracurricular activity, sometimes a send-up or parody, in which the voices are anything but professional, but eventually merging music and theatre departments into joint enterprises to the benefit of both, the musical theatre enterprise succeeds where straight drama sometimes falls short. Useful for studies of academic theatre in America, collaboration among departments, and similar work. Appendices of musical theatre offerings of the four institutions; short bibliography.

Biner, Pierre. *The Living Theatre*. New York: Horizon Press, 1972.
Originally written in French, this study of Julian Beck's company is one of the first full-length examinations of Beck and Malina's group. Treated as a biography of the group itself. The writing is lucid and insightful and accompanied by photographs of the performances, many of which have been reproduced in virtually every other study of the group. The beginning study for performance theatre of the 1960's and 1970's, heavily cited by all subsequent scholars. Two appendices give dates of performances and a chronology of the European tour; index.

Blau, Herbert. *The Impossible Theater: A Manifesto*. New York: Macmillan, 1964.
It can be said that contemporary theatre began with the publication of this

startling statement of principle by the then producer-director of the Actors' Workshop in San Francisco. From chapter to chapter, Blau clears the ground, erects new idols of existential and nihilistic aesthetics, faces the entropic facticity of current theatre, and, "trusting to the clearest gods," confronts the absence of ritual with the possibilities of the impossible theatre. "In Search of Identity," the second section's title, sums up Blau's attempts to find what contemporary theatre will be about for the rest of the century. This is a manifesto unanimously shouted into law by the next three decades of experimentalists, from Julian Beck to Robert Wilson.

_____. *Take Up the Bodies: Theater at the Vanishing Point.* Urbana: University of Illinois Press, 1982.
The foremost scholar-critic of avant-garde theatre and theatrical aesthetics, Blau writes this "remembering of a theory" after decades of producing "the impossible theatre" (the name of his first important manifesto). His theories came to life with KRAKEN, an experimental theatre group designed to realize some of his best ideas. As he points out, however, "the kraken dies when it surfaces." This is the highly sophisticated and philosophical chronicle of that experiment as it worked through the "House of Atreus" story and other Greek myths. One of the truly seminal works on contemporary theatre, fully illustrated, beautifully expressed, and highly recommended. "My body, my time: that end."

Braun, Thomas Charles. *The Theory of "Aesthetic Distance" and the Practice of "Audience Participation."* Ann Arbor, Mich.: University Microfilms, 1978 (Ph.D. dissertation, University of Minnesota, 1972).
An examination of performance groups, notably Julian Beck's Living Theatre (*Paradise Now*) and Richard Schechner's Performance Group (*Dionysus in 69*), in the 1960's performances involving audiences in the participatory aesthetic experience. In a good position to observe experimental theatre (under the guidance of Arthur Ballet), Braun is one of the first to try to construct the principles of this kind of theatre and to assess its artistic value, using news accounts and other direct observations. Mentions Firehouse Theatre and Norah Holmgren's *Still Falling.* Bibliography; anatomical "map" of *Paradise Now.*

Brecht, Stefan. *The Original Theatre of the City of New York from the Mid-Sixties to the Mid-Seventies. Book 4: Peter Schumann's Bread and Puppet Theatre.* London: Methuen, 1988.
A continuing project of Brecht's, this book covers the puppet theatre of Peter Schumann in two volumes. Schumann came to New York in 1963; his stay is divided into puppet making, religious observances and children's theatre from 1963-1969, the Vietnam War and street agitation during the 1960's, and indoors theatre during the 1960's. Volume 2 covers 1970-1974 (The Goddard period), 1975-1978 (on Dopp Farm), and the 1979-1983 period of "prophetic theatre of

doom condemning civilization." Comprehensive and authoritative study, with bibliography, appendices, and photos of the puppets.

Chapel, Robert Clyde. *The University of Michigan Professional Theatre Program, 1961-1973*. Ann Arbor, Mich.: University Microfilms, 1978 (Ph.D. dissertation, University of Michigan, 1974).
A very close look, replete with models and manifestos, at one of the successful professional theatre training programs currently feeding American and international theatre. Although the conditions under which Robert C. Schnitzer, Ellis Rabb, and their colleagues created this program are unique, their problems and the solutions they invented serve as a textbook for aspiring theatre administrators, for theatre scholars studying the relationship between academic and professional theatre, and for anyone trying to repair present, less prosperous, programs. One warning: This is theatre history, and the conditions and solutions no longer prevail.

Cioffi, Robert Joseph. *Al Carmines and the Judson Poets' Theater Musicals*. Ann Arbor, Mich.: University Microfilms, 1982 (Ph.D. dissertation, New York University, 1979).
From 1962 to 1978, a very unusual off-off-Broadway theatre called Judson Poets' Theater, "under the leadership of Al Carmines, a minister and musician," offered more than forty zany musicals, "written quickly, hurriedly rehearsed, and hectically designed and produced." Some were transferred to commercial houses, but the process and product of creation at the Judson Poets' Theater, as recorded and documented, were uniquely off-off-everything: "the Coke bottle as phallic symbol . . . wet dreams . . . sexual troilism . . . lesbian longing . . . and male hustling." An excessively academic look at a Dionysian delight.

Coleman, Janet. *The Compass*. New York: Alfred A. Knopf, 1990.
Few nontheatre people have even heard of The Compass, David Shepherd's storefront improvisational theatre of the Chicago Radical 1960's. Yet from its serious intent—to examine the questions of its day—came a new form of comic theatre, one that fed the present generation of iconoclastic stage performers. Coleman's style is that of the new journalism, entertaining and rhetorical, almost novelistic, but she is intensely interested in her subjects: Paul Sills, Viola Spolin, Shelley Berman, the inestimable (Mike) Nichols and (Elaine) May partnership, a hundred others. No study of Chicago theatre—or politicocomic theatre, for that matter—is complete without this highly readable account. Index and photographic illustrations.

Croyden, Margaret. *Lunatics, Lovers, and Poets: The Contemporary Experimental Theatre*. New York: McGraw-Hill, 1974.
After a review of European roots, Croyden describes Happenings, the Living

Theatre ("The mother of them all"), the Open Theatre, environmentalists (including the Performance Group and Robert Wilson), and the influence of Peter Brook and Jerzy Grotowski on the movement, with about fifty illustrations of the more visually outrageous performances. Stylistically, this is a layperson's introduction to American experimentation, but the research and insights are highly professional. Excellent for comparing and contrasting the American manifestations with their European origins. Notes, bibliography, and index.

Davy, Kate. *Richard Foreman and the Ontological-Hysteric Theatre*. Ann Arbor, Mich.: UMI Research Press, 1981.
Full-length study of Foreman as director, playwright, "scenographer," inventor, and spectator (the unique element in his work). Contains 78 plates of performances, a necessary accompaniment to discussions of postscriptive texts. Davy's clear-headed intellectual analysis, dividing Foreman's work by the facets of Foreman's theatrical energy, is followed by a chronology, list of characters and performers, notes, bibliography, and index. The best kind of scholarship UMI has to offer.

Dent, Thomas C., Richard Schechner, and Gilbert Moses, eds. *The Free Southern Theater by the Free Southern Theater*. Indianapolis: Bobbs-Merrill, 1969.
Its subtitle describes this book as "a documentary of the South's radical black theater, with journals, letters, poetry, essays and a play written by those who built it." As part of the racial desegregation of the South and an offshoot of an SNCC campaign, the Free Southern Theater was started by Doris Derby, John O'Neal, Gilbert Moses, and others. A general prospectus drafted in 1963 describes the project: "to establish a legitimate theater in the deep South . . . to stimulate creative and reflective thought among Negroes in Mississippi and other Southern states." Told through letters, interviews, photographs. "And the hell with what the white critics say or expect. It's as simple as that."

Evans, Thomas George. *Piscator in the American Theatre: New York, 1939-1951*. Ann Arbor, Mich.: University Microfilms, n.d. (Ph.D. dissertation, University of Wisconsin, 1968).
The influence of "new theatre" design, innovations in expressionistic staging, film projection, and agitprop theatrical presentations, as filtered through Erwin Piscator's relationship with American theatre during and after World War II. Earlier collaborations in Germany (1919-1932) and the "interim" years of the 1930's are dealt with as well, but the body of the study deals with Piscator's visit in 1939 and his work with the Dramatic Workshop, the Studio Theatre, and elsewhere. Notes and bibliography.

Fabré, Genevieve. *Drumbeats, Masks, and Metaphor: Contemporary Afro-American Theatre*. Translated by Melvin Dixon. Cambridge, Mass.: Harvard University Press, 1983.

The chapter on historical precedent is particularly useful in this full-length study of such a diverse group as Amiri Baraka, Ed Bullins, Edgar White, Douglas Turner Ward, Paul Carter Harrison, Mikki Grant, J. E. Gaines, and Melvin van Peebles. By dividing the study further into "Militant Theatre" and "Theatre of Experience," Fabre has succeeded in separating what may never have been separated before: the private life of the American Afro-American theatre artist and the public expression of his or her anguish and anger. Some production stills; notes and index.

Gard, Robert E., and Gertrude S. Burley. *Community Theatre: Idea and Achievement.* New York: Duell, Sloan and Pearce, 1959.
The pre-Kennedy years do not yield many studies of community theatre, so this little book is valuable for getting an idea of what community theatre was like before the chaos of the 1960's. By means of a series of conversations with community theatre practitioners, mostly directors, the authors outline a "direction" ("manifesto" is too strong a word for this courteous statement of principle) for future theatres to follow. "A Note on Courage" tells one what to fight: "Most Community Theatres try to bring good plays to their audiences, but not at the expense of the recreational function of the organization." Bibliography and list of American community theatres, with addresses.

Gibbs, David Andrew. *The Architectural Programming of Six Selected University Performing Arts Centers.* Ann Arbor, Mich.: University Microfilms, 1982 (Ph.D. dissertation, University of Illinois at Urbana-Champaign, 1980).
"Program" for architects means "the written or graphic description of an intended building, as conceived by the architect, client, or intended user." Six academic facilities are described and (sometimes too abruptly) compared and contrasted, with examples of small, medium, and large multitheatre facilities, accommodating professional as well as student theatre, and offering space for all the performing arts. A good history of these buildings and a model of how theatre complexes are thought out. Documents not reproduced in this edition.

Grotowski, Jerzy. *Towards a Poor Theatre.* New York: Simon & Schuster, 1968.
As a primary text, the first to describe in some detail the methods of Polish director and teacher Grotowski, this book is now theatre history. Because of Grotowski's overwhelming influence on American experimental theatre in the 1960's and 1970's, this book has become part of the history of American theatre's transformation during that period. A simple text, neither didactic nor apologetic, in short paragraphs of direct quotation, outlines, and "rules": "Bodily activity comes first, and then vocal expression." The illustrations of self-masking techniques, classroom training exercises, audience-stage arrangements, and especially of the late Ryszard Cieslak in *The Constant Prince* make the book unforgettable at first reading.

Guerrilla Theater Essays: 1. San Francisco: San Francisco Mime Troupe, 1970.
Printed in response to requests for information for theatre workshops and semi-
nars, this pamphlet explains what guerrilla theater is and how it works with the
Mime Troupe. One interesting feature is the dialogue that brought the pamphlet
to a vote, and another is a list of "the people responsible for creation of San
Francisco Mime Troupe": about three hundred names, from Sandra Archer and
Susan Darby to Ron Davis, Lee Breuer, Lawrence Ferlinghetti, and Bill Graham.
Strange, creative mix of free enterprise and collectivism, but an exciting format
of news clips, photographs and essays dated 1962 to 1969. The facts and flavor
of guerrilla theater in about eighty unnumbered pages.

Handel, Beatrice, ed. *The National Directory for the Performing Arts/Educational*.
3d ed. New York: John Wiley & Sons, 1978. Updated biannually.
Arranged alphabetically by state and then by school, this directory gives basic
information on major schools and institutions that offer performing arts training.
Good for profiles of schools contributing to theatre history, but lacking historical
information such as date of corporation or years in performing arts curricula.
Faculty sizes, student sizes, degrees offered, departments, and performing groups
are given, but not accreditations; some URTA affiliations are mentioned. A new
feature is the identification of artists in residence, valuable but ephemeral.

Hardy, Camille Combs. *The Contributions of Samuel Selden to Educational Theatre*.
Ann Arbor, Mich.: University Microfilms, 1976 (Ph.D. dissertation, University
of Michigan, 1971).
Selden taught at the University of North Carolina in 1968 (Hardy was a pupil)
but spent thirty-six years at the University of California at Los Angeles. He
helped to develop and legitimize educational theatre, "convinced that it should
be established and maintained as an institution of high artistic and academic
standards." This study traces his aesthetics and pedagogy through his career,
from scenic design assistant at the Provincetown Playhouse (1922) to his retirement in 1971. Bibliography.

Houghton, Norris. *Entrances and Exits: A Life In and Out of the Theatre*. New
York: Limelight Editions, 1991.
This autobiography covers the career of the practical theatre man as well as the
academic and scholarly theorist, whose book *The Exploding Stage* is much cited
among contemporaries. In describing his long life (1909-1980 is discussed), from
Broadway successes as a stage designer to regional theatre experiments (founder
of the Phoenix Theatre) to university campuses (Princeton's McCarter Theatre),
Houghton drops names on the way to his next energetic project. Photographs of
productions and snapshots of celebrity events. Indispensable index.

Huerta, Jorge A. *Chicano Theater: Themes and Forms*. Ypsilanti, Mich.: Bilingual Press, 1982.
Mexican-American theatre—in particular the rise of Chicano theatre groups in the 1960's—forms the subject of this reflective, often moving analysis. At the center is El Teatro Campesino, the Farmworker's Theater, founded by Luis Valdez and often tied to the larger farm labor union work of Cesar Chavez. By 1977, a Chicano Theater Festival was "exposing the sociopolitical conditions of the Mexican-American community." Focusing on "the more developed *teatros*" but not neglecting the newer troupes, "the only true people's theaters," this study encourages expansion while asking to keep the revolution "on stage." Valuable bibliography and index.

Kerr, Walter. *God on the Gymnasium Floor and Other Theatrical Adventures*. New York: Simon & Schuster, 1971.
Kerr gets his credentials from Broadway journalism reviews, but he pays his respects to "living" theatre, including The Living Theater and the Open Theatre and all their kin. No idolater in this new, almost religious, theatrical experience, Kerr nevertheless sees what is lively, honest, and funny in it, and what in it is worth keeping and adopting into legitimate theatre. Because he paid attention so early to this highly experimental theatre, what he has to say about it rings truer than the opinions of latecomers. Good firsthand accounts of some earlier work, including the Living's *Paradise Now*. Index.

Kostelanetz, Richard. *The Theatre of Mixed Means: An Introduction to Happenings, Kinetic Environments, and Other Mixed-Means Performances*. New York: Dial Press, 1968.
Interviews with nine major experimental environment artists, musicians, and practitioners of "happenings" and other alternative art/theatre forms. Collectively, these interviews and Kostelanetz's two essays constitute a manifesto of contemporary aesthetic thought in the three arenas of visual art, theatre, and music. Strong introductions to the variations on the performance/fine arts interface. Bibliography and index.

Lahr, John. *Astonish Me: Adventures in Contemporary Theater*. New York: Viking Press, 1973.
Bert Lahr's son, reviewer for *Evergreen Review* and *Village Voice*, reflects on the impact of experimental theatre in three divisions: pageants (spectacular "liberating forces of three-dimensional space"), playwrights (he compares Jules Feiffer and Sam Shepard, for example), and performances (including *Terminal* and Muhammad Ali's career). Always an American perspective, even when dealing with European theatre.

_____. *Up Against the Fourth Wall: Essays on Modern Theater*. New York: Grove Press, 1970.

The trendy style of *Evergreen Review* informs these essays on experimental theatre, by which is meant the assaults on the "fourth wall" theatre of naturalism. Lahr, who was one of the first critics to acknowledge the potential importance of street theatre, the Open Theater, theatre of the absurd, and other "underground" movements, used the *Evergreen Review* as a forum for his first impressions. His writing and his insights become more sophisticated later in his career. Notes and index.

Levine, Mindy N. *New York's Other Theatre: A Guide to Off-Off Broadway*. New York: Avon Books, 1981.
A handy little book, written with the cooperation of the Off-Off Broadway Alliance, on the small lofts, basements, churches, and other gathering places of New York's low-rent (?) districts: the lower East Side, Soho, West and East Village, Chelsea, and others. Joseph Papp's introduction supplies the justification and encouragement: "It takes the playgoer off the beaten track . . . it is an idea about theatre, a commitment to theatre as an art form." Outdated now but valuable for the history of the movement; includes artistic profiles, typical productions, ticket prices, even which subway to take. Reference appendix with such headings as "Theatres that accept unsolicited manuscripts."

The Living Book of the Living Theatre. Greenwich, Conn.: New York Graphic Society, 1971.
A photo collection with some text graphics, this "is" the Living Theatre, and its contributors are listed alphabetically in the front of the book. Strong visual images of the work of the Living Theatre, with little documentation or dates to place the information in context. Ends with the "Living Theatre Action Last Declaration": The structure is crumbling." It divided into four cells, located in Paris (political), Berlin (cultural), India (spiritual), and presumably America (no specific orientation mentioned). An interesting adjunct to the study of the group; not many light moments photographed, and not much humor.

McCaslin, Nellie. *Theatre for Children in the United States: A History*. Norman: University of Oklahoma Press, 1971.
Beginning with a poignant history of children's theatre, with valuable accounts of early productions, McCaslin leads her readers into present-day conditions, many of which are tinted and tainted by political and economic strictures. Whenever federal funding and corporate donations feed children's entertainment projects, however praiseworthy in the abstract, a hidden censorship and a restrictive atmosphere threaten free expression. With production stills and strong, organized description, McCaslin draws the fine line between them and provides valuable facts along the way. Good bibliography and index.

McNamara, Brooks, and Jill Dolan, eds. *"The Drama Review": Thirty Years of Commentary on the Avant-Garde*. Ann Arbor, Mich.: UMI Research Press, 1986.

TDR, originally housed at Tulane, has been the official record of avant-garde—especially nonscripted—performance for several decades. This selection of articles makes available the more general and the more theoretical essays, discussing the large ideas of new theatre, although occasionally a specific essay (such as Jerzy Grotowski's on *Doctor Faustus*) provides details of a specific performance event. The best observers of alternative theatre—Kate Davy, Michael Kirby, Theodore Shank, Arnold Aronson—are well represented, as is the semiotic analyst Patrice Pavis. Useful index.

Malina, Judith. *The Diaries of Judith Malina, 1947-1957.* New York: Grove Press, 1984.
Years before the Living Theatre hit the theatre news, Judith Malina and her husband, Julian Beck, were theorizing, brainstorming, observing, and otherwise preparing to revolutionize the way theatre was done in the United States. These journal entries chronicle the thinking and conversations between them and among their colleagues, leading toward the manifesto of Beck's *Life in the Theatre*, but passing through much of the experimental theatre world in the process. Much that is personal, even intimate, is related here, and it makes for exciting reading in the light of where Malina's creativity eventually manifested itself. Index and notes (too few, however).

_____. *The Enormous Despair.* New York: Random House, 1972.
Without preamble, Malina launches into a subjective, highly charged, almost frightened account of the Living Theatre's return to America in 1968 after five years of exile. In telegraphic style she records the events of the tour, giving an immediacy to the experience and placing it squarely in the revolutionary spirit of the times. Includes such documents as her lawyer's written instructions in the event of arrest. Records her colleagues' responses, resistances, and reflections on the events around her as well. A sparse book, yet intimate and daring in its nakedness, not unlike Malina's theatre work. The book's title is taken from a letter from Martin Buber to Malina and Beck, dated 1961, about the "inevitable failure" of a European general strike. Index.

Malpede, Karen. *Three Works by the Open Theatre.* New York: Drama Book Specialists, 1974.
Postscriptive texts, sometimes fragmented and enigmatic, and stunning photographic portfolios by Max Waldman, Mary Ellen Mark, and Inge Morath of the important creations of Joseph Chaikin's Open (as opposed to Broadway's "closed") Theatre: *Terminal, Mutation Show,* and *Nightwalk.* Descriptive introduction serves as Malpede's interpretation of the group's aesthetic performance theory; a chronology and beginning bibliography demonstrate how deeply the group's work has affected all future theatre experimentation.

Mantegna, Gianfranco. *We, the Living Theatre*. New York: Ballantine, 1970.
This is "a pictorial documentation . . . of the life and the pilgrimage of The Living Theatre in Europe and the U.S.," concentrating on their four major works of the period. An introductory panel discussion is printed, with the subject among Malina, Beck, and Aldo Rostagno being Theatre as Revolution. An appendix of selected documents and American reviews. A small book, to be compared with the *Living Book of the Living Theatre*.

Neff, Renfreu. *The Living Theatre: USA*. Indianapolis: Bobbs-Merrill, 1970.
"The Living Theatre laid rightful claim to a significant and influential position in the cultural vanguard" and "sustained that pre-eminence for two generations," Neff explains in the introduction to this touring record of the Living's return to America in 1968. After a decade of international success, "this young generation had never heard of the Living Theatre." Neff follows their tour through New England, the Midwest, the West Coast, and the Southwest (they refused bookings in the South in protest). Fully chronicled, with itineraries 1968-1969; index.

Pasolli, Robert. *A Book on the Open Theatre*. Indianapolis: Bobbs-Merrill, 1970.
Joseph Chaikin's energies in the theatre, coupled with those of his friends and fellow performers in the Open Theatre, created a new kind of performance experience, captured as well as can be hoped in photographs, exercises, methods, and group activities. This little book about a large idea serves as an introduction to further study of alternative theatre methods of the 1960's and 1970's. "Sound and movement" procedures, built from Nola Chilton's work, oriental meditations, and physical techniques of American and European clowning and masking, are described, along with many other graceful ways into the performance art. History of the group interspersed with exercises. Highly recommended.

Robertson, Cosby Warren. *The Theatre as a Vehicle for Community Action*. Ann Arbor, Mich.: University Microfilms, 1975 (Ph.D. dissertation, Florida State University, 1972).
A study of how (and whether) community development includes theatrical entertainments, carried on in the Tampa area as part of a development project for Florida Agricultural and Mechanical University. As much a sociological profile of the city as it is a theatre history document, this work is most valuable as a methodology for subsequent studies of the same type, with copies of questionnaires, surveys, and results. Most interesting are two "dramatic events" scripts, one on voter registration (*People Got To Be Free*) and one on drug dependence (*Turning On For Real*), which merit disinterment and reperformance in other communities.

Sainer, Arthur. *The Radical Theatre Notebook*. New York: Avon Books, 1975.
A lively first look at some of the germinal theatre experiments of the 1950's and

1960's by an insider who thoroughly understands the impulses that drove his subject into theatre history. Besides covering the better-known groups such as the Living Theatre and the Performance Group, Sainer records the histories and the chaotic, often postscriptive stage texts of such temporary aberrations as the Firehouse Theater (Minneapolis), the OM-Theatre Workshop (Boston), and the Bridge Collective (New York), with which Sainer was connected as playwright.

Schechner, Richard. *Environmental Theater*. New York: Hawthorn, 1973.
A statement of principles as well as an authorized record of the activities of The Performance Group, Schechner's laboratory for theatrical experimentation, from his meeting designer Jerry Rojo in 1966 to the ongoing work on Sam Shepard's *Tooth of Crime* (first "seen by an audience" in 1972). Profusely illustrated with production photographs and diagrams, this work stands at the center of all intellectual inquiry into the nature of the theatrical event, especially its relationship to audience. Strong bibliography and index.

_____. *Essays on Performance Theory, 1970-1976*. New York: Drama Book Specialists, 1977.
Coming from the most creative and intense of modern theorists, this collection is as much a manifesto as was his 1973 work, *Environmental Theater*. A series of ideas on contemporary American theatre history, which began with the Becks but found its most articulate proponent in Schechner. Here are the connections among European, Asian, and primitive stage practices and American manifestations of the same impulse to explode the stage beyond its realistic limitations. Bibliography mixes anthropological and theatrical sources.

Schroeder, Robert J., ed. *The New Underground Theatre*. New York: Bantam Books, 1968.
Although essentially a book of short dramatic pieces from the "non-academic American artistic community of the 1960's," these texts are the history of avant-garde theatre in America. From these modest beginnings came the best work of Irene Maria Fornes, Jean-Claude van Itallie, and Sam Shepard. Schroeder preserves the germ from which grew this decade's best contemporary theatre. Short bibliography of works by represented playwrights.

Shank, Theodore. *American Alternative Theater*. New York: Grove Press, 1982.
The Grove Press Modern Dramatists series is particularly informative in this instance, as the performances discussed are not script oriented but examples of postscriptive documentation. This book adds both facts and insights to what one can know (without being there) about The Living Theatre, Open Theatre (his spelling), Performance Group, Snake Theater, Robert Wilson, Richard Foreman, The Wooster Group, Squat Theatre, and a half dozen other artists and groups of this ilk. Shank knows this work well, from a career-long interest. Many

photographs, mostly his own, but poorly reproduced and mostly to be found elsewhere, notably in *The Drama Review*.

Shyer, Laurence. *Robert Wilson and His Collaborators*. New York: Theatre Communications Group, 1989.
A valuable and extensive review of Wilson's work to date, with a fully illustrated text, notes, and chronology from The Byrd Hoffman School of Byrds to *La Nuit d'avant le Jour* in 1989. A glance at Wilson's collaborators, from Sheryl Sutton to Christopher Knowles to Robert Applegarth, is all the proof needed that Wilson is a major artistic force today. Strong chronology and bibliography but no index. Highly recommended for keeping track of Wilson's prodigious accomplishments.

Smith, Michael. *Theatre Journal: Winter, 1967*. Columbia: University of Missouri Press, 1968.
Smith, who was writing for the *Village Voice* during a crucial time in off-off-Broadway history, records in about fifty pages his visceral impressions (not all off-off-Broadway) of productions destined to become the history of theatre in the 1960's: Lanford Wilson's *Rimers of Eldritch*, Sam Shepard's *La Turista*, Barbara Garson's *MacBird!*, Carolee Schneemann's *Snows*, and more. This dynamic collection of first impressions is perhaps more valuable than any other document for getting the feel of an impending eruption of new theatrical ideas. A final tribute to Joe Cino; index.

Sumpter, Clyde G. *Militating for Change: The Black Revolutionary Theatre Movement in the United States*. Ann Arbor, Michigan: University Microfilms, 1971.
Though originally a doctoral dissertation in drama from the University of Kansas, Sumpter's study is at the same time a full review of what he calls "the Black Revolutionary stage," meaning the concerted effort to change the social black image by using the stage to negate and then replace black stereotypes with true depictions of black life and history. From the Federal Theatre Project, through LeRoi Jones (Amiri Imamu Baraka) and his Black Arts Repertory Theatre/School in Harlem (1965), to his almost Meyerhold-driven Spirit House Movers in Newark, the best of the movement is chronicled. Strong bibliography.

Szilassy, Zoltan. *American Theater of the 1960's*. Carbondale: Southern Illinois University Press, 1986.
Part of a Crosscurrents series, this short but intensive study divides into the "Rebellious Drama" (Edward Albee), and "The Intermedia" (happenings and performance theories), with "Conclusion, Outlook, and Reminiscences." Most valuable is a discussion of the regional alternative theater movement, notably the Minneapolis Playwright's Laboratory, Provisional Theatre, Los Angeles, and the San Francisco Mime Troupe. This Hungarian critic ends his study with the hope that the American Theatre Today exhibit he saw in Budapest in 1983 is not the last word on experimental theatre. Notes and index.

Trefny, Beverly Robin, and Eileen C. Palmer. *Index to Children's Plays in Collections 1975-1984*. Metuchen, N.J.: Scarecrow Press, 1986.
Continuing the series (1972, 1977 by Barbara A. Kreider), this third volume brings the total entries to almost two thousand. Subject headings, cast analysis, directory of publishers, and bibliography of collections complete this small but effective guide to children's plays, a theatre history source in the making but designed for the potential producer of theatre for children.

Watts, Billie Dean. *Arch Lauterer: Theorist in the Theatre*. Ann Arbor, Mich.: University Microfilms, 1976 (Ph.D. dissertation, University of Oregon, 1970). Undeservedly little known in professional theatre circles, Lauterer was an innovative scene designer, lighting designer, director, and architectural consultant working coast to coast, mostly in academic theatre—Bennington, Sarah Lawrence, and Mills. Watts came by Lauterer's theories while studying at the University of Oregon, especially the idea (new at the time) of "discovering the action of the play, then fitting to that action the design of the space, the setting, the lighting, and the movement of the actors in time." A thorough study, useful for historians of academic theatre as a laboratory for contemporary theatre in the professional arena. Plates do not reproduce well.

Williams, Mance. *Black Theatre in the 1960's and 1970's: A Historical-Critical Analysis of the Movement*. Contributions in Afro-American and African Studies 87. Westport, Conn.: Greenwood Press, 1985.
This study, which is more analytical than descriptive, assumes a familiarity with the primary material. After chapters on political-cultural writers, it concentrates most productively on black theatre companies, producers ("Hustling the Muse" is the irreverent title of this chapter), and "non-polemical structuralists," by which is meant Edgar White and Adrienne Kennedy. Strong bibliography and index.

PERIODICALS

American Theatre. Since the early 1980's a publication of Theatre Communications Group, this monthly news magazine communicates among the members of the League of Resident Theatres, university students in the arts, and the decentralized theatre community in general. Covers Broadway events on a general basis, emphasizing the work of the approximately two hundred LORT theatres in every major city. New playwrights, new directors and artistic directors, and new theatrical ideas are noted and reported; collectively, *AT* is the storehouse of the history of regional theatre. Complete play scripts are offered several times each year. Plenty of production stills, editorials, "front lines" commentators, "trends," and similar feature columns.

Black Theatre: A Periodical of the Black Theatre Movement. From 1969 to the mid-1970's, during a period of strong growth, the black theatre community, led by the New Lafayette Theatre, published articles on the dramatic creative output of both playwrights and performers, edited by Ed Bullins. It has since become a good source of historical information on the movement and period, with interviews, reviews, scripts, illustrations, and feature articles articulating the energies of black theatre artists during a volatile time. LeRoi Jones (as he was still called), Langston Hughes, Ben Caldwell, Otis Redding, Black Nativity, and a poem to Dionne Warwick are representative subjects. Woodcuts, etchings, and other very interesting illustrations invite investigation as well.

Dramatics. The magazine of the International Thespian Society, the high school drama organization, this is a richly illustrated current-events magazine connecting professional theatre to its potential young audiences. Plenty of how-to articles, advice to young talent, reviews of Broadway and experimental fare, and a yearly overview of the International Thespian Festival held in Muncie, Indiana. Interviews with working playwrights such as August Wilson and Lee Blessing, and occasional play scripts suitable for high school production.

International Bibliography of Theatre: 1982, 1983. Books, articles, dissertations, and so on. Classed entries are numbered and very briefly annotated; subject entries then refer to the numbers. A good way to find sources of specific information. For example, Eva Le Gallienne's American Repertory Theatre from 1945 to 1947 is discussed in item 652, which is Nancy McClave's case study. Comes with a guide for users, explanation of terms, and a very interesting "taxonomy" of eleven categories, divided subsequently into dozens of smaller sections. Edited by Benito Ortolani and published by Theatre Research Data Center of Brooklyn College, CUNY.

The Mask: A Monthly Journal of the Art of the Theatre. "So long as the theatres in
    America are run like bargain counters, with the management continually on the
    outlook for easy sellers, the drama in America will remain at a low ebb." This,
    from the initial volume in 1908 of *The Mask*, speaks volumes for London's and
    Europe's opinions of turn-of-the-century American theatre fare, even though the
    sentiment is voiced here by G. B. Baker of Harvard. Each issue of this interna-
    tional theatre review deals at some length with American theatre, especially
    shows that are crossing the Atlantic to try their hand at wooing American
    audiences. The journal proves "how deeply the possibilities of the drama are now
    impressing some of the most eager and imperative minds in Europe" and in
    America. Best for the European-American connection but also interesting in its
    own right. Plenty of American readers, as witness the ad for Walter Prichard
    Eaton's book, *The American Stage of To-day.*

New York Theatre Critics' Reviews, 1940-   . New York: Critics' Theatre Reviews,
    1940-
    The complete reviews, photocopied, from about a dozen New York print sources
    (television reviews included in later issues), published weekly and bound yearly.
    Note that the issues are bound (in binder form at first, but library bound even-
    tually) in reverse order, the latest on top. A cumulative table of contents grows
    from issue to issue and begins anew at the beginning of each year. Indexed in
    several ways: by cast, authors, dance directors, managers or producers, scenic
    designers, stage directors, composers, and so on. A complicated system, but once
    mastered, a primary source of educated opinion on living theatre under one
    cover, with full production and award information included.

Performing Arts Journal (PAJ). Begun in 1976 as an alternative to *The Drama
    Review,* concentrating on experimental theatre, especially political, international,
    nonscripted, feminist, and gay theatre. International in scope, but particularly
    valuable for documenting and reporting American experiments in the 1980's to
    the present. Many theoretical articles on performance theory, theatre semiotics,
    audience theory, and the like. Special reports, festival roundups, and so on are
    regular features. Some, but not all, issues center on a theme, such as the intercul-
    turalism double issue 33/34.

Performing Arts Review. Begun in 1969 as "the journal of management and law of
    the arts," this quarterly covers "relevant commercial, nonprofit and academic
    sectors of the performing arts...including theatre, motion pictures, television,
    music and the dance, as well as the literary and artistic works underlying them."
    Editor Joseph Taubman is a lawyer whose success with his books *Financing a
    Theatrical Production* and *The Business and Law of Music* prompted him to start
    this journal. Typical articles are Clive J. Davis' "They're Not All 'My Fair
    Lady'" (1969) and Luanne Aronen Rosenfeld's "The Showcase Code: Evolution

and Revolution" (1980). Good source of legal information on controversies of the stage.

Players: The Magazine of American Theatre. Started in the mid-1920's as the outlet for the National Collegiate Players of Northern Illinois University. No longer in publication. Articles such as "Show Me Showtime" (on the Missouri Repertory Theatre, 1968) and The Alice Liddell Theatre Company (April, 1975) are handy for historians of other than Broadway fare.

Plays in Process. Since about 1980, the Theatre Communications Group has made available in an inexpensive format the new play scripts from regional theatre productions in the United States, to promote the proliferation of productions of scripts that might otherwise be lost to the rest of the country. These are new plays, translations and adaptations, separately bound, primarily but not exclusively by American playwrights; each text adds a brief biography of the playwright and a first production history. No critical apparatus otherwise. The series is an indispensable source for keeping up with current work, and the collection will be valuable when scholarship on new play development begins to find its way into theatre journals.

Studies in American Drama, 1945-Present. Begun in 1986, this journal from Pennsylvania State University edited by Philip C. Kolin and Colby H. Kullman "presents scholarly articles on theatre history, dramatic influences and technique, original interviews, theatre documents, useful bibliographies, and theatre reviews." Some insights into the unique character of post-World War II American theatre, but top-heavy on the literary side.

TDR. The Drama Review. This journal, which has undergone several changes of name and venue, began as the *Tulane Drama Review* but is currently edited by New York University and published by MIT Press. Experimental theatre, especially postmodern performance art and mixed-media presentations, is the focus; much of the journal's coverage deals with international theatre festivals and experimentation, but the New York avant-garde scene is thoroughly examined through performance "reports," nonevaluative descriptions of experimental performance. Each issue features a theme, country, or theatrical subgenre, such as "East Village performance" or "Processional performance." Quickly becoming the official document of record for fugitive, nonscripted performances, theoretical manifestoes, and production stills of unrepeated events such as "Happenings" and stagings in nontraditional performance spaces.

Theater. Formerly *Yale/Theater.* Begun in 1968 "to examine contemporary American theater through the activities of the Yale School of Drama," but expanded in 1977 to publish "essays, interviews, and retrospectives that reflect . . . larger concerns, and not simply documentation that is time-bound to particular productions." Typical articles: "Sam Shepard's *Inacoma* at the Magic Theatre" by William Kleb (1977) and "The Song-Lines of Kevin Kling" by Mark Bly (Fall, 1990). Best on experimental theatre, political issues on stage, and sociological implications of performance.

The Theatre. A monthly commercial magazine that brings New York theatre news to the entire country. Began publication in 1958. Part self-promotion, part internal communication among the theatre people of Broadway. Feature articles on new plays and actors, pictorials of productions, special features, and departments such as "Playguide" and "Books and Records." Newsy and inviting. Good source for research into opening-night reactions and promotional blurbs.

Theatre Arts. Beginning with an article entitled "Acting and the New Stagecraft," this periodical has been the forum for new ideas and communication among theatre professionals and scholars since its inception in 1916. It underwent many format changes until its demise in the mid-1960's. Cited by virtually every theatre historian, it contains (in later issues) full texts of modern dramas. A cross between a weekly news magazine and a journal of record for the American (and world) theatre. Back issues are being republished by Arno Press, thus allowing libraries to obtain complete collections. Typical articles: "The Newest Art" by Rollo Peters (Summer, 1918), a response to the "New Art of the Theatre" controversy of Gordon Craig; less typical but indicative of changes is "Oklahoma's Mummers Theatre" by Aline Jean Treanor (December, 1963), on a non-New York production effort. Departments include Theatre Bookshelf, Calendar, and (in later years) Theatre USA, a roundup of theatre news west of the Hudson River.

Theatre Arts Monthly. Editor Edith J. R. Isaacs and associate editors Kenneth Macgowan, Ashley Dukes, and Stark Young turned this monthly into the center of the creative theatre world for several decades, from the early 1920's to the mid-1940's. "Eugene O'Neill and This Big Business of Broadway" by Robert Garland (January, 1925) is often cited in O'Neill scholarship; Norris Houghton's article on Laurette Taylor (December, 1945) is a famous tribute to her unforgettable Amanda Wingfield. Many illustrations of productions, listed in the table of contents of each issue. Regular features include Theatre Arts Bookshelf and Rosamond Gilder's Broadway in Review (she edited later years of this publication). Note: *Theatre Arts* and *Theatre Arts Monthly* are often shelved together and, when rebound, named fairly arbitrarily one or the other.

Theatre Crafts. Begun 1967 and published monthly. Comparable to *Theatre Design and Technology* but aimed at shop foremen, theatre technicians, and designers of practical sets for real-life situations. Full of design articles, reviews of new theatre facilities, special design and technology projects (such as rock concerts and theme parks), and riddled with full-color photographs and advertisements (with ad index). Many handy tips on prop making, set construction, fabric dyeing, and similar hands-on, everyday problems of play production (example: "Grids: Problems and Solutions" by Robert Long, in his regular "Architecture" column). Typical articles: "Authentic Kabuki, American Style" by Samuel L. Leiter (volume 2, September/October, 1968) and "Jennifer Tipton: Architect of the Air" by Michael Sommers (October, 1990). Other regular features are a how-to column, Callboard, and editorials.

Theatre Design and Technology. Quarterly journal of the U.S. Institute for Theatre Technology. Specializes in informative, often technical reports of new products, innovations in theatre hydraulics, lighting, drum revolves, computer-assisted stage designing, and other hardware, as in "Scenic Wagon Restraint Systems" by Frank Silberstein (Summer, 1977), as well as essays on scenography and design reports, such as "A Roundup of Recent Theatre Buildings" (Winter, 1968). Sophisticated publication that assumes considerable expertise on the part of the reader. Back issues are good for researching technical innovations. Book reviews and obituaries are regular features, along with editorials, a new products column, and technical reports. Advertisements for the trade.

Theatre Documentation (TD). "An international medium of communication between theatre scholars and theatre collection curators, and a reference tool for everyone interested in the performing arts." Published twice yearly by the Theatre Library Association. The scope of this invaluable periodical is bibliography, classification, collections, theatre practice and education, and news of international theatre scholarship. Begun in fall, 1968. Once the intimidation is overcome, a priceless source. Example: a much-needed index to William Clapp's *A Record of the Boston Stage* is provided by Sister Carol Blitgen in the initial volume; volume 3 offers an index to photographs of scene designs in *Theatre Arts* from 1916 to 1964, and Clyde G. Sumpter provides a bibliography on the "Negro in Twentieth Century American Drama."

Theatre History Studies. An annual publication of the Mid-America Theatre Conference. Contents include articles on all aspects of theatre and drama, but a good source for American theatre articles with a regional slant, such as "Wooing a Local Audience: The Irish-American Appeal of Philadelphia's Mae Desmond Players" by Mari Kathleen Fielder (1981), and "The Living Newspaper's *Power* in Seattle" by Barry B. Witham (1989). An interesting regular feature is "Theatre History Obscurities," a kind of nest for short articles on otherwise lost information; a section of book reviews is particularly helpful to the historian.

Theatre Journal. (TJ). Formerly *Educational Theatre Journal* (the name changed in 1979). The official organ of the Association for Theatre in Higher Education, but originally published quarterly by the disbanded American Theatre Association. Yearly updates on Scholarly Works in Progress. Articles of high-quality scholarship reflecting a wide range of subjects, international in nature, but with preference to American productions. Not exclusive to American theatre history, but full of informative, scholarly articles on such subjects as David Henry Hwang's *M. Butterfly* and Philip Kan Gotanda's *Yankee Dawg You Die* (by James S. Moy, March, 1990), and Deborah R. Geis's "Wordscapes of the Body," on Maria Irene Fornes's plays (October, 1990). Typical American theatre articles: "Notes from the Avant-Garde" by Xerxes Mehta (March, 1979); "Appropriation and Transgression in Contemporary American Performance: The Wooster Group, Holly Hughes, and Karen Finley" by Jon Erickson (May, 1990). Issues often built around a theme, as in "Women and/In Drama" (October, 1990). Kate Davy edits the theatre review regular feature, which provides much historical data on performances by regional and experimental theatres. Katherine E. Kelly edits the book review section.

Theatre News. Newsletter of the American Educational Theatre Association. Originally monthly, then quarterly, beginning with volume 1, October, 1968. Carries news to members of AETA, convention announcements, and similar news items. Back issues useful for research in educational and academic theatre, such as "First American College Theatre Festival Sets Top Standard Precedent for Succeeding Events," appearing in June, 1969; subsequent issues are slicker, more essay oriented, as with "Dramatizing Black Poetry" by Vera J. Katz (Summer, 1981).

Theatre Profiles: The Illustrated Guide to America's Nonprofit Professional Theatres. New York: Theatre Communications Group, 1974-
Indispensable guide to and history of regional theatre published biannually as a service to TCG members and the American theatre community in general. Gives personnel, dates of seasons, facilities information, financial overview, annual attendance and subscriber figures, past production information (with directors and set/costume/lighting design credits), and more. Alphabetical entries are introduced by essays from theatre community spokespersons and interspersed with photograph sections of production stills. Name and title index and chronology of the growing regional theatre movement.

Theatre Quarterly. Rejuvenated in 1985 as *New Theatre Quarterly*, *Theatre Quarterly* is essentially a British publication (copublished by the University of Southern California); yet, because it deals with international theatre as well, such articles as R. G. Davis's "Directing in Underdeveloped California: The Watsonville Experience," David Hirst's "The American Musical and the American

Dream: From 'Show Boat' to Sondheim," (February, 1985), and Stanley Kauff-mann's "Broadway and the Necessity for 'Bad Theatre'" can be found there (all in the 1985 volume).

Theatre Studies. The Journal of the Ohio State University Theatre Research Institute. Yearly. Book reviews, OSUTRI news and notes are regular features. Reports research within the institute. International subjects, highly scholarly. No adver-tisements or promotions. Typical articles: "The Activist Theatre of the Thirties" by Howard Burman and Joseph Hanreddy (number 18, 1971/1972); "The Yiddish Theatre in New York, 1880-1920: A Secular Ritual" (number 30, 1983/1984).

Theatre Survey. An annual (later semiannual) publication of the American Society for Theatre Research. Volume 1 published in 1960. Articles on international topics, but concentrating on performance aspects rather than literary analysis. Typical articles: "Revolution in the American Theatre: Glimpses of Acting Conditions on the American Stage, 1855-1870" by E. J. West (1960); "The Omaha Magic Theatre: An Alternative Theatre for Mid-America" by Judith Babnich and Alex Pinkston (volume 30, May 1989). Occasional specialized issues, such as the "Eugene O'Neill Centennial Issue" (May 1988). Review essay and short book reviews in each issue.

Theatre Today. An annual begun in 1968. Published by the Advanced Insititue for Development of American Repertory Theatre. The term *repertory* sometimes refers to resident theatre but more often refers to a company of actors who stay together through several productions. A good source for the history of repertory theatre as it emerges and disappears in America, especially on campus.

Ulrich's International Periodicals Directory. A general source of information for all kinds of periodicals, but under "theatre" are listings for currently circulating periodicals, more than one hundred in number. Some libraries carry back issues to the 1930's, so out-of-print issues can be located. Look under "theatre" to find current in-print periodicals, including newsletters; gives originating dates for currently active periodicals and a brief description of contents.

Variety. The weekly newspaper of the entertainment industry, begun in 1905, when the stage held the lion's share of print space. Now, with live performances of dramatic works confined to a "Legit" section, the newspaper concentrates on financial matters, openings and closings, touring revenues, and producers' hype, with some reviews thrown in. Still valuable as a historical document. Indexes to past issues will lead the reader to obituaries, openings, and so forth. Usually on microfilm, since newsprint was not designed for posterity.

AMERICAN
THEATRE
HISTORY

INDEX

INDEX

INDEX

Mostel, Zero, Jack Gilford, Kate Mostel, and Madeline Gilford 108
Moussinac, Leon 81
Mowatt, Anna Cora 7, 46
Murdoch, James E. 36
Murphy, Donn B., Douglas Bennett Lee, and Roger L. Meersman 30
Musical theatre 3, 17, 33, 53, 57, 64, 65, 80, 87, 92, 98, 101, 104-106, 111, 113, 114, 132

Nadel, Norman 81
Nathan, George Jean 81, 82, 109
National Theatre, The 30
Neff, Renfreu 141
Negro theatre. *See* African-American theatre.
Nelson, Benjamin 109
New Stagecraft and Art Theatre, The 57
New York Cultural Consumer 109
New York Times Theater Reviews, 1920-1970 82
Niblo's Garden Theatre 13
Novick, Julius 125
Nugent, Elliott 109
Nugent, J. C. 36

O'Connor, John, and Lorraine Brown, eds. 82
Odell, George C. D. 36
Odets, Clifford 57, 62, 82
O'Donnol, Shirley Miles 109
Off Broadway 2, 95, 99, 101, 102, 105, 126
Ogdon, Jess, and Jean Carter 60
Old Drury. *See* Chestnut Street Theatre, The.
Oldenburg, Chloe Warner 125
Open Theatre, The 140-142
Open-Air theatre 61
Overmyer, Grace 37
Overstreet, Robert Lane 37
O'Neill, Eugene 1, 59, 60, 90, 151
O'Neill, Eugene, and George Jean Nathan 86
O'Neill, James 18
O'Neill family, The 41

Palmer, Eileen C., and Beverly Robin Trefny 144
Palmieri, Anthony F. R. 82
Papp, Joseph 120, 123
Parola, Gene Joseph 83
Pasolli, Robert 141
Patrick, John Max 37
Patterson, Lindsay, ed. 83
Payne, Ben Iden 126
Payne, John Howard 37
Pemberton, Brock 69
Performing Arts Journal (PAJ) 146

Performing Arts Review 146
Perry, Jeb H. 110
Phelps, William Lyon 83
Philadelphia theatre, The 38
Pike, Frank, and Lee Alan Morrow 125
Pinkston, Claude Alexander, Jr. 38
Piscator, Erwin 135
Players 147
Plays in Process 147
Playwrights Producing Company, The 91, 100
Plotkins, Marilyn Jane 84
Poggi, Jack 84
Pollock, Thomas Clark 38
Porter, Cole 84
Porterfield, Robert 91
Postlewait, Thomas, and Bruce A. McConachie, eds. 38
Powers family, The 35
Preminger, Erik Lee 110
Prince, Harold 103
Provincetown Players, The 1, 86

Quinn, Arthur Hobson 38
Quintero, Jose 2, 126

Rabb, Ellis 3, 122
Raider, Roberta Ann 84
Redfield, William 110
Rehan, Ada 5, 49
Reignolds-Winslow, Catherine Mary 39
Rialto at Union Square, The 18
Rice, Elmer 82, 84
Rice, Thomas D. 10
Richmond stage, The 42
Rickert, William, and Jane Bloomquist 126
Ridge, Patricia Lin 85
Rigdon, Walter, ed. 85
Ritchey, Robert David 39
Robbins, Jhan 110
Robbins, Phyllis 39
Roberts, J. W. 85
Roberts, Kenneth Harris 111
Roberts, Vera Mowry, Milly S. Barranger, and Alice M. Robinson, eds. 126
Robertson, Cosby Warren 141
Robertson, Roderick 86
Robinson, Alice M., Vera Mowry Roberts, Milly S. Barranger, eds. 126
Rodgers, Richard 111
Rodgers, Richard, and Oscar Hammerstein 104
Roman, Lisbeth Jane 39
Ross, Hellen, and Lillian Ross 111
Ross, Lillian, and Hellen Ross 111
Ross, Theophil Walter, Jr. 86
Ruggles, Eleanor 40

INDEX